CRIMINOLOGICAL AND CRIMINAL JUSTICE RESEARCH METHODS

ASPEN COLLEGE SERIES

CRIMINOLOGICAL AND CRIMINAL JUSTICE RESEARCH METHODS

WESLEY G. JENNINGS
University of South Florida

JENNIFER M. REINGLE
University of Texas School of Public Health

Wolters Kluwer
Law & Business

Published by Wolters Kluwer Law & Business in New York.

Wolters Kluwer Law & Business serves customers worldwide with CCH, Aspen Publishers, and Kluwer Law International products. (www.wolterskluwerlb.com)

To contact Customer Service, e-mail customer.service@wolterskluwer.com, call 1-800-234-1660, fax 1-800-901-9075, or mail correspondence to:

> Wolters Kluwer Law & Business
> Attn: Order Department
> PO Box 990
> Frederick, MD 21705

Printed in the United States of America.

1 2 3 4 5 6 7 8 9 0

ISBN 978-1-4548-3306-2

Library of Congress Cataloging-in-Publication Data

Jennings, Wesley G., author.
   Criminological and criminal justice research methods / Wesley G. Jennings and Jennifer M. Reingle.
      pages cm
   Includes bibliographical references and index.
   ISBN 978-1-4548-3306-2—ISBN 1-4548-3306-8 1. Criminal justice, Administration of—United States. 2. Criminology—United States. 3. Criminology—Research—Methodology. I. Reingle, Jennifer M., author. II. Title.
   KF9223.J46 2014
   364.072—dc23

                                                                    2013044466

About Wolters Kluwer Law & Business

Wolters Kluwer Law & Business is a leading global provider of intelligent information and digital solutions for legal and business professionals in key specialty areas, and respected educational resources for professors and law students. Wolters Kluwer Law & Business connects legal and business professionals as well as those in the education market with timely, specialized authoritative content and information-enabled solutions to support success through productivity, accuracy and mobility.

Serving customers worldwide, Wolters Kluwer Law & Business products include those under the Aspen Publishers, CCH, Kluwer Law International, Loislaw, ftwilliam.com and MediRegs family of products.

CCH products have been a trusted resource since 1913, and are highly regarded resources for legal, securities, antitrust and trade regulation, government contracting, banking, pension, payroll, employment and labor, and healthcare reimbursement and compliance professionals.

Aspen Publishers products provide essential information to attorneys, business professionals and law students. Written by preeminent authorities, the product line offers analytical and practical information in a range of specialty practice areas from securities law and intellectual property to mergers and acquisitions and pension/benefits. Aspen's trusted legal education resources provide professors and students with high-quality, up-to-date and effective resources for successful instruction and study in all areas of the law.

Kluwer Law International products provide the global business community with reliable international legal information in English. Legal practitioners, corporate counsel and business executives around the world rely on Kluwer Law journals, looseleafs, books, and electronic products for comprehensive information in many areas of international legal practice.

Loislaw is a comprehensive online legal research product providing legal content to law firm practitioners of various specializations. Loislaw provides attorneys with the ability to quickly and efficiently find the necessary legal information they need, when and where they need it, by facilitating access to primary law as well as state-specific law, records, forms and treatises.

ftwilliam.com offers employee benefits professionals the highest quality plan documents (retirement, welfare and non-qualified) and government forms (5500/PBGC, 1099 and IRS) software at highly competitive prices.

MediRegs products provide integrated health care compliance content and software solutions for professionals in healthcare, higher education and life sciences, including professionals in accounting, law and consulting.

Wolters Kluwer Law & Business, a division of Wolters Kluwer, is headquartered in New York. Wolters Kluwer is a market-leading global information services company focused on professionals.

BRIEF CONTENTS

CONTENTS

Chapter 3
MEASUREMENT AND INSTRUMENTATION

Chapter 4
CRIME MEASUREMENT

PREFACE

We are well aware that the research methods course is usually not eagerly anticipated by the majority of students who are often required to take it as part of their criminology or criminal justice studies. Most students in these programs enroll in the course to prepare for work as police officers, parole officers, or perhaps, after law school, defense or prosecuting attorneys. Such students may see research methods as unnecessary and irrelevant to their future careers. This book was created largely in response to this misperception and to demonstrate that the study of research methods in criminology and criminal justice can be interesting, relevant, and at times even humorous. But although the text is directed toward criminology and criminal justice undergraduates with no particular interest in research methods and no plans to attend graduate school, it also offers additional, more challenging material that may be integrated at the instructor's discretion for use in advanced undergraduate or even graduate-level research methods classes.

This book stands out among the many research methods texts available because it focuses on delivering the essential core materials with a vivid and consistent sense of their practical, real-world application to issues and situations central to practice in criminology and criminal justice. The text offers methods and formats with direct application to situations and issues students will encounter in the field, and it illustrates these using scenarios based on actual conditions and events. This approach not only facilitates student learning and understanding of the research methods studied, but it also helps students envision the utility of the methods and thus, we hope, motivates them to read, retain, and even enjoy the material.

As authors who are both heavily involved in theoretical, methodological, empirical, and practical evaluations and applications of criminology and criminal justice research methods, we bring a range of relevant, current experience to the content, organization, and writing of this text. We were able to identify outmoded, inessential methods that are no longer standard practice or that are impractical or irrelevant in the field. We also place a heavy emphasis on research methods that are in very frequent use among researchers in criminology and criminal justice—such as survey data and secondary analysis—and that produce results widely disseminated among and considered by police, prison, and criminal justice officials and policy makers.

This text includes both classical criminology and criminal justice research methods in continuing use and cutting-edge approaches that are quickly proving their usefulness in the field. Both are presented clearly and directly, so undergraduate students can easily absorb and build on their understanding of the content as they explore increasingly complex material and learn to put it to practical use. Stand-alone chapters are devoted to such essential topics as ethics, measurement, survey research, secondary data analysis, and sampling. Emerging approaches, such as case-control and longitudinal designs and experiments in criminology and criminal justice settings, are covered as well. Because most criminology and criminal justice agencies have an in-house or contracted analyst, we specifically focus on research design, rather than the nuts and bolts of coding and analysis. This places the emphasis on students' likely future needs as consumers rather than producers of research.

In response to the predilections of a new generation of college students, this text employs innovative pedagogical techniques designed to engage as they instruct. To this end, the textbook approaches its topics like a series of short stories. Each chapter employs its own scenario, based on one or more real-world situations, showing how criminology and criminal justice research methods, terminology, and techniques work in the field to help practitioners analyze developments and resolve problems. By engaging the reader in these stories, the text helps students absorb and retain more of the material in ways that mirror how it is actually put into action.

Our goal was to develop a criminology and criminal justice research methods textbook that used new approaches while remaining true to the important and relevant core material, that did not resort to jargon or overly abstract concepts, and that both undergraduate and graduate students would find accessible and informative. We wanted to attract and keep the attention of the next generation of criminology and criminal justice practitioners so that they are prepared and eager to implement in their agencies evidence-based policies based on sound, up-to-date criminology and criminal justice research methods. We feel that we have succeeded in meeting these goals. We sincerely hope that both instructors and students will agree and will find this text refreshing to use and to be an effective guide to proficiency in criminology and criminal justice research methods.

ACKNOWLEDGMENTS

We would like to thank our families and dear friends for their love, patience, and support during the development of this textbook. We also would like to thank David Herzig, our associate publisher, for providing us the opportunity to write this textbook, and Susan Boulanger, our developmental specialist, for her detailed edits, comments, and assistance in moving this textbook into production. Finally, we wish to thank the reviewers of the initial book proposal and the reviewers of the original (and revised) draft of our textbook as their helpful advice and comments undoubtedly improved the overall quality of this publication.

—Wesley G. Jennings, Ph.D., and Jennifer Reingle, Ph.D.

CRIMINOLOGICAL AND CRIMINAL JUSTICE RESEARCH METHODS

INTRODUCTION TO RESEARCH DESIGN IN CRIMINAL JUSTICE

Why study research methods in criminal justice? You probably decided to major in criminal justice or criminology to work as a police officer, investigator, probation officer, parole officer, or supervise one of these roles. Although research methods may not apply directly to your daily work, a working knowledge of research methods will be necessary for you to stay on the leading edge of research in your field. This will be handy when it comes to promotion, as supervisors should be able to interpret **evidence-based practices** in the field. Therefore, taking this class and reading this text may make you stand out from other workers also in line for promotion. Alternatively, you may decide that you enjoy research methods and pursue graduate school.

Although research may seem daunting, unmanageable, and tedious, once you get the hang of it, you may find that you enjoy the challenge. The benefits are constant learning, freedom to research topics of interest to you, and professional autonomy. We hope that this text will inspire you to apply research in your professional life and will be directly applicable and useful to you. We want to provide you with a solid knowledge of core concepts directly applied to the field of criminal justice. Each chapter will include *one* story line that introduces all of the relevant concepts in each chapter. We hope that this technique will make the text more readable and easy to absorb. In fact, you should thank your professor for choosing the most engaging text in the field of criminology.

Research methods is a broad term that refers to the variety of tools and techniques available to research to add to a body of knowledge. There is a very specific scientific method that allows us to learn more about the causes of crime. Given that criminal justice is known as a "soft" science (or social science), it is more difficult to isolate the effect of one activity, behavior, or personality characteristic on crime. In the "hard" sciences, such as chemistry and biology, the controlled environment of a petri dish will directly allow conclusions to be drawn as to whether a given treatment will destroy bacteria. This is not the case in criminal justice.

The prospect of research in criminology does have merit, despite the complex environment that we live in. We have theories, which guide our understanding of the causes of criminal behavior and guide development and testing of hypotheses (i.e., ideas based upon theory that will serve as a guideline for our research agenda). We have a comprehensive body of literature that we use to guide future research. We base our conclusions upon results of a strong research design, using rigorous statistical methods of analysis. Although this is challenging and requires a great deal of preparation and planning on the front end of the project, a strong design can add to knowledge in the field of criminal justice just as findings from a laboratory can add to the field of biology (Rynes, Bartunek, & Daft, 2001). In other words, we conduct research in criminology to describe crime (and criminals), explain why some people are criminals (and how to make them stop offending), and use this information to prevent crime from happening (and criminals from becoming offenders) in the first place. That is the purpose of research in criminal justice and criminology.

When Dr. Reingle first began studying research methods and statistics, she was surprised to learn that everything she took for granted as knowledge is based upon probability. In other words, the information she assumed to be factual actually had 90 to 95 percent probability of being true. We think everything we learned in high school is true; however, these findings are based upon samples of people and statistics. Rarely in criminology can something be proven. Instead, we just take a body of evidence in support of a finding and come to the conclusion that something is true. This chapter will provide an overview and introduction to concepts discussed in this text.

IDENTIFYING A PROBLEM

How does one begin doing research? First, you need to evaluate the circumstances surrounding you (e.g., access to data) and your area of interest. These two things may coincide, or they may directly conflict. For instance, your employer may ask you to conduct research in an area that you are not at all interested, but the data is readily available. Alternatively, you may wish to answer an interesting **research question**, but you may be unable to find a suitable data source. Hopefully, access and interest will coincide for you to make research a rewarding and entertaining process.

You may stumble across an idea for a research project in several ways. You may be employed in a private corporation seeking to use your own data to answer specific questions. You may be interested in evaluating whether or not some government or organization policy is working. Finally, in more and more fields, the research priorities of researchers reflect the research priorities of the funding agencies. This is because research funding is often required before a research study can be initiated. Research is an expensive endeavor, and very few criminal justice agencies have adequate funds to conduct research on their own. Particularly in criminal justice agencies and universities, a research project cannot be initiated without external funding, making research priorities of the funding agencies (Office of Juvenile Justice and Delinquency Prevention, National Institute of Justice) central to devising research studies.

Once we have identified a broad area of interest (e.g., social media in policing), we must narrow down specific hypotheses. We will search the literature extensively to find all research that has been conducted to evaluate the utilization and effectiveness of social media in policing. This is commonly called the **literature review**. We will seek to make ourselves an expert in the field. We will look for gaps in the research that has already been conducted. We will see which questions we can answer that are left unanswered by the existing research. We will see if our data are better (e.g., more representative of the population, have better measurement of key concepts) than the data collected for the previous work (Green, Johnson, & Adams, 2006). If we have data that is different in some way from what has been used previously, we may seek to **replicate** the work that has already been done. In addition to replication, we must build on the findings in some way. Therefore, identifying a gap in the literature is the primary step in narrowing down an interest area to a hypothesis.

The literature review is conducted using various methods. We should be thankful that the overwhelming majority of the scientific research literature is available online, and we have no longer have need to track down each article manually in a library. Instead, we are able to access tens of thousands of scientific articles using major databases, such as EBSCOhost, Web of Science, Criminal Justice Abstracts, and Google Scholar. These databases will retrieve the exact article (in a PDF format) that is physically printed in a journal. Because the paper copies of journals are becoming obsolete, many publishers are using online-only formats. Regardless of the format, the opportunity for an exhaustive literature search lies at your fingertips, and there is no longer an excuse for a less-than-thorough literature review.

HYPOTHESIS DEVELOPMENT AND TESTING

The majority of scientific inquiry is driven by **hypothesis** (with the exception of exploratory qualitative research, as we will describe later in the text). This means we need to have some evidence (or reason to believe) that a cause is resulting in a given effect before we can initiate a study. These are specific, testable, and directional in nature. Hypotheses are generated using **theories**, or testable explanations, of criminal behavior. In most cases, we wouldn't set out with a broad research question, or a broad nondirectional question, such as, "What causes crime?" Instead, we might test the hypothesis that elementary-school-aged children who are friends with delinquent peers are more likely to be violent offenders in high school than are those without friends who are delinquent peers. This is based upon our working knowledge of social learning theory. It has a given direction (more likely to be violent) that fits with our knowledge of this theory, and it has the potential to be rejected.

Research questions, on the other hand, do not have the potential for rejection. Using a research question to assess the same behavior, we might ask, "What behavior in elementary school is associated with violent behavior in high school?" This does not imply any directionality, and it is not clear exactly which early behavior we are looking for. Using this research question, we might find that elementary-school students with lower grades are more likely than those with better grades to be violent in high school. These research questions are used in exploratory studies when no theoretical guidance is available. Therefore, research questions and hypotheses are used in different settings and for different purposes. In most criminological research, we have a theoretical explanation for behavior. All hypotheses should be guided by these established theories.

There are two possible outcomes in any given study: A hypothesis may be rejected or we may fail to reject a hypothesis. When we are testing a hypothesis, we assume that there is no difference or association between the variables (i.e., a cause measure and an effect measure) that we are evaluating. This is referred to as the **null hypothesis** (there is no relationship between delinquent peers and high school delinquency). If, after our statistical analysis, we find that there is a difference, the null hypothesis is rejected in favor of the **alternative hypothesis** (there is a relationship between delinquent peers and high school delinquency). The **test statistic** from the statistical analysis will tell us the magnitude and direction of the relationship (positive or negative, delinquent peers are positively/negatively associated with violence in high school). This directionality may be reflected in the alternative hypothesis, but this is not always necessary.

SCIENTIFIC LANGUAGE

As you may have noticed already, there is a specialized language used in research that is distinct from most Americans' vocabularies. The language of research is often called **researchese**. For instance, the distinction between **causation** and **correlation** may seem artificial and unimportant to you at the moment. However, the differences in the meaning and interpretation of these concepts are tremendous in researchese (Lee, 2012). If someone said that two variables were correlated, we do not know which one comes first, if the association is due to an unmeasured third variable, or if the cause is present every time the effect is present. These things are entirely unknown when we discuss correlation. When we discuss causation, however, we understand that variable A *always* comes before B. We also know that the relationship is not **spurious**, or due to any other variable that may be associated with A or B. Finally, we must have demonstrated that B is present whenever A is present. Clearly, the criterion for causation is much stronger than that for correlation. Therefore, as students of research methods, we should be able to interpret a study that differentiates between "water bottles cause cancer" and "water bottles are correlated with cancer." Clearly, the national media frequently misinterprets these correlations as causes. Because you are in this class, you will not make the same mistake.

In this introduction, we will discuss a few terms that are important to understand before we begin a more in-depth discussion of research methods.

Variables

In order for us to examine a relationship between two things, we must first have measures of those two things (Hausman, 2001). These measures are known as **variables**, and they are the basic building blocks of any research project. If we want to measure association with delinquent peers and high school delinquency, we must first find out from elementary-school-aged children how many of their friends engage in activities that we consider delinquent (variable A, or cause). Then we must assess violence and delinquency in high school, either by administering a questionnaire or using juvenile justice or school records (variable B, or effect). If we are missing either measure (variable), we could not answer these questions.

Operationalization

There are several ways to measure a variable. To measure variable B from our example above, we could have passed out a survey and asked high schoolers about their delinquent behaviors. Alternatively, we could have looked for official records of behavior. There are pros and cons associated with each type of measure. However, the way that we choose to measure a variable is known as its **operationalization** (Wolfe, 1994). In describing the research method, we might say something like, "We operationalized delinquency as the self-reported engagement in at least one of the following seven criminal and status offenses. . . . "

Aggregation

Researchers rarely speak in certainties, even when a causal relationship between two variables is present. Instead, researchers speak in probabilities. A researcher (or consumer of research) should never attribute research findings that are based on a group of people to a single person who participates in that behavior. For example, we know that smoking cigarettes causes cancer. Although we can encourage people not to smoke, we cannot tell one person that they need to quit smoking or they will develop lung cancer. We all have stories of Great-Aunt Martha who smoked two packs of cigarettes per day for 80 years and died from a fall, not lung cancer. Instead, we could say something like, "Smoking two packs a day increases your risk of lung cancer by 1,000 percent." This does not directly affect an individual; rather, it affects a population. The findings do not tell us what will happen to each individual person.

This is known as being reported in the **aggregate** (or large population from which the findings were derived), compared to the individual level (each person who is a member of the population) (Ramanathan & Ganesh, 1994).

Qualitative and Quantitative Research

There are two umbrella terms describing two distinct methods of research. In criminal justice, quantitative research is used most commonly (Tewksbury, 2009). These methods seek to quantify criminal behavior, code **predictors**, and statistically determine a relationship between variable A and variable B. All research that generates a numeric **effect size**—or the strength of the relationship—is quantitative (Kotrlik, Williams, & Khata, 2011). Quantitative research provides us the opportunity to assess precisely how much risk is associated with a behavior that we think is associated with criminal behavior. For instance, we might say that an elementary student who has more than one delinquent friend is 40 percent more likely than those with no delinquent friends to be violent in high school. This *quantifies* the extent of the relationship between variables A and B.

Qualitative research, on the other hand, enhances the depth of the information that we can obtain about a given subject. If we wanted to conduct a qualitative study about the same behavior, we could identify people who are violent in high school and people who are not (Hawkins, McIntosh, Silver, & Holman, 2004). Then we could conduct an in-depth interview of both sets of youth, asking questions such as, "What do you think influenced your [criminal or violent] behavior?" or "Did anything happen in your early life that influenced your current behavior?" These questions are often free-flowing and lead in a general direction. They are sometimes developed beforehand; however, trained interviewers may **probe**, or ask follow-up questions, to investigate a single topic in greater depth if they believe it may provide insight (McKinnon, 1988). Specialized packages exist for managing analysis of qualitative research, but these samples are generally much smaller due to the large time commitment involved in long, in-depth interviews. Qualitative methods reveal the *depth* of information, while quantitative methods reveal the *width* of information. It is easy to find out a little bit about a wide variety of topics using a survey. Qualitative methods allow us to find out a lot of information about one specific topic. Given the complementary strengths of both methods, many funding agencies are giving priority to mixed-methods research, or projects that incorporate both qualitative and quantitative research methods (Johnson & Onwuegbuzie, 2004).

Participatory Research

There are several ways to refer to people who participate in our research studies. Historically, these people were referred to as *subjects*. The movement toward **community-based participatory research** recognizes that the people providing data in a study have needs and agendas just as the researchers do (Wallerstein & Duran, 2008). The use of the word *subjects* has made some research participants feel that the researcher is *subjecting* them to something, causing unnecessary anxiety and creating the impression that researchers do not care about the people who are participating in their studies. Community-driven research, on the other hand, ensures some benefit to the population of study participants. Regardless, people who participate in research are generally referred to as *participants* or *respondents* rather than *subjects*.

Induction/Deduction

One last terminology distinction is the difference between *induction* and *deduction*. These two methods allow us to reason about information in two different ways. **Inductive reasoning** moves from the specific to the general (Shye, 1988). In other words, we might take several specific findings—for example, about substance abuse among criminals (criminals tend to use marijuana, or incarcerated people, when not jailed, use alcohol more frequently than does the general population)—and we conclude from them that, say, substance use is associated with (or potentially causes) crime. Alternatively, **deductive reasoning** takes a top-down approach, first developing a theoretical explanation for a behavior, then operationalizing that behavior into specific variables, and finally testing whether the explanation is true in a selected sample (Rodriguez-Moreno & Hirsch, 2009).

Applying this type of reasoning, we might start by planning to test a particular theory emphasizing the role of risk behavior (including drug use) in increasing crime rates. We want to test this theory to see if drug use is really an important predictor of criminal behavior. A deductive investigation might start by finding a sample of criminal offenders and asking them specifically about their drug use in the past, which types of drugs they used, how often they were used, and so on. The results of this inquiry will either support the theory or provide evidence that does not support the theory.

These are two methods of developing a research question, and one is no better or worse than the other. Rather, they apply in different situations. Inductive reasoning is frequently used when data is readily available—for example, when your supervisor tells you to analyze a given set of already gathered data (Heit & Rotello, 2010). In such cases, we take specific findings from the data, and we attempt to generalize a conclusion from them. Alternatively, when no data is available, devising a theoretically important research question becomes necessary. Once the research question has been identified, a source of data must be identified that will allow us to examine our question: We must find specific items that measure the **constructs** of interest derived from our theory (Fornell & Larcker, 1981). This is a top-down approach.

SUMMARY

This chapter included a basic introduction to research methods in the field of criminal justice, focusing on the more prominent designs. We began by defining research methods, theories, and hypotheses to lay the foundation for research project development in criminal justice. We discussed an application of hypothesis development, correlation and causation, and hypothesis testing, using our example of delinquent peer association as a risk factor for violence among high school students. Several key terms and brief overviews of the research process were identified and discussed. The chapter concluded with a discussion of the different types of research methods utilized in the field of criminology and criminal justice. The concepts of quantitative (statistically based research) and qualitative (more in-depth research) methods were discussed, and the importance of mixed-methods research (research designs involving both qualitative and quantitative methods) and community-based participatory research was detailed.

KEY TERMS

Aggregate   A collection of items (in this case research items) gathered to form a total quantity, rather than individual responses reported specifically (e.g., the completion rate for a course may aggregate data from several terms).

Alternative hypothesis   The opposite of the null hypothesis, the *alternative hypothesis* indicates the idea or possibility that an observed effect between variables or phenomena is real and not occurring due to chance alone.

Causation   The notion that events occur in a predictable manner and that one event leads to or is caused by another event. To infer causation, we must be sure that the variables are statistically associated, are ordered properly in time, and that all possible other causes are ruled out.

Community-based participatory research   Research conducted cooperatively between the community and experts in the field, with the community participating fully in all aspects of the research process.

Construct   A concept, model, or schematic idea established in a theory and examined through research.

Correlation   A functional or qualitative correspondence between two items, or a statistical statement that two variables are related to each other.

Deduction/Deductive reasoning   Thinking about a research question from a stated premise to a conclusion—that is, reasoning from the general to the specific.

Effect size   The measure of the strength of the relationship between two variables in a population.

Evidence-based practices   Interdisciplinary approaches to clinical practice. Evidence-based practice requires that applications or use of programs in practice be based on scientifically sound research.

Hypothesis   A tentative explanation for an observation, phenomenon, or scientific problem.

Induction/Inductive reasoning   A way of thinking about a research question that represents the process of deriving general principles (general information) from particular facts or instances (specific information).

Literature review   A researcher's examination of a body of texts intended to thoroughly review the knowledge on a specific topic. This review of the literature includes substantive findings, as well as theoretical and methodological contributions to a particular topic.

Null hypothesis   The general or default research hypothesis indicating that no relationship exists between two measured phenomena or that a potential treatment has no effect.

Operationalization   Represents the process of defining a concept for the purpose of making the concept measurable and understandable in terms of empirical observation.

Predictor   Measures risk factors, or explanatory variables, for the dependent variable (e.g., crime).

Probe   Indicates the interviewing approach that prods respondents with follow-up comments or questions to dig deeper into their experiences and to elicit more depth and detail in their responses.

Replication   As a primary principle of the scientific method, *replication* of a finding or an experiment verifies or expands upon the results of a previous study.

Researchese   The specific language, terminology, and way of talking and writing used by researchers and the research community.

Research methods   The toolbox of processes used to collect information and data for the purposes of obtaining scientifically sound results.

Research question   The methodological point of departure in scholarly research, the broad question that a researcher is seeking to answer during a research study.

Spurious   A false or factitious claim.

Test statistic   A numerical value that summarizes the information contained in the sample data, which is the primary basis for testing a given hypothesis.

Theory   A set of statements or principles devised to explain a group of facts or phenomena that have typically been widely tested and accepted.

Variable   A condition that is subject to change—specifically, a characteristic that is allowed to vary during a scientific experiment to test a hypothesis.

REVIEW QUESTIONS

1. What is the difference between deductive and inductive reasoning? Provide an example of a situation in which deductive reasoning would be more useful and one in which inductive reasoning would be preferable.

2. Define *community-based participatory research*. Provide an example of when this type of research would be good to use.
3. What is aggregation? Give an example from criminology of an appropriate use of aggregation in research.
4. What does the term *operationalization* mean in research? Provide an example.
5. What is the difference between hypothesis testing and theory? How do these two terms relate to each other?

Useful Websites

www.socialresearchmethods.net/. Website dedicated to research methods in social science research.

https://wrds-web.wharton.upenn.edu/wrds/. The Wharton Research Data Services website is a well-known tool for global research.

www.research.gov/research-portal/appmanager/base/desktop?_nfpb=true&_page Label=research_page_who_We_Are. Research website from the National Science Foundation.

http://obssr.od.nih.gov/scientific_areas/methodology/community_based_ participatory_research/index.aspx. Information on community-based participatory research from National Institutes of Health.

www.youtube.com/watch?v=6dVQra1Ea4k. A YouTube video taking a humorous look at deductive and inductive reasoning.

References

Fornell, C., & Larcker, D. F. (1981). Evaluating structural equation models with unobservable variables and measurement error. *Journal of Marketing Research, 17*, 39–50.

Green, B. N., Johnson, C. D., & Adams, A. (2006). Writing narrative literature reviews for peer-reviewed journals: Secrets of the trade. *Journal of Chiropractic Medicine, 5*(3), 101–117.

Hausman, J. (2001). Mismeasured variables in econometric analysis: Problems from the right and problems from the left. *Journal of Economic Perspectives, 15*(4), 57–67.

Hawkins, N. A., McIntosh, D. N., Silver, R. C., & Holman, E. A. (2004). Early responses to school violence: A qualitative analysis of students' and parents' immediate reactions to the shootings at Columbine High School. *Journal of Emotional Abuse, 4*(3/4), 197–223.

Heit, E., & Rotello, C. M. (2010). Relations between inductive and deductive reasoning. *Journal of Experimental Psychology: Learning, Memory, and Cognition, 36*(3), 805–812.

Johnson, R. B., & Onwuegbuzie, A. J. (2004). Mixed methods research: A research paradigm whose time has come. *Educational Researcher, 33*(7), 14–26.

Kotrlik, J. W., Williams, H. A., & Khata, J. M. (2011). Reporting and interpreting effect size in quantitative agricultural education research. *Journal of Agricultural Education, 52*(1), 132–142.

Lee, J. J. (2012). Correlation and causation in the study of personality. *European Journal of Personality, 26*(4), 372–390.

McKinnon, J. (1988). Reliability and validity in field research: Some strategies and tactics. *Accounting, Auditing, and Accountability, 1*(1), 34–54.

Ramanathan, R., & Ganesh, L. S. (1994). Group preference aggregation employed in AHP: An evaluation and an intrinsic process for deriving members' weightages. *European Journal of Operational Research, 79*(2), 249-265.

Rodriguez-Moreno, D., & Hirsch, J. (2009). The dynamics of deductive reasoning: An FMRI investigation. *Neuropsychologia, 47*(4), 949–961.

Rynes, S. L., Bartunek, J. M., & Daft, R. L. (2001). Across the great divide: Knowledge creation and transfer between practitioners and academics. *Academy of Management Journal, 44*(2), 340–355.

Shye, S. (1988). Inductive and deductive reasoning: A structural reanalysis of ability tests. *Journal of Applied Psychology, 73*(2), 308–311.

Tewksbury, R. (2009). Qualitative vs. quantitative methods: Understanding why qualitative methods are superior for criminology and criminal justice. *Journal of Theoretical and Philosophical Criminology, 1*(1), 38–58.

Wallerstein, N., & Duran, B. (2008). The theoretical, historical, and practice roots of CBPR. In *Community-based participatory research for health: From process to outcomes* (pp. 25–46). San Francisco: Wiley.

Wolfe, R. A. (1994). Organizational innovation: Review, critique, and suggested research directions. *Journal of Management Studies, 31*(3), 405–431.

ETHICS IN SCIENTIFIC RESEARCH

R esearch in criminology and criminal justice is conducted with a theoretical and empirical focus on the causes of, explanations for, and consequences of criminal behavior. Many studies are conducted in
residential settings (such as a jail or prison), and this presents several
fundamental problems in the ethical conduct of research (Byrne, 2005).
Because incarcerated persons are especially susceptible to exploitation and
abuse by researchers compared to the average research participant, they are
known as a **vulnerable population** (Code of Federal Regulations, Title 45,
Part 46; Pont, 2008). For instance, an inmate has little to benefit from participating in a survey conducted among prisoners at their institution, as payments
and amenities are not normally provided as an incentive for participation. The
prisoners may also feel that participating in the survey may help them be
released early (Cumberland & Zamble, 1992), when in reality research participation does not influence their "good time." The historical discussion below
further illustrates the processes in place to prevent exploitation and explains
why exploitation of research participants is problematic.

THE HISTORY OF CONCERN OVER THE ETHICAL TREATMENT OF PRISONERS

Let's imagine that you are incarcerated in a federal prison after being arrested
for a drug-related offense. You have completed just 1 year of your 5.5-year
sentence, and you are tired of the daily prison routine. You would do anything
to be released early, even if only 1 or 2 days. You have accumulated some good
time, but you still have over 3 years until your release date. A situation then
presents in which the people who are in charge of the jail talk to you about an
opportunity to participate in research. These administrators are people you
don't know, who seem to have power in the institution. They want to talk
to you about your experiences that were related to your most recent arrest.
If you tell these people that you do not want to talk to them, do you think
they may make note of this noncompliance in your record? To you, this
could mean that you may wind up staying in jail longer. These people mention
that saying no would not change the length of your sentence, but do you trust

them? As you can see, this presents a clear dilemma in which incarcerated people may be convinced to participate in research under false pretenses (e.g., the illusion that they may be released early). This problem is further illustrated in the discussion below.

The Stanford Prison Experiment

The Stanford Prison Experiment (Zimbardo, 1971) was originally intended to understand the psychological consequences of becoming a prisoner or correctional officer (called *prison guards* at the time). To do this, a "prison" was created on the campus of Stanford University, in the basement of the psychology building. Advertisements were placed in newspapers and more than 70 students applied to participate in this research opportunity. Each applicant was given a thorough psychological examination, and any applicants with a history of criminal behavior, drug use, or psychological or medical disability were excluded from participating, ensuring that the "best and the brightest" of college students comprised the sample. These exclusions resulted in a final sample of 24 well-adjusted, middle-class male students from universities all over the country and Canada, who happened to be in the Stanford area at the time of the study. Each participant was offered an **incentive**—payments of $15 per day as remuneration for incarceration in this pseudo-jail.

Each participant was assigned to be either a guard or a prisoner by the flip of a coin. Prisoners were stripped, searched, issued a uniform, and assigned a number. Guards were not trained; rather, they were instructed to do whatever was necessary to maintain order within the institution. Guards wore sunglasses to promote their anonymity and were issued uniforms and police-grade nightsticks. Prisoners were woken up at night for "counts," and physical repercussions were imposed on prisoners who broke rules (e.g., talking back to a prison guard was punishable by having the inmate do push-ups and calisthenics).

After only 1 day of incarceration, the prisoners revolted. They barricaded themselves inside their cells, cursed at the guards, and removed their prisoner ID numbers (Zimbardo, 2007). The guards used a fire extinguisher to back the prisoners away from the doors of their cells, and they stripped, harassed, and placed the inmates in solitary confinement. The guards began using psychological tactics to control the inmates, by allowing those who were not involved in the rebellion to be clothed again and have some special privileges instituted. The guards' behavior became more and more coercive and controlling, until push-up sessions lasted hours. Each prisoner was offered three bland meals and the opportunity to use the toilet three times each day. In less than 36 hours after the study began, the first prisoner was released due to major emotional disturbances, crying, and rage.

During this experiment, brief questionnaires were administered to evaluate the emotional and behavioral changes of guards and inmates as a result of their incarceration. The initial study was intended to last 2 weeks; however, it was terminated after only 6 days due to the "unexpectedly intense reactions" of the participants (Haney, Banks, & Zimbardo, 1973:88).

The purpose of this study was to examine whether it was the structure and nature of the prison itself that was dehumanizing and brutal, or whether this was caused by the types of people who work in and are incarcerated in prisons. In this case, it was immediately apparent that the prison environment could transform well-adjusted college students into abusive and brutal guards and could cause serious psychological harm in a short amount of time to inmates. The prisons themselves were the problem, not the inmates or the guards.

This experiment illustrates several concepts in the responsible conduct of research. First, participants did not give formal **informed consent** before the research was conducted. This document would have provided prospective research participants a summary of the purpose of the research and a list of prospective benefits and potential harm that may result from participation in the study (Cahana & Hurst, 2008). Even if the authors had informed the participants about the potential harms, they may not have foreseen the severe emotional distress that occurred as a result of incarceration in this pseudo-prison. Today, all participants would be required to sign a document (or verbally consent, in some cases) indicating a full understanding of all the study's potential ramifications and benefits.

Second, the behavior of the guards was not controlled. The guards during the study were given no training or guidance on how to act as prison guards and maintain order in the facility. Their behavior became more abusive, manipulative, and controlling throughout the study. The researchers did not attempt to control the guards' behavior. Finally, participants in a research study must be afforded the opportunity to cease participation at any point. The first participant was dismissed from the research after *severe* emotional distress was observed, and participants were not led to believe that participation was voluntary. The investigators halted the research earlier than expected due to their observations of deleterious behavior. These ethical predicaments, in part, resulted in the development of formal guidelines detailing appropriate characteristics and requirements for ethical research.

The Belmont Report

On July 12, 1974, the National Research Act (Pub. L. 93-348) was codified, creating a commission charged with creating guidelines that outline ethical human subjects research. The commission (named the National Commission for the Protection of Human Subjects of Biomedical and Behavioral Research) was intended to consider four ethical domains: (1) the distinction between routine practice and research (e.g., at what point is a new community policing model considered research and when is it routine practice?); (2) the role of the risk-benefit ratio to the participants in research (e.g., how important is it that those who participate in research gain something from the experience in comparison to the risk that is undertaken?); (3) guidelines for the selection of research participants (e.g., women, juveniles, prisoners, etc.); and (4) the nature and extent of informed consent in various research settings. This final report was known as the **Belmont Report** (National Commission for the Protection of Human Subjects of Biomedical and Behavioral Research, 1979).

To distinguish research and practice, this report stated that *practice* refers to interventions developed for the purpose of benefiting the participant, client, or citizen, with reasonable expectation of success. Conversely, *research* tests a hypothesis and contributes to knowledge. To illustrate, a police chief might implement a drug prevention program in his city school district to reduce drug use. The purpose of this program is to help students say no to drugs, which directly benefits the students. Therefore, this would be considered practice. If, instead, the chief decides to implement the program in comparison with another program implemented in a different school to see which one is better at reducing drug use, this would be considered research.

The Belmont Report also dictated three basic ethical principles that should guide all research: respect for persons, beneficence, and justice. *Respect* for persons dictates that individuals must elect to participate in research, and participation may not be coerced in any way. Those with limited capacity (e.g., mentally handicapped) to make decisions are afforded additional protections from exploitation. *Beneficence* asserts that research should reduce or eliminate the harms associated with research and increase the benefits whenever possible. Finally, *justice* requires that the benefits and burdens of participation in research should be equally distributed across all participants.

These principles led to the processes of informed consent, or the ability for persons to choose what they will and will not allow to happen to them during the course of research; the assessment of risks in relation to benefits of the research from the participants' standpoint; and fairness in selection of research participants (e.g., researchers cannot systematically exclude one particular race or age group without justifiable cause). This report has led to the creation of a code of professional ethics and **institutional review boards** at all research enterprises.

CODES OF PROFESSIONAL ETHICS

There are several formalized codes of professional ethics, including those issued by the American Psychological Association (2002) and the American Sociological Association (1999). Specific to criminal justice, the Academy of Criminal Justice Sciences (ACJS) and the American Society of Criminology (ASC) share a common code of ethics, adapted from the American Sociological Association code. The code states that "[criminal justice researchers and practitioners will] not knowingly place the well-being of themselves or other people in jeopardy in their professional work" (ACJS, 2000).

For researchers, the ACJS (2000) details 22 specific ethical guidelines:

1. Members should adhere to the highest possible technical standards in conducting their research.
2. Researchers should acknowledge the limitations of their work.
3. Research findings should be presented fully, without bias toward significant or against unexpected findings.
4. Members should disclose financial conflicts of interest and sponsors of their research.
5. Members should not make commitments to persons, groups, or organizations without the intent on following through with the commitments.
6. Whenever possible, after full analysis has been completed, raw data should be made available to other scientists at a reasonable cost, except when confidentiality or privacy may be violated.
7. Scales and measures used in the course of research should be adequately cited.
8. Members should not accept grants, contracts, or research assignments that may violate the principles detailed in this code of ethics, and if a violation is suspected, the relationship or agreement should be terminated.
9. When financial support for a project has been accepted, the researcher should make an effort to complete the proposed work.
10. When a member is collaborating on a project, the division of labor, compensation, access to data, and authorship should be clearly delineated at the onset of the project. If these roles change throughout the course of the project, these modifications should be known and understood by all collaborators.
11. Members have the right to disseminate the results of their research, except when the findings are likely to cause harm (e.g., in the case of a confidentiality breach).
12. Members of the Academy will not misuse their position for the purposes of gathering information about others, organizations, or government.
13. Human subjects (i.e., research participants) have the right to understand the purpose of the research project in which they are participating as soon as it is appropriate. Participants should be informed about any aspect of the process that may influence their desire to participate, including risks, discomfort, or any unpleasant experiences.
14. Research participants have the right to confidentiality unless it is waived (confidentiality will be discussed more thoroughly below).
15. Information about research participants that is public record cannot be protected by guarantees of confidentiality or privacy.

16. Respondents may not be exposed to greater than minimal harm as a result of the research, and informed consent will be obtained when risks are greater than that encountered in daily life.
17. Culturally appropriate steps should be taken to secure informed consent and avoid privacy invasion, when necessary.
18. Researchers should anticipate privacy threats and take all steps necessary to avoid these threats.
19. Information provided by research respondents should be treated as confidential by research staff.
20. Members should recognize and respect a collaborators' need for anonymity on a research project.
21. All research conducted should meet the ethical requirements of the funding agency; however, study design and data collection should respect general protections of human rights regardless of funding.
22. Members should comply with federal and institutional guidelines pertaining to the conduct of their research.

These guidelines clearly dictate general ethical guidelines for research in criminology and criminal justice for members of ACJS. In addition to professional codes of conduct, colleges and universities generally have their own codes of ethics, and researchers must comply with all standards imposed upon them. Failure to comply with professional codes of ethics may result in termination of employment, retraction of research, and/or termination of membership in professional organizations. Codes of research conduct are generally reviewed and policed by each university's institutional review board (IRB).

THE INSTITUTIONAL REVIEW BOARD

The concept of the IRB was created by the Code of Federal Regulations (Title 45, Part 46). All government and nongovernmental agencies (including colleges and universities) that conduct research involving human subjects must create a review board known as the IRB. These IRBs have two purposes: (1) to create an unbiased pool of reviewers who will determine whether the risk to study participants is reasonable considering the possible benefits and (2) to assess whether the procedures used in the study adequately protect the confidentiality, safety, and welfare of participants.

Responsibilities of the IRB

Before a researcher can begin a study, it must be approved by the institution's IRB (or an independent IRB, as many private for-profit IRBs have emerged in recent years). The IRB will review several aspects of the research project.

Anonymity and Confidentiality.   Protection of research subjects' anonymity and/or confidentiality is a central concern of the IRB. When a researcher assures participants that responses are **confidential**, they will not reveal the responses to anyone. For instance, if a researcher is collecting self-reported data on a juvenile's criminal history and illegal drug use, the researchers must be certain that this information will not be leaked to parents, a school, or the police.

There are several ways to ensure confidentiality. The first option is for the survey to be **anonymous**, meaning that the participant's name (or any other identifying information) is not attached to the survey. Instead, surveys may be labeled using a number and all other identifying information deleted from study records. Using this method, no one will be able to determine whether any specific survey response belongs to any individual participant. If the purpose of the research makes anonymous responses impractical (e.g., the same respondents will be re-surveyed 1 month later and the two surveys linked together), it is still possible to maintain the confidentiality of research participants. In such cases, names, addresses, and other identifiers should be disassociated from the survey as soon as possible. Following the second interview with respondents, researchers can link the two surveys with a number instead of a name, thus protecting participants' confidentiality.

If the information required for participation in research is especially sensitive (as in the case of illegal drug use or addiction), a **certificate of confidentiality** may be obtained from the federal government. This certificate prevents anyone, even by subpoena, from obtaining the results of a person's confidential information provided in a survey (Earley & Strong, 1995). This assurance may help respondents feel better about providing researchers with the truth, rather than inaccurately reporting behavior in fear of getting in trouble.

Deceiving Participants.   An IRB will also review the appropriateness of deception in research. In most cases, it is unethical to give participants inaccurate information about the purposes of the research trial; however, there are some instances when this may be acceptable (Miller & Kaptchuk, 2008). For instance, Widom, Weiler, and Cottler (1999) collected data using a sample of child abuse victims several years after their cases were concluded in court. They were specifically interested in whether victims of child abuse were more likely than those who were not abused to use illicit drugs; however, they could not inform the participants that this was the purpose of the study for fear of inaccurate responses. Instead, they explained that the study was to collect information on human development. Although this may seem unethical, when the risks are limited and deception is necessary for the purposes of the research project, minimal deception may be deemed acceptable by the IRB.

Voluntary Participation.   The IRB will make sure that an informed consent document is read and understood by all research participants (or their parents, if under the age of 18). For participation to be voluntary, potential participants must be cognitively able to understand the purpose of the research project, the harms and benefits associated with their participation, and any procedures that will be used. They must also understand that they are free to leave the study at any point, and contact information for the IRB should be made available. Use of children in research (less than 18 years) provides a unique example of consent, as parental consent is required for participation. In special circumstances, only parental assent may be required, in which cases parents must be notified of the study and may elect to exclude their child from participating in the research (Fletcher & Hunter, 2003).

All permission to participate in research must be either **active consent** or **passive consent**. Active consent requires that respondents directly affirm that they understand the research project, the harms and benefits, and the procedures. They must sign and date a physical informed consent document to "opt in" to the study. Passive consent requires participants to "opt out" of a study (Range, Embry, & MacLeod, 2001). For instance, in a classroom, a survey may be passed out to all students with the informed consent document printed on the first page of the survey. The students are instructed to read the informed consent and sign if they agree to participate in the survey. This is an example of active consent. In the same classroom, students may receive a letter the week before the survey will be administered. This letter will detail the purpose of the research and other required information, and it will let students know that consent is inferred by completing the survey. If they do not care to participate in the research, they may either opt out or not complete the survey on the day it is administered. Generally, the active consent procedures are more widely used in research settings and are more likely to be approved by IRBs (Esbensen et al., 1996).

Vulnerable Populations.   In criminal justice research, juveniles and prisoners, referred to as **vulnerable populations**, are afforded special provisions to ensure that they are protected from exploitation (Thompson & Spacapan, 1991). As noted above, in most cases, parental consent is required for juveniles to participate in research. Prisoners are protected because they have been historically exploited in biomedical research (Mitford, 1973), resulting in serious harm or even death. To protect the rights of prisoners, the Department of Health and Human Services required that prisoners must not be subjected to greater harms than the general population. Prisoners are also protected from coercion, and the informed consent document must detail that participation in research will not influence a prisoner's parole, privileges, or work release assignment. When a research proposal involving prisoners (or another incarcerated population) is reviewed by the IRB, a prisoner or prisoner representative is required to be present at the meeting (Carnahan & McFarland, 2007). This process ensures that the research project will not unnecessarily exploit prisoners or expose them to excessive harms.

Incentives.   Incentives are payments (monetary or nonmonetary) made to a research participant for one of two purposes: to remunerate (pay) them for the time and effort it takes to participate in the research or to increase the likelihood that they will participate. These payments may be in the form of cash, a gift card, a lottery for a prize or money, or some other tangible item (Harhoff, 1996). The IRB will review the incentives to ensure that they are not excessive given the amount of effort required to participate in the research, as this may indicate some degree of coercion.

Additional Concerns Regarding IRBs

Some research does not need to be reviewed by the IRB and is considered exempt from review. For instance, when the information being used for research is already public record, or the information has already been collected, the risk to subjects is minimal. In these cases, a less intensive IRB application may be completed in which the researchers must demonstrate that they have either anonymous or confidential information to be analyzed for a new purpose. They must justify that the harms are minimal and there is no threat of a confidentiality breach. One method of protecting confidentiality is by reporting aggregated responses only. By using this method, the results of all participants who completed surveys will be pooled, and no information from one particular participant will be reported. It is possible that one behavior is so rare that someone could potentially be identified due to its rarity. Referring to participants only in the aggregate protects the whole sample from identification. In addition, research conducted for educational purposes (cognitive or aptitude testing) is generally exempt from review by the full IRB board. However, for studies that propose direct data collection, sampling, and informed consent, a review by the full IRB board must be conducted.

It is worth noting that most large universities have several IRBs (Klitzman, 2011), and depending on the topic, criminological research may fall under more than one IRB. For instance, some large research universities with a medical center will have a health science IRB and a traditional social science IRB. If a criminologist is interested in collecting genetic data from a population to see if a particular gene is related to offending, this project may be referred to the health science IRB for review rather than the social science IRB (Nygaard, 1997). In many cases, these IRB applications for review comprise hundreds of pages of paperwork before data collection may be initiated.

APPLICATIONS: ETHICAL EXAMPLES AND WHAT WENT WRONG

Josef Mengele

During World War II, Josef Mengele performed medical procedures on prisoners of war. These prisoners were infected with disease, injected with untested medications, poisoned, and exposed to extreme temperatures in the name of science (Katz, 1972). After the war, the Nuremberg Code was developed to govern the rights of human subjects in research, including the concept of "voluntary" participation (*Permissible Medical Experiments*, October 1946–April 1949).

Tuskegee Syphilis Study

In Alabama, a study was conducted among black male sharecroppers to understand the natural history of syphilis (Brandt, 1978). Approximately midway through the study, penicillin was discovered as a cure for this disease; however, the medication was purposely withheld from participants in the study. The participants were told that they were treated for "bad blood," and between 28 and 100 men died as a result of their untreated syphilis (Final Report of the Tuskegee Syphilis Study Legacy Committee, 1996). Informed consent was not obtained, and for 40 years participants were deceived as to the purpose of the study.

University of California Schizophrenia Study

In a study conducted at the University of California, youth diagnosed with schizophrenia were taken off their medication. This resulted in cases of severe violence, confusion, poor school performance, and one suicide. This case is the result of inappropriate protections for vulnerable populations (e.g., poor, mentally ill youth).

SUMMARY

In this chapter, we discussed the ethical problems that are unique to criminal justice research, including the potential for coercion among incarcerated or institutionalized research participants. We then provided key examples of ethical violations, including the Stanford Prison Experiment, Tuskegee, and the Nazi World War II scientific trials. In an attempt to prevent further exploitation of research participants, the Belmont Report was codified. Specifically, the report dictates the three basic ethical principles guiding all research: respect of persons, beneficence, and justice. The professional ethics statement for the Academy of Criminal Justice Sciences was detailed, and the structure and function of the institutional review board was discussed.

KEY TERMS

Active consent Requires the participant to directly acknowledge (via signature) the purpose of the research study, any harms and benefits associated with their participation, and their role in the research.

Anonymous   Keeping a person's identity unknown and their personal information personally unidentifiable and publicly unknown.

Belmont Report   The purpose of the September 1978 report was and still is to protect research participants and subjects in clinical trials and research studies involving ethics and health care research. This report consists of three principles: respect for persons, justice, and beneficence.

Certificate of confidentiality   A legal document issued to researchers by federal agencies for the purpose of protecting the privacy and welfare of subjects. The release of identifiable information and sensitive information about subjects who are participating in a research project is prohibited with this certificate.

Confidential   Research results or data that must remain privileged or secret.

Incentives   Anything that motivates an individual to participate in research. Incentives may take the form of cash, gift cards, or other compensation for participating in research.

Informed consent   The process in which research participants are informed of their role in a research study and the purpose of the research. Research participants must be informed of their role in a research study and the possible risks (and benefits) associated with participating in a given study.

Institutional review board   A committee that has been formally designated to approve, monitor, and review medical and behavioral research involving human subjects and participants.

Passive consent   Implies consent to participate in research. A signed refusal to participate in a study will retract consent. Otherwise, consent is assumed.

Voluntary participation   Refers to the information provided to research participants so that their participation is voluntary and that failure to participate in the study or withdraw will not result in any penalty or loss of benefits.

Vulnerable populations   Groups of people who are typically excluded, marginalized, or disadvantaged due to certain characteristics. These characteristics may include environmental, economic, social, or cultural characteristics. Women, children, and prisoners are examples of vulnerable populations.

REVIEW QUESTIONS

1. What were the primary findings from the Stanford Prison Experiment? Why would this type of research be prohibited in today's world?
2. What is informed consent? Please define the term and give an example of a research project involving informed consent. How would informed consent be used in this project?
3. What is the difference between active and passive consent? Please provide examples of research involving active consent and passive consent.
4. What is the purpose of the institutional review board? Are there any circumstances in research in which IRB approval is not necessary?

5. What is the purpose of professional ethical codes, such as those made by the American Sociological Association? Please provide details with your answer.

Useful Websites

www.asanet.org. The official website of the American Sociological Association.

www.research.usf.edu/dric/hrpp/. Official website of the University of South Florida's institutional review board.

www.prisonexp.org. Official website of the Stanford Prison Experiment.

www.hhs.gov/ohrp/humansubjects/guidance/belmont.html. Online access to the Belmont Report from the Department of Health and Human Services.

http://grants.nih.gov/grants/policy/coc/. Online resource from National Institutes of Health (NIH) to obtain certificates of confidentiality.

References

Academy of Criminal Justice Sciences. (2000). Code of ethics. Retrieved on November 14, 2013 from www.acjs.org/pubs/167_671_2922.cfm.

American Psychological Association. (2002). *Ethical principles of psychologists and code of conduct.* Washington, DC: American Psychological Association.

American Sociological Association. (1999). *Code of ethics.* Washington, DC: American Psychological Association.

Brandt, A. M. (1978). Racism and research: the case of the Tuskegee syphilis study. *Hastings Center Report, 8*(6), 21-29.

Byrne, M. W. (2005). Conducting research as a visiting scientist in a women's prison. *Journal of Professional Nursing, 4,* 223–230.

Cahana, A., & Hurst, S. A. (2008). Voluntary informed consent in research and clinical care: An update. *Pain and Practice, 8*(6), 446–451.

Carnahan, T., & McFarland, S. (2007). Revisiting the Stanford prison experiment: Could participant self-selection have led to the cruelty? *Personal Social Psychological Bulletin, 33*(5), 603–614.

Code of Federal Regulations. (2009). Department of Health and Human Services. Retrieved from www.hhs.gov/ohrp/humansubjects/guidance/45cfr46 .html#subpartc.

Cumberland, J., & Zamble, E. (1992). General and specific measures of attitudes towards early release of criminal offenders. *Canadian Journal of Behavioural Science, 24*(4), 442–455.

Earley, C. L., & Strong, L. C. (1995). Certificates of confidentiality: A valuable tool for protecting genetic research. *American Journal of Human Genetics, 57*(3), 727–731.

Esbensen, F., Deschenes, E. P., Vogel, R. E., West, J., Arboit, K., & Harris, L. (1996). Active parental control in school based research: An examination of ethical and methodological issues. *Evaluation Review, 20*(6), 737–753.

Final Report of the Tuskegee Syphilis Study Legacy Committee—May 20, 1996. Retrieved from www.hsl.virginia.edu/historical/medical_history/bad_blood/ report.cm.

Fletcher, A. C., & Hunter, A. G. (2003). Strategies for obtaining parental consent to participate in research. *Family Relations, 52*(3), 216–221.

Haney, C., Banks, W. C., & Zimbardo, P. G. (1973). Interpersonal dynamics in a simulated prison. *International Journal of Criminology and Penology, 1*, 69–97.

Harhoff, D. (1996). Strategic spillovers and incentives for research and development. *Management Science, 42*(6), 907–925.

Katz, J. (1972). *Experimentation with human subjects.* New York: Russell Sage Foundation.

Klitzman, R. (2011). The myth of community differences as the cause of variations among IRBs. *AJOB Primary Research, 2*(2), 24–33.

Miller, F. G., & Kaptchuk, T. J. (2008). Deception of subjects in neuroscience: An ethical analysis. *Journal of Neuroscience, 28*(19), 4841–4843.

Mitford, J. (1973). *Kind and unusual punishment: The prison business.* New York: Random House.

National Commission for the Protection of Human Subjects of Biomedical and Behavioral Research (1979). The Belmont Report: Ethical Principles and Guidelines for the Protection of Human Subjects of Research. Washington, DC: US Department of Health, Education, and Welfare.

Nygaard, R. L. (1997). The ten commandments of behavioral genetic data and criminology. *Judges Journal, 36*(3), 59–64; 94–96.

Permissible Medical Experiments. Trials of war criminals before the Nuremberg military tribunals under control council law no. 10: Nuremberg October 1946–April 1949. Washington: U.S. Government Printing Office (n.d.), vol. 2, pp. 181–182.

Pont, J. (2008). Ethics in research involving prisoners. *International Journal of Prison Health, 4*(4), 184–197.

Range, L., Embry, T., & MacLeod, T. (2001). Active and passive consent: A comparison of actual research with children. *Ethical Human Social Services, 3*(1), 23–31.

Thompson, S. C., & Spacapan, S. (1991). Perceptions of control in vulnerable populations. *Journal of Social Issues, 47*(4), 1–21.

Widom, C. S., Weiler, B. L., & Cottler, L. B. (1999). Childhood victimization and drug abuse: A comparison of prospective and retrospective findings. *Journal of Consulting and Clinical Psychology, 67*, 867–880.

Zimbardo, P. G. (1971). The power and pathology of imprisonment. *Record.* (Serial No. 15, 1971-10-25). Hearings before Subcommittee No. 3, of the Committee on the Judiciary, House of Representatives, Ninety-Second Congress, *First Session on Corrections, Part II, Prisons, Prison Reform and Prisoner's Rights: California.* Washington, DC: U.S. Government Printing Office.

Zimbardo, P. G. (2007). Revisiting the Stanford prison experiment: A lesson in the power of a situation. *Chronicle of Higher Education, 53*(30), 1.

Zimbardo, P., Haney, C. W., Banks, C., & Jaffe, D. (1971). The Stanford prison experiment: A simulation study of the psychology of imprisonment. Retrieved from http://dams.stanford.edu/depts/spc/uarch/exhibits/spe/Narration.pdf.

3 MEASUREMENT AND INSTRUMENTATION

This chapter provides an in-depth look into the process by which crime can be conceptualized and operationalized, or measured. Furthermore, levels of measurement and scaling procedures are reviewed. The chapter concludes with a detailed discussion on the **instrumentation** components of crime measurement as it relates to the different types of *validity* and *reliability*.

CONCEPTUALIZATION AND OPERATIONALIZATION

Regardless of the source of crime data, a critical issue to be aware of when being a consumer of research or when producing research is the process of conceptualizing and operationalizing the variables that are measured and reported. The first step in measurement is to identify the concepts that are being used to represent mutually agreed upon mental images (LaFree & Kick, 1986). This is the process of **conceptualization**. For example, the word *crime* generates specific mental images for people when they hear it. Although the thoughts and images may vary for some people, where some may immediately think of murder or some may think of burglary, crime as a concept has a general and mutually agreed image associated with it.

Operationalization refers to the method of identifying specific question(s) that serve as indicators of the concepts that are being measured and determining how these concepts should be measured. For instance, if you are reading an article in the newspaper that states crime in your community is on the rise, then you need to have a critical eye for what the reporter is reporting as a crime. Once you give the article a closer look, you learn that the reporter is referring only to a rise in the number of arrests for open alcohol container violations on your local college campus. In this case, the concept of crime was operationalized as open alcohol container arrests, and after identifying this operationalization of the key concept of crime, you are likely less fearful or alarmed about the "crime wave" cited by the reporter. This so-called crime wave is merely related to an increasing number of underage college kids getting arrested for very minor forms of criminal behavior. In contrast, if the reporter had operationalized crime as an increase in the number of arrests for violent crime, the operationalization would likely be a cause for concern. These differences in operationalization account for many of the sensational headlines that constantly draw our attention to violence and crime in the popular media.

TYPES OF VARIABLES

In most criminological or criminal justice research, crime is considered a **dependent variable**. A dependent variable is the outcome variable in research or the variable that is assumed to depend on or be caused by another variable. The **independent variable** in research is the variable that is expected to cause or determine the dependent variable. Independent variables can come in two forms: **explanatory variable**, which is derived directly from an explicit theoretical or conceptual model, or **control variable**, which means they are being used to take other alternative explanations into account but are not of central importance or interest to the theory that is being tested or the research question.

Let's say you are interested in studying the relationship between impulsivity and crime. In this particular case, impulsivity would be your independent explanatory variable and crime would be your dependent variable. However, from reading through prior research, you know that even some antisocial and impulsive people may not always commit crime, especially when the opportunity does not exist. For instance, even an impulsive person sitting near the college dean is unlikely to light up a marijuana joint. Thus, it would be important for you to include opportunity as a control variable in your research because opportunity (or lack thereof) can serve as an alternative explanation for why people are committing or not committing crime beyond their impulsivity. Interestingly, while crime is generally referred to as a dependent variable, it can at times be an independent variable as well. An example of crime as an independent variable can be found in gang research. Individuals involved in crime at age 13 may become gang members at age 14; in such cases, crime is the independent variable assumed to influence the individual's decision to join a gang, while gang membership is the dependent variable (or outcome). Gang membership could also be considered an independent variable in a subsequent analysis measuring crime as the dependent variable among individuals at age 15: Criminal involvement at age 13 leads to gang membership at age 14, and joining a gang at age 14 leads to greater involvement in crime at age 15. In other words, the research question drives your selection of the independent and dependent variables.

Variables can be measured as qualitative or quantitative variables. **Qualitative variables** are usually designated as words or labels, and the differences between the categories cannot be expressed numerically. For instance, gang membership in the above example is a qualitative variable; either the individual reports having joined a gang (yes) or the individual reports not having joined a gang (no). In this case, there is no numerical difference between a yes or a no response; the difference is whether or not the individual has the label of a gang member. In contrast, **quantitative variables** are variables whose values are defined by numbers, and the differences between adjacent numbers or categories of number can be expressed numerically. In the above example, crime could be considered a quantitative variable, assuming it measures the number of arrests for crime. Relatedly, variables can either be **discrete measures**, meaning they have a relatively fixed set of values of categories (e.g., religion measured as Catholic, Protestant, or other), or they can be **continuous measures**, which have an infinite number of values and these values can be further divided into smaller increments.

LEVELS OF MEASUREMENT

The four main levels of measurement for variables, ordered here as the level providing the least amount of information to the level providing the most detailed data, are nominal, ordinal, interval, and ratio (detailed below). Regardless of the level of measurement, it is critical that the measures are exhaustive and mutually exclusive. **Exhaustive** measures classify every observation in the data. For example, if a survey question asked, "What is your race/ethnicity?" and provided only the response options "white" or "Hispanic," the survey results would not be a exhaustive, because black, Asian, biracial, and other respondents would not be classifiable. In addition, without a "biracial" or "multiracial" category, mixed-race individuals might check multiple response options to describe themselves. **Mutually exclusive** measures, on the other hand, classify every observation in the data in terms of only one attribute. For example, in the instance above describing racial/ethnic identity, we would want to be sure that each person could select only one option. This may include "biracial" rather than "Asian" and "African American." In this case, "biracial" provides for mutually exclusive response options, while selecting multiple responses does not satisfy this requirement.

Nominal measures represent the lowest level of measurement possible. **Nominal measures** merely offer names or labels for certain characteristics, and these names and labels indicate only a qualitative difference between the categories. The most common example of a nominal level measure is biological sex: male or female. Other examples found in some research include race measured as "white" or "nonwhite"; religion measured as "Catholic" or "non-Catholic"; and political affiliation measured as "Republican," "Democrat," or "Independent."

Ordinal measures are the second level of measurement; these variables indicate different attributes representing ordered levels of a variable and the different attributes/categories, which *must* be able to be logically ordered or ranked. This ranking is what differentiates nominal and ordinal-level variables. For example, level of education measured as less than a high school diploma, high school diploma, some college, or college degree represents an ordinal measure, as "some college" means the respondent has more education than someone who has either or high school diploma or less than a high school diploma. Low-, middle-, and upper-class and rookie, sergeant, and police chief are also examples of ordinal measures.

The third and fourth levels of measurement are **interval measures** and **ratio measures**, respectively. These levels of measurement are very similar in that there is a specified numerical difference between the categories expressed in the measure (e.g., the distance between 3 and 5 is the same as the distance between 5 and 7), but in ratio measures there is a true and meaningful 0. The number of arrests represents a ratio measure, since its baseline of 0 indicates the absence of any arrest.

Keep in mind that each advancing level of measurement includes all qualities of the lower levels of measurement. In other words, number of arrests is a ratio measure, since it has a true and meaningful 0 (ratio measure property). The distance between categories can be expressed numerically, such that the difference between 2 and 4 arrests is the same as the distance between 6 and 8 arrests (interval measure property), and the values can be ranked logically (1, 2, 3, 4, etc., arrests; ordinal measure property). The arrests greater than 0 mean that the respondent has accumulated an arrest relative to not having accumulated an arrest (nominal measure property). In addition, higher levels of measurement can be recoded and expressed as lower levels of measurement. For instance, number of arrests can be recoded from its ratio level into an ordinal measure (0 arrests, 1 to 2 arrests, or 3 or more arrests) or into a nominal measure (arrested, yes or no).

SCALING PROCEDURES

Scaling refers to the general procedures that can be applied to increase the complexity of the level of measurement from nominal to at least ordinal and preferably interval or ratio. There are a variety of methods that can be used to construct scales, but the most general method would be an additive scale of a series of nominal (yes/no) **dummy variables** (variables with only two possible responses, coded as 0=no crime/no, 1=crime/yes, also known as binary variables) to create what is called a **variety index**. The delinquency variety index created by Elliot, Huizinga, and Ageton (1985) is one of the most well-known scales of this type in criminology and criminal justice research. A list of items that can be used to create this variety index can be found in Table 3.1. As it currently stands, you would just have a series of nominal variables representing whether the respondent answered yes or no to whether they had committed one or any number of these delinquent acts. Thus, in order to construct the variety index, you would simply add up the number of yes responses for each respondent. You would now have an interval/ratio level measure of the respondents' criminal involvement constructed from a list of nominal variables.

Table 3.1   Variety Index Example Items

For the following questions please indicate your response by checking Yes or No.

	Yes	No
1. Run away from home?	☐	☐
2. Skipped classes or school without a good excuse?	☐	☐
3. Lied about your age to get into some place or to buy something, for example, lying about your age to get into a movie or to buy alcohol?	☐	☐
4. Hitchhiked where it was illegal to do so?	☐	☐
5. Carried a hidden weapon?	☐	☐
6. Been loud, rowdy, or unruly in a public place so people complained about it or you got into trouble?	☐	☐
7. Asked for money or things from strangers?	☐	☐
8. Drunk in a public place?	☐	☐
9. Purposely damaged or destroyed property that did not belong to you, for example, smearing or pouring paint on something, writing graffiti on walls, or breaking, cutting, or marking up something?	☐	☐
10. Purposely set fire to a house, building, car, or other property or tried to do so?	☐	☐
11. Avoided paying for things such as movies, bus or subway rides, food or computer services?	☐	☐
12. Gone or tried to go into a building to steal something?	☐	☐
13. Stolen or tried to steal things worth less than $5?	☐	☐
14. Stolen or tried to steal things worth between $5 and $50?	☐	☐
15. Stolen or tried to steal something worth between $50 and $100?	☐	☐
16. Stolen or tried to steal something worth over $100?	☐	☐
17. Taken something from a store without paying for it?	☐	☐
18. Snatched someone's purse or wallet or picked someone's pocket?	☐	☐
19. Taken something that did not belong to you from someone's car, for example, the car radio or a hubcap?	☐	☐
20. Knowingly bought, sold, or held stolen goods for someone else?	☐	☐
21. Gone joyriding, that is, taken a motor vehicle, such as a car or motorcycle, for a ride or a drive without the owner's permission?	☐	☐
22. Stolen or tried to steal a motor vehicle, such as a car or motorcycle?	☐	☐
23. Used checks illegally or used a slug or fake money to pay for something?		
24. Used or tried to use someone else's credit card or ATH/ATM card without the owner's permission?	☐	☐
25. Tried to cheat someone by selling them something that was worthless or not what you said it was?	☐	☐
26. Attacked someone with a weapon or to seriously hurt or kill them?	☐	☐
27. Hit someone on purpose to hurt them?	☐	☐

continued on next page

	Yes	No
28. Used a weapon, force, or strong-arm methods to get money or things from people?	☐	☐
29. Thrown objects at people that could have hurt them, such as rocks or bottles?	☐	☐
30. Been involved in a gang fight?	☐	☐
31. Been paid for having sexual relations with someone?	☐	☐
32. Had, or tried to force someone to have, sexual relations with you against their will?	☐	☐
33. Physically hurt, or threatened to hurt, someone to get them to have sex with you?	☐	☐
34. Sold drugs to anyone?	☐	☐
35. Been arrested or picked up by the police for anything other than a minor traffic offense?	☐	☐
36. How many times in your life have you been convicted in court or by a judge for doing something against the law or a delinquent act? (0 = never, 1 = one or more times)		_____

Source: Elliot et al. (1985).

Oftentimes researchers rely on *Likert scales* to measure their key concepts. We are sure that you all have had some experience with answering questionnaires with these types of questions, at least experience with filling out teaching evaluations, which use these types of questions! **Likert scales** are scales that have a predetermined set of response options that generally range from "strongly disagree" to "strongly agree" with some neutral response option in the middle, such as "neither agree nor disagree" (Bayens & Roberson, 2010). For instance, a survey question might ask, "On a scale of 1 to 5, with 1 being 'strongly disagree' and 5 being 'strongly agree,' rate the degree to which you agree with the death penalty as a sanction for punishing murderers." Likert-scale-type questions can also be summed, similar to variety indexes, to create a larger scale where responses to several questions—such as support for the death penalty for murderers, rapists, and child molesters—could be added together (each item ranging from 1 to 5) to produce a scale that ranged from 3 (strongly disagree to the use of the death penalty as a sanction for all three types of criminals) to 15 (strongly agree to the use of the death penalty as a sanction for all three types of criminals) (Croasmun & Ostrom, 2011).

Arbitrary scales are scales created from several variables (usually a sum) that have different values, in the sense they are not all nominal (like variety indexes) or Likert-scale-type responses (Dantzker & Hunter, 2011). The Uniform Crime Reports (UCR) total crime index is an example of an arbitrary scale where the number of homicides, larceny thefts, forcible rapes, motor vehicle thefts, robberies, burglaries, and aggravated assaults are added together. It is arbitrary due to the fact that murder is a much rarer event than larceny theft but both of these crimes are just added together along with the other crimes, ignoring the differences in frequency and/or crime seriousness.

In contrast, **seriousness scales** are commonly used in criminology and criminal justice research to account for the fact that some crimes are more

Table 3.2 Sellin-Wolfgang Seriousness Scale with Hypothetical Data			
Crime Types	Seriousness Scores	Number of Crimes	Scale Score After Accounting for Crime Seriousness
Murder	26	15	390
Rape	11	40	440
Robbery (with weapon)	5	100	500
Larceny ($5,000)	4	120	480
Motor Vehicle Theft (no damage)	2	400	800
Larceny ($5)	1	1,000	1,000
Assault (minor)	1	750	750
TOTAL		2,460 crimes	4,360 (crimes* seriousness)

serious than others. One of the most classic examples of a crime seriousness scale is the Sellin-Wolfgang Index developed by Sellin and Wolfgang (1964), which is displayed in Table 3.2. This table also presents hypothetical crime count data to demonstrate the effect of accounting for crime seriousness and crime frequency. Less frequently occurring crimes, such as murder, are given more weight due to their seriousness, and less serious but more frequently occurring crimes such as simple assault are weighted less.

VALIDITY AND RELIABILITY

Validity and reliability as they relate to measurement are two fundamental concepts that affect all research results to varying degrees (Gertz & Talarico, 1977). **Validity** refers to whether the measure being used or reviewed in other research or presented in media is accurately measuring the concept that it claims to be measuring (Jansson, Hesse, & Fridell 2008). For instance, if you are studying the relationship between crime and video games and you measure crime by self-reported violence among teenagers who self-report playing video games, then these measures seem valid. On the other hand, **reliability** is focused on the stability or consistency of your measurement, or whether your question would generate the same answer upon remeasurement.

Validity

There are four main types of validity: face validity, criterion-related validity, construct validity, and content validity. Face validity is arguably the easiest to establish and recognize. Specifically, a measure that has **face validity** appears to be measuring what it is attempting to measure—in essence, the measure makes sense and intuitively appears to measure the phenomenon of interest. For example, if you were listening to the news and they reported that their sources indicate that there is a relationship between unemployment and crime, but you find out that the sources are using the number of hours spent watching television each week to measure unemployment and the number of times people swear in a week to measure crime, then it is fairly obvious that these measures lack face validity. Measuring unemployment by asking neighborhood residents to self-report whether they were currently employed and to report their criminal activity (Lindstrom, 2005) would be better measures that arguably have face validity.

Criterion-related validity is focused upon whether the results of your measure behave similarly to those of some trustworthy alternative measure. Consider that you are interested in administering a self-report survey to examine the link between self-control and crime to your fellow majors in criminology and criminal justice, but you know that your professors are going to give you only 5 minutes out of their class time to administer your survey. You are well aware that the self-control scale of Grasmick, Tittle, Bursik, and Arneklev (1993) is the most widely utilized way to measure Gottfredson and Hirschi's (1990) self-control and that Elliot et al.'s (1985) variety index is used frequently to measure crime. However, the Grasmick et al. scale has 24 questions and the Elliot et al. variety index scale has more than 30 questions. What you could do is consider alternative measures of self-control and crime with fewer questions and then administer both forms of these measures to one class where the professor was not as strict on the 5-minute time constraint. You could then compare the results from your revised and abbreviated measures of self-control and crime to those of the more established measures. If the results are similar, then your revised and abbreviated measures may have criterion-related validity.

Construct validity is the most theoretically informed type of validity in the sense that it concerns whether the instrument you are using to measure your concepts is actually measuring the concepts and that your measures related to the phenomenon you are investigating are in the expected direction. Let's assume you would like to study the difficulties that prisoners face dealing with their prison experience by mailing a survey questionnaire to 100 inmates in the local prison. You begin by constructing your survey using the knowledge you have gained in your coursework and include questions such as, "Is your being in prison accompanied with deleterious consequences, and if so, please describe these deleterious consequences?" or "Is fragmented interpersonal relationship a collateral consequence of your prison experience?" While these questions on their face seem to be valid measures of difficulties prisoners may face or report as a result of their imprisonment, it is highly likely that only a small minority of prisoners (particularly those with college and more advanced educational backgrounds) would even be able to read and understand these questions. So the questions have face validity, but the results may lack construct validity because these questions are better measures of educational background, as a high level of education is needed to be able to read and accurately respond to these questions.

The final type of validity, **content validity**, centers on the degree to which your measure covers the complete range of meanings included with the concept that you are intending to measure (Beck & Gable, 2001). For example, consider that you and your classmates just completed your first exam in your research methods class. The exam consisted of 40 multiple choice questions with 10 questions related to sources of crime data, 10 questions related to crime measurement, 10 questions related to validity and reliability, and 10 questions about how the police respond to calls-for-service. Obviously, the class performs poorly on the 10 questions about how the police respond to calls-for-service, as this material would not be covered in a course on research methods. Therefore, the exam that was administered lacks content validity as a measure of the class's knowledge of research methods because the questions about police response to calls-for-service do not cover/assess the content in the course. Once these 10 questions are deleted from the exam, then the exam could be considered to have content validity as a measure of knowledge of research methods.

Reliability

There are also four main types of reliability: test/retest reliability, representative reliability, split-half reliability, and inter-rater reliability. **Test/retest reliability** is the most commonly used method of evaluating reliability and considers the stability and consistency of your measure over time (Silverman, Saavedra, & Pina, 2001). In other words, this type of reliability addresses whether your measure provides the same results when applied repeatedly over time. Test/retest reliability is easily established because all you need to do is administer your measure of self-control and crime to your fellow classmates at the beginning and the end of the semester (Kivetz & Zheng, 2006). Assuming that you use the same items measuring self-control at both time points, identical results on the survey responses at the beginning of the semester and at the end of the semester indicate that your measures demonstrate test/retest reliability.

Representative reliability concerns the degree to which your measures demonstrate stable and consistent results across subgroups or populations (Beaver, Wright, Delisi, & Vaughn, 2008). A classic example of this is the IQ test. Although this instrument has long been used as a measure of intelligence and has produced valid and reliable results, there has been considerable discussion that this measure of intelligence is biased toward those with middle-class backgrounds. Thus, the traditional IQ tests may lack representative reliability (Lawler, 1978) because it disadvantages or does not equally apply to subgroups of the population, particularly those from non-middle-class backgrounds. In order to establish representative reliability, it is important to administer and test your measures across relevant subgroups such as males and females, whites and nonwhites, and low-, middle-, and upper-class persons.

While the former two types of reliability focus on applying a measure repeatedly to the same individuals or to different subgroups, **split-half reliability** is applied at one point in time and relates to the internal consistency of the measure. For instance, returning to the example of measuring self-control and crime, you would take the responses to the items measuring self-control and crime from your survey and randomly split the items that comprise the measure in halves. So, assuming your self-control measure had 10 items and your crime measure had 10 items, you would randomly split the items into halves (e.g., one measure of self-control with five items and a second measure of self-control with five items and one measure of crime with five items and a second measure of crime with five items). After having randomly split the measures into equal halves, you would then examine the relationship between the halves. If the halves of the self-control measure are correlated with each other and the halves of the crime measure are correlated with each other, then you have established split-half reliability (Thompson, Green, & Yang, 2010). Generally, some type of reliability coefficient, such as Cronbach's (1951) coefficient alpha, is used to statistically assess the degree of reliability of your measure as it relates to internal consistency.

The final measure of reliability that we will discuss is known as *inter-rater reliability*, or intercoder reliability. **Inter-rater reliability** concerns the situation in which there are multiple raters or coders who are attempting to measure the same phenomenon (Van der Knapp, Leenarts, Born, & Oostervold, 2012). If you are interested in studying bullying among preschoolers, but you only have time to observe the kids in the class one time yourself, you could ask one of your fellow students to observe the kids in the class a second time. After you both have observed the kids and their classroom bullying behavior, you could compare your results to determine the degree to which your measurement of bullying was consistent. Typically, the Kappa statistic is used to determine the inter-rater reliability across multiple raters/coders (Cohen, 1960).

Comparing Validity and Reliability

It is important to recognize that validity and reliability are distinct, yet an interrelationship does exist between these concepts (Maxfield & Babbie, 2011). Figure 3.1 depicts all of the possible ways in which validity and reliability can intersect. The first dartboard demonstrates a measure that is reliable but not valid because although the measure is hitting the target consistently in the same spot, all of the hits are missing their mark, so the measure is reliable but not valid. In the second dartboard, the measure is considered valid because the target is hit every time the concept is measured and the measurement is

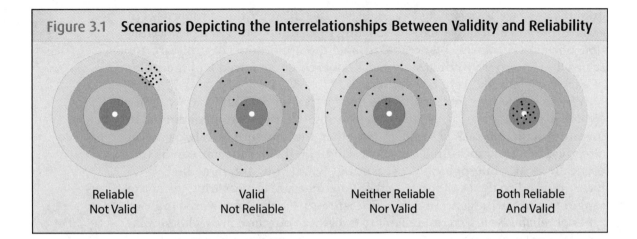

Figure 3.1   Scenarios Depicting the Interrelationships Between Validity and Reliability

Reliable
Not Valid

Valid
Not Reliable

Neither Reliable
Nor Valid

Both Reliable
And Valid

relatively equally distributed around the target; however, there is no consistency in where the target is hit (i.e., no reliability). Generally speaking, a measure can be reliable but not valid, but a measure cannot be valid if it is not reliable. In the third scenario, the measure is hitting the target, though not consistently near the center. The hits are unevenly distributed around the target, so this measure is neither valid nor reliable. Finally, the final dartboard displays the perfect real-world scenario: the measure is hitting the center of the target and doing so consistently; therefore, the measure is both valid and reliable.

SUMMARY

This chapter examined the basics for developing the methods and procedures for conceptualizing and operationalizing the measures of the crime you might study in criminal justice. Conceptualization draws upon shared mental images that come to mind when a particular concept like *crime* is mentioned, and this conceptualization process leads to operationalization. Operationalization involves identifying indicators and arriving at important decisions on how you are going to measure your concepts.

There is specific measurement terminology that delineates the role of different variables in a research project. Dependent variables (outcome variables) serve as the outcome, independent variables serve as the predictor of interest, and control variables, provide alternative explanations of an observed link between an explanatory variable and a dependent variable. The levels of measurement for different types of variables were also described (nominal, ordinal, interval, and ratio), as well as the distinction between quantitative (involving numbers) and qualitative variables (involving words) and discrete versus continuous variables. We detailed the qualities of well-constructed variables—specifically, the properties of exhaustive and mutually exclusive. Scaling procedures, such as the construction of variety indexes, Likert scales, and the application of arbitrary (or scales that incorporate crime seriousness) were also reviewed and examples of each type of scale were provided.

We concluded by discussing the four types of validity: face validity (whether the measure on its face is measuring what you are intending it to measure), criterion-related validity (whether the measure is related to an already established measure), construct validity (whether the measure is theoretically and philosophically measuring what you are intending it to measure), and content validity (whether your measure is measuring the entire range of values in the concept you are measuring). Finally, we covered the four types of reliability: test/retest reliability (whether your measure yields similar results over time), representative reliability (whether your measure applies to subpopulation or subgroups), split-half reliability (once split, whether the halves of your measure are related to one another), and inter-rater reliability (whether ratings by more than one person are related to one another). The relationship between reliability and validity, as well as examples of how these concepts are related, was discussed.

KEY TERMS

Arbitrary scales Scales that can be computed that are summations of several variables, in the sense that they have different variables (are only all nominal); these are similar to the variety index.

Conceptualization The process in which concepts are formed out of experience, observation, and data.

Construct validity Refers to whether a scale measure correlates with the psychological constructs it is theorized and purported to measure.

Content validity The extent to which a measure represents all facets of a given construct that it is intended to measure.

Continuous measure A measure that can take on any range of values and is not discrete.

Control variable Also known as *covariate*, this is a construct or measure that is held constant and unchanged within the course of an experiment.

Criterion-related validity A measure of how well one variable or a set of variables predicts an outcome based on information from other variables.

Dependent variable A measure that is modified during an experiment. The dependent variable responds in some manner to the independent variable.

Discrete measures Variables that exist as part of a countable set—that is, they are not continuous.

Dummy variable A *dummy variable* is coded as 1 or 0, indicating either the presence or the absence of a quality (e.g., individuals who live in the United States can be coded as 1 and individuals who do not live in the United States can be coded as 0).

Exhaustive   Refers to the ability to cover the entire spectrum of a situation. For example, measuring gender as male or female is an exhaustive category that covers all possibilities.

Explanatory variable   A variable that may be manipulated to explain the response variable. Often this type of variable is also called an *independent variable* or a *predictor variable*.

Face validity   A property of a measure. An item on a survey has face validity if it measures what it is intended to measure.

Independent variable   A concept (age, height, etc.) whose variation does not depend on that of another variable. Also known as a *risk factor*, *predictor*, or *explanatory variable*.

Instrumentation   Refers to the formation and development of measurement instruments for scientific purposes.

Inter-rater reliability   The degree of agreement or concordance among raters. This type of reliability gives us an indication of how much homogeneity or consensus there is in ratings given by judges.

Interval measures   These tell researchers about the order of data points and the size of intervals in between data points.

Likert scales   A scale commonly used in survey research and involves scaling of responses from "strongly disagree" to "strongly agree."

Mutually exclusive   *Mutually exclusive* variables occur when response options to a measure (or variable) are contradictory and unable to both be true at the same time.

Nominal measures   Those that enable the classification of variables in relation to its quality feature (i.e., grade, school, etc.).

Ordinal measures   Those in which it is possible to classify and rank the value of the variable from its lowest to highest value.

Qualitative variables   Measures that have no natural set of ordering. Typically these variables are measured on a nominal scale.

Quantitative variables   Naturally measured as numbers for which meaningful arithmetic operations make sense.

Ratio measures   The same thing as interval measures, except that they include a meaningful zero.

Reliability   Refers to the consistency of a measure. Does the item consistently measure what it is intended to measure?

Representative reliability   The degree to which a measure demonstrates stability across subgroups or populations.

Scaling   The branch of measurement that involves the construction of a numerical instrument that associates qualitative construct with quantitative measurements.

Seriousness scales   Often used in criminology and criminal justice to account for the fact that some crimes are more serious than others. An example of this type of scale is the Sellin-Wolfgang Index.

Split-half reliability   The consistency of a measure when it is split in two, and the scores of each half of the test are compared with one another. If the scores are comparable, they are likely measuring the same concept.

Test/retest reliability   Assesses the degree to which test scores are consistent from one time period to the next.

Validity   Refers to the idea that a concept, conclusion, or measurement corresponds accurately to the real world or measures what it is intended to.

Variety index   A type of composite measure that summarizes and rank orders specific observations to represent a more generalized dimension.

REVIEW QUESTIONS

1. What are the four levels of measurement? Define and give an example of each type.
2. What is the process of operationalization? Identify a construct and operationalize it.
3. Define, compare, and contrast the different types of validity.
4. What is inter-rater reliability? Give an example of this concept.
5. What is difference between reliability and validity? Compare and contrast these two concepts.

Useful Websites

www.socialresearchmethods.net/ Website dedicated to social science research methods.

http://en.wikipedia.org/wiki/Level_of_measurement Wikipedia entry dedicated to levels of measurement.

www.counseling.org/Publications/FrontMatter/72914-FM.PDF A helpful article on scale validation.

http://explorable.com/operationalization.html Helpful website for how to operationalize variables.

www.crim.cam.ac.uk/ Institute of Criminology at Cambridge University.

References

Bayens, G. J., & Roberson, C. (2010). *Criminal justice research methods: Theory and Practice* (2nd ed.). Boca Raton, FL: CRC Press.

Beaver, K. M., Wright, J. P., Delisi, M., & Vaughn, M. G. (2008). Genetic influences on the stability of low self-control: Results from a longitudinal sample of twins. *Journal of Criminal Justice, 36,* 478–485.

Beck, C. T., & Gable, R. K. (2001). Ensuring content validity: An illustration of the process. *Journal of Nursing Measures, 9*(2), 201–215.

Cohen, J. (1960). A coefficient of agreement for nominal scales. *Educational and Psychological Measurement, 20,* 37–46.

Cronbach, L. J. (1951). Coefficient alpha and the internal structure of tests. *Psychometrika, 16,* 297–334.

Croasmun, J. T., & Ostrom, L. (2011). Using Likert-type scales in the social sciences. *Journal of Adult Education, 40*(1), 19–22.

Dantzker, M. L., & Hunter, R. D. (2011). *Research methods for criminology and criminal justice* (3d ed.). Sudbury, MA: Jones and Bartlett Learning.

Elliott D. S., Huizinga, D., &, Ageton, S. S. (1985). *Explaining delinquency and drug use.* Beverly Hills: Sage Publications.

Gertz, M. G., & Talarico, S. M. (1977). Problems of reliability and validity in criminal justice research. *Journal of Criminal Justice, 5*(3), 217–224.

Gottfredson, M. R., & Hirschi, T. (1990). *A general theory of crime.* Stanford, CA: Stanford University Press.

Grasmick, H. G., Tittle, C. R., Bursik, R. J., & Arneklev, B. J. (1993). Testing the core empirical implications of Gottfredson and Hirschi's general theory of crime. *Journal of Research Crime and Delinquency, 30*, 5–29.

Jansson, I., Hesse, M., & Fridell, M. (2008). Validity of self-reported criminal justice involvement in substance abusing women at five-year follow up. *BMC Psychiatry, 8*(2).

Kivetz, R., & Zheng, Y. (2006). Determinants of justification for self-control. *Journal of Experimental Psychology: General, 135*(4), 572–587.

Lafree, G. D., & Kick, E. L. (1986). Cross national effects of development, distributional and demographic variables on crime: A review and analysis. *International Annals of Criminology, 24*, 213–236.

Lawler, J. M. (1978). Reliability and validity of IQ tests. In *I.Q., heritability, and racism,* New York: International Publishers.

Lindstrom, M. (2005). Psychosocial work conditions, unemployment, and self-reported psychological health: A population based study. *Occupational Medicine, 55*(7), 568–571.

Maxfield, M. G., & Babbie, E. R. (2011). *Basics of research methods for criminal justice and criminology* (3d ed.). Belmont, CA: Wadsworth.

Sellin, T., & Wolfgang, M. E. (1964). The measurement of delinquency. Oxford: Wiley.

Silverman, W. K., Saavedra, L. M., & Pina, A. A. (2001). Test-retest reliability of anxiety symptoms and diagnoses: With the anxiety disorders interview schedule for DSM-IV: Child and Parent Versions. *Journal of American Academy Child Adolescent Psychiatry, 40*(8), 937–944.

Thompson, B. L., Green, S. B., & Yang, Y. (2010). Assessment of the maximal split-half coefficient to estimate reliability. *Educational and Psychological Measurement, 70*(2), 232–251.

Van der Knapp, L. M., Leenarts, L. E. W., Born, M. P., & Oostervold, P. (2012). Reevaluating interrater reliability in offender risk management. *Crime and Delinquency, 58*(1), 147–163.

4 CRIME MEASUREMENT

C rime measurement and instrumentation are arguably two of the most critical issues to consider when studying crime. There are three major sources of crime data that are commonly used to discern the nature and extent of crime: official statistics, victimization surveys, and self-report offender surveys. These sources are each reviewed in detail and are discussed in terms of their similarities and differences.

OFFICIAL STATISTICS

With regard to crime measurement, what we consider **official statistics** are information about the nature and extent of crime, gathered from administrative or agency records or data (Skogan, 1977). Some examples that are readily used and referred to throughout criminal justice research and practice, including the Uniform Crime Reports, the National Crime Victimization Survey, and the National Incident-Based Reporting System, are described below.

Uniform Crime Reports

The **Uniform Crime Reports (UCR)** is the most widely recognized official source of criminological and criminal justice data. The UCR originated in 1930 from a meeting and related discussions of the International Association of Chiefs of Police held during the 1920s (Rosen, 1995). These discussions revolved around the issue that there was no uniform or systematic way of crime reporting across all of the jurisdictions in the United States, and this lack of uniformity precluded the ability to compare and contrast crime across jurisdictions or arrive at national level estimates of crime.

UCR data is compiled and reported annually in the crime reporting handbook by the Federal Bureau of Investigation (FBI) and is derived from the data provided by local jurisdictions and agencies. For example, the local police department in your city collects their UCR data for any given year and sends it directly to the FBI (although in some states the local police agencies collect their UCR data, send it along to a state-level UCR program, and then this information is sent to the FBI). Once all of the agency-level UCR data is collected by the FBI, the FBI combines all of this information in order to publish annual national estimates and the nature and extent of crime in the United States. While the collection of UCR data and the reporting of this data to the FBI on an annual basis is entirely voluntary, there has been considerably high participation rates across the United States since UCR's inception. Although participation rates fluctuate somewhat from year to year, annual crime estimates generated from the compilation of agency-level UCR data reported by the FBI generally represent nearly 98 percent of the U.S. population living in metropolitan areas and roughly 90 percent of the U.S. population living in rural areas.

Data reported in the UCR are divided into Part 1 and Part 2 offenses. The full list of Part 1 and Part 2 crimes appears in Table 4.1. The **Part 1 crimes** are further categorized into a **violent crime index** (including murder and non-negligent manslaughter, forcible rape, robbery, and aggravated assault) and a **property crime index** (including burglary, larceny theft, and motor vehicle theft). These particular crimes were selected as the basis of the UCR because they represent the crimes most likely to be reported to police nationwide, and police investigations can easily establish whether the reported crimes in fact occurred. Other reasons these crimes are listed include their geographical distribution, their inherent seriousness, and the sheer volume of their occurrence.

Historically, the FBI reported seven crimes in the annual crime index. Because larceny theft occurred more frequently than other crimes in the index, such as murder, the FBI decided to stop reporting the aggregate annual crime index in 2004, instead separating the statistics into a violent index and a property index. Researchers interested in examining long-term trends and fluctuations in the UCR crime estimates over time now simply sum these two post-2004 indexes to generate figures comparable to those reported in the pre-2004 indexes.

In contrast, there are 22 other crimes (21 after excluding arson) listed among the Part 2 crimes. **Part 2 crimes** are considered nonindex crimes; examples of these crimes are listed in Table 4.1.

The Part 1 crime rates can be observed in Figure 4.1 on page 46. The **crime rate** is reported as the total number of crimes that occur per 100,000 persons in the U.S. population (Myers, 1980). Similarly, the violent crime rate is the number of violent crimes per 100,000 persons in the U.S. population, and the property crime rate is the number of property crimes per 100,000 persons in the U.S. population (excluding arson). When reviewing estimates presented in research and the media, it is always important to pay close attention to how the crime rate is expressed in terms of per 1,000, 10,000, or 100,000 persons in the population. For example, a violent crime rate of 100 per 10,000 persons (or $100/10,000 = 1$ per every 100 persons) is much higher than a violent crime rate of 100 per 100,000 persons (or $100/100,000 = 1$ per every 1,000 persons).

The UCR data includes crimes that are known to the police and/or have been cleared by arrest. Usually these crimes are reported in the UCR and become known to the police through three main sources: victim reports,

Table 4.1   UCR Part 1 and Part 2 Offenses

Part 1 Offenses	Part 2 Offenses
Murder and nonnegligent manslaughter	Other assaults (simple)
Forcible rape	Forgery and counterfeiting
Robbery	Fraud
Aggravated assault	Embezzlement
Burglary (breaking or entering)	Stolen property: buying, receiving, possessing
Larceny theft (except motor vehicle theft)	Vandalism
Motor vehicle theft	Weapons: carrying, possessing, etc.
Arson	Prostitution and commercialized vice
	Sex offenses (except forcible rape, prostitution, and commercialized vice)
	Drug abuse violations
	Gambling
	Offenses against the family and children
	Driving under the influence
	Liquor laws
	Drunkenness
	Disorderly conduct
	Vagrancy
	All other offenses
	Suspicion
	Curfew and loitering laws (persons under age 18)
	Runaways (persons under age 18)

witness reports, and crimes detected by the police. Of these sources, the majority of the crime data are generated through victim reports.

Limitations of the UCR.   As with any measure of crime, the UCR has a series of inherent limitations that must be acknowledged and considered when this source is relied on to provide estimates on the nature and extent of crime. UCR data provides offense-level data and not individual-level data. Furthermore, the data provided by the FBI for public use is only available at the agency level as the lowest level of aggregation. So although crime estimates are reported by the FBI for other aggregations such as cities, counties, states, metropolitan areas, and regions of the United States, you would not be able to use UCR data to analyze how many offenders had multiple offenses or how many crimes occurred on a particular street in a neighborhood. Also, it

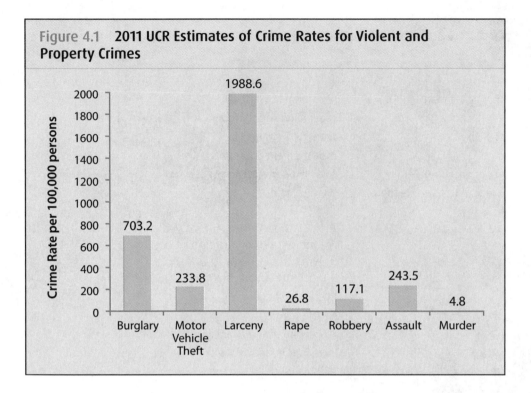

Figure 4.1 **2011 UCR Estimates of Crime Rates for Violent and Property Crimes**

would not be possible to identify a certain offender or offenders and track their progression through the criminal justice system to see if their arrest led to a conviction or a subsequent incarceration. Characteristics of the offenders are not reported when an arrest has not been made, as offender characteristics are not known to the police until they have arrested someone. Similarly, victim characteristics are not reported. Homicide is an exception, as some agencies do fill out what is referred to as a **supplemental homicide report (SHR)**, which can include information such as offender characteristics (i.e., age, gender, race), relationship between victim and offender, the weapon used, the location of the incident, and the circumstances surrounding the offense (Braga, Piehl, & Kennedy, 1999).

Perhaps one of the largest and most documented limitations of UCR data lies in its use and application of the hierarchy rule. In following the **hierarchy rule**, agencies reporting crime data to the FBI report only the most serious crime that occurred, not all offenses or crimes that may have occurred in one particular incident. Suppose, for example, that an offender stole a bicycle from someone's backyard (larceny theft) and rode it to the local McDonald's, where the offender held the cashier at gunpoint and took $1,000 from the register (robbery) before running into the parking lot, hitting a motorist on the back of the head with the firearm (aggravated assault), stealing the motorist's car (motor vehicle theft), and shooting and killing a pedestrian who tried to stop the car (murder). Of all the crimes committed—larceny theft, robbery, aggravated assault, motor vehicle theft, and murder—only one would be reported in the UCR data: the murder.

Beyond these limitations, a number of other factors affect the reporting of crime, which in turn affects the crime estimates available from UCR data. In general, crimes usually come to the attention of the police through a "reactive mobilization process"; in other words, the police are dependent upon citizens to report crime to them and then the police react in response to the crime that is reported. It is very rare for a police officer to catch a criminal in the act of committing an aggravated assault or a burglary. Crime reporting varies considerably as a function of the seriousness of the crime. Crimes such as larceny theft are much less reported than are motor vehicle thefts, largely due to the importance of a motor vehicle to a victim's livelihood and the requirement of insurance agencies to have a police report to pay out a claim.

The type of crime can also affect the reporting of a crime. For instance, rape often goes unreported for a variety of reasons, such as the victim's fear or shame. Police agencies frequently may become involved in "crackdowns" on certain types of offenses or may implement organizational changes in how to combat certain crimes that can affect their occurrence. If officers are cracking down on drinking and driving by having DUI checkpoints, then it is logical to assume that the number of DUIs at least in the immediate time would increase because of the increased likelihood of detecting intoxicated motorists. Or, a police chief may decide that he wishes to change the way his department handles unruly teenagers whose parents have called the police. In this scenario, the chief may instruct his officers to charge the teens with simple assault (delinquent/criminal offense) instead of a status offense (nondelinquent/noncriminal offense). There are also differences across police departments in their level of professionalism, style of enforcement (community policing, problem-oriented policing, zero tolerance policing), and the number-of-police-per-citizen ratio that can affect the crime rate.

National Incident-Based Reporting System

In the late 1970s, the International Association of Chiefs of Police and the National Sheriffs' Association began discussing how to undertake a massive redesign of the UCR system, a system that had been in place for nearly five decades. After much discussion, this process led to the creation of the **National Incident-Based Reporting System (NIBRS)**, which is an official source of crime data where agencies report all of the crime that occurs within each incident rather than just the most serious crime within any particular incident. NIBRS divides the data into two parts, like the UCR, but refers to these parts as Group A offenses and Group B offenses. A complete list of these offenses can be found in Table 4.2.

NIBRS vs. UCR

There is a series of key distinctions (namely, expected improvements) between NIBRS and the UCR. The most important difference between the two reporting

Table 4.2 NIBRS Group A and Group B Offenses

Group A Offenses	Group B Offenses
1. Arson	1. Bad Checks
2. Assault Offenses—Aggravated Assault, Simple Assault, Intimidation	2. Curfew/Loitering/Vagrancy Violations
3. Bribery	3. Disorderly Conduct
4. Burglary/Breaking and Entering	4. Driving Under the Influence
5. Counterfeiting/Forgery	5. Drunkenness
6. Destruction/Damage/Vandalism of Property	6. Family Offenses, Nonviolent
7. Drug/Narcotic Offenses—Drug/Narcotic Violations, Drug Equipment Violations	7. Liquor Law Violations
8. Embezzlement	8. Peeping Tom
9. Extortion/Blackmail	9. Runaway
10. Fraud Offenses—False Pretenses/Swindle/ Confidence Game, Credit Card/Automatic Teller Machine Fraud, Impersonation, Welfare Fraud, Wire Fraud	10. Trespass of Real Property
11. Gambling Offenses—Betting/Wagering, Operating/Promoting/Assisting Gambling, Gambling Equipment Violations, Sports Tampering	11. All Other Offenses
12. Homicide Offenses—Murder and Non-negligent Manslaughter, Negligent Manslaughter, Justifiable Homicide	
13. Kidnapping/Abduction	
14. Larceny/Theft Offenses—Pocket-picking, Purse-snatching, Shoplifting, Theft from Building, Theft from Coin-Operated Machine or Device, Theft from Motor Vehicle, Theft of Motor Vehicle Parts or Accessories, All Other Larceny	
15. Motor Vehicle Theft	
16. Pornography/Obscene Material	
17. Prostitution Offenses—Prostitution, Assisting or Promoting Prostitution	
18. Robbery	
19. Sex Offenses, Forcible—Forcible Rape, Forcible Sodomy, Sexual Assault With An Object, Forcible Fondling	
20. Sex Offenses, Nonforcible—Incest, Statutory Rape	
21. Stolen Property Offenses (Receiving, etc.)	
22. Weapon Law Violations	

systems is that NIBRS data includes crime data on each and every crime that occurred within any given crime incident as opposed to imposing the hierarchy rule as is done with the UCR data and reporting only the most serious crime within any crime incident. NIBRS also collects and reports detailed demographic information on the offender and victim (i.e., age, sex, and race) along with information related to the type of injury, the victim-offender relationship, offender's alcohol/drug history, type of weapon used during the offense, and so on.

In addition to expanding the list of crimes and including important victim and offender information, NIBRS data is based on revised and improved definitions for some crimes, such as homicide and rape (Roberts, 2007). In the UCR's definition of rape, this particular crime refers to "the carnal knowledge of a female forcibly and against her will," which excludes male victims, refers only to sexual penetration of a male penis of a female vagina, and requires that force is used. Whereas, NIBRS definition of rape is as follows: "carnal knowledge of a person, forcibly and/or against that person's will; or, not forcibly or against a person's will where the victim is incapable of giving consent because of his/her temporary or permanent mental or physical incapacity." In 2012 the FBI announced that it is going to revise its age-old definition of rape to "the penetration, no matter how slight, of the vagina or anus with any body part or object, or oral penetration by a sex organ of another person, without the consent of the victim." In addition, while the UCR distinguishes between crimes against persons (violent crime index) and crimes against property (property crime index), NIBRS also provides the added distinction of "crimes against society." Offenses in this new categorization are drug offenses, gambling violations, pornography, and prostitution. NIBRS also makes a distinction between attempted and completed offenses.

Ultimately, although the intention of the originators to revamp the UCR and develop the NIBRS system was well intended, there has been a degree of reluctance from law enforcement agencies to adopt this new system. Currently, roughly half of U.S. states have agencies that participate in and provide NIBRS data to the FBI, and these data represent approximately 20 to 25 percent of the U.S. population. Reluctance is due to a variety of factors such as law enforcement's resistance to change, lack of personnel/resources to enter in all of the detailed data that NIBRS requires, and the considerable increase in the potential for clerical error based on the vast amount of information that has to be coded and inputted. Finally, there is also some concern about inflation in the national crime estimates if NIBRS data was suddenly reported in the media versus UCR data without sufficiently informing the public of the differences. For instance, the crime rate could multiply 10s to 100s of times because all of the crimes within incidents are reported in NIBRS, not just the most serious crimes as reported in the UCR.

VICTIM SURVEYS

The UCR was considered the only definitive source of national-level crime data until the 1970s, when research conducted by the National Opinion Research Center, the President's Commission on Law Enforcement, and the Administration of Justice noted that many crimes were not reported by police. Researchers needed better estimates on the **dark figure of crime**, crime that is not reported to the police and is not found in UCR data.

National Crime Victimization Survey

This concern over how much crime was really occurring in the United States led to the creation of the **National Crime Victimization Survey (NCVS)** in 1973. The NCVS, sponsored by the U.S. Justice Department's Bureau of Justice Statistics, is conducted by the U.S. Census Bureau. Trained NCVS interviewers collect data each year from a nationally representative sample of approximately 76,000 households comprising nearly 130,000 persons on the nature and extent of criminal victimization in the United States.

The NCVS involves a panel design wherein individuals who are invited and agree to participate in the survey are involved in the project for 3 years. Participants are interviewed twice a year for 3 years and are asked about victimizations that occurred in the past 6 months. The initial interview is referred to as the **bounding interview**, which serves to provide a benchmark for a reference period for subsequent interviews. For example, in the first interview a participant may report one previous simple assault victimization. Then in their first follow-up interview (second overall interview), they may report one prior simple assault victimization in the previous 6 months. The trained interviewer can then ask additional questions in reference to the reported assault victimization in the first bounding interview to make sure this second reported victimization is distinct from the previously reported victimization and occurred during the 6 months between the first and the second interview. This strengthens the quality of the measurement and therefore may provide some benefits in the accuracy of self-reported victimization. Keep in mind that the NCVS design is a **household survey**, which means that every person in the household that is over the age of 12 is interviewed separately. Although participation rates vary across years, in any given year the respondents to the NCVS represent 95 percent of eligible households and 99 percent of eligible persons within those households.

The NCVS includes a number of **screening questions**, or questions that are asked about particular victimization experiences. Should the respondent answer yes to any of these screening questions, additional follow-up and detailed questions about each incident are asked subsequently. The following is an example of one such screening question:

"Has someone attacked or threatened you in any of these ways?"

- With a weapon such as a gun or knife
- With anything like a baseball bat, frying pan, scissors, or stick
- By something thrown, such as a rock
- Include any grabbing, punching, or kicking
- Any rape, attempted rape, or other type of sexual assault
- Any face-to-face threats or
- Any attack or threat or use of force by anyone at all. Please mention if you were not certain it was a crime.

The NCVS provides a wealth of information based on the data obtained from crime victims, including crime type, location of crime, date/time of crime, victim-offender relationship, offender characteristics, costs and consequences of the victimization, whether the crime was reported to the police, whether a weapon was used, and alcohol and/or drugs involved in the victimization. Victim demographic information is also collected (i.e., age, gender, race, income; Hashima & Finkelhor, 1999). Similar to the UCR's reporting of crime rates, the NCVS reports a **victimization rate**. Specifically, the NCVS reports a victimization rate per 1,000 households. This is the number of victimizations that reportedly occur per 1,000 households. For example, if the victimization rate was 10 per 1,000 households for burglary, then this would indicate that 10 households out of every 1,000 households had been burglarized in the particular reference year. Figure 4.2 reports the violent crime and property crime victimization rates per 1,000 households.

The NCVS is a valuable source of crime data, but there are some limitations associated with it. A single incident often involves multiple victims, so the extent to which multiple people are reporting the same incident could lead

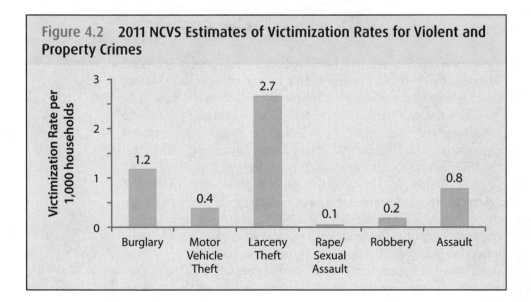

Figure 4.2 2011 NCVS Estimates of Victimization Rates for Violent and Property Crimes

to an overestimation of the number of victimizations and the corresponding victimization rate. Having said this, **series victimizations**, or victimizations that are reported to occur frequently and even at times daily, are removed from the annual national victimization estimates (Garofalo, Siegel, & Laub, 1987). Even though the interviews are confidential, there still is the potential for **underreporting** of victimizations, or a lack of willingness to report certain victimizations largely due to embarrassment and/or fear of consequences. Also, **testing effects** can influence the victimization estimates (Meithe & Meier, 1990). *Testing effects* refer to the issue where after the participant has been interviewed previously, they will remember that the last time they answered yes to one of the NCVS screening questions asking about their prior victimization experience it led to a series of additional questions that lengthened the time of the interview. Finally, **recall problems** refer to inaccuracies in memory, such as a respondent thinking/remembering that his wallet was stolen 2 months ago when it really was stolen 8 months ago. This can affect the estimates as well (Widom & Shepard, 1996). The use of the bounding interview described earlier reduces some of the potential for recall problems, but they still exist to some extent.

NCVS vs. UCR

Considering that the NCVS was specifically created to address the problem of some crimes not being reported to the police, it is important to review some direct comparisons and contrasts between these two sources of data. Specifically, UCR data only includes crimes known and/or reported to the police, whereas NCVS data includes crime reported to the police and unreported crime along with detailed victim and offender information (Decker, 1977). As far as Part 1 crimes, homicide and arson are included in the UCR but not in the NCVS (Ansari & He, 2012). You cannot call up a place that was the victim of arson just as you cannot get a response from a dead victim (Chilton & Jarvis, 1999).

Other than these two Part 1 crimes, both sources measure aggravated assault, rape, robbery, larceny theft, burglary, and motor vehicle theft. However, there are some definitional differences in how these sources define rape and burglary. The UCR defines rape as "the carnal knowledge of a female forcibly and against her will," while the NCVS defines rape as "the carnal knowledge through the use of force or threat of force, including attempts" (e.g., heterosexual and homosexual rapes are included in this definition) (Muehlenhard, Powch, Phelps, & Giusti, 1992). With regard to burglary, the UCR defines burglary as "the unlawful entry or attempted entry of a structure to commit a felony or theft," compared with the NCVS defining burglary as "the entry or attempted entry of a residence by a person who had no right to be there." As mentioned earlier, the UCR reports annual and national per capita crime rates based on the number of crimes per 100,000 *persons*, and the NCVS reports annual and national per capita victimization rates based on the number of victimizations per 1,000 *households*. This minor distinction in the denominator can make a drastic difference in the prevalence rate of criminal behavior. In addition, the UCR includes commercial crimes and crimes against children under the age of 12, while the NCVS does not.

SELF-REPORT OFFENDER SURVEYS

A **self-report survey** is a survey that is administered to a participant who is asked to report and write down her responses to any questions that the surveyor deems relevant for the survey (Hindelang, Hirschi, & Weis, 1979). Austin Porterfield (1943) is generally regarded as the first person to have published a paper on delinquency utilizing a self-report survey among college students. This seminal study along with the work of Nye and Short (Nye, 1958; Nye, Short, & Olson, 1958; Short, 1957) in the 1950s led to a considerable surge in self-report offender surveys in the 1960s and later decades, and now self-report surveys are considered one of the main sources of crime data. These studies have contributed to the extant criminological and criminal justice knowledge in a number of areas such as delinquency theory, the relationship between social class and delinquency, and the identification of correlates of crime and delinquency (Krohn, Thornberry, Gibson, & Baldwin, 2010; Thornberry & Krohn, 2000). Additionally, some of the well-known self-report surveys that have been widely used in criminological and criminal justice research include the General Social Survey (Smith, Marsden, & Hout, 1972–2010), the National Longitudinal Survey of Youth (www.bls.gov/nls/nlsy79.htm), and the Monitoring the Future Survey (http://monitoringthefuture.org).

SUMMARY

This chapter opened with a discussion of official statistics as a primary source of crime measurement. The history of the Uniform Crime Reports (UCR), Part 1 and Part 2 crimes, and the strengths and limitations were also covered. Some of the most notable limitations of the UCR include the hierarchy rule, the inability to track an offender through the criminal justice system, limited or absent offender and victim characteristics, the reactive nature of policing, crime reporting varying as a function of seriousness, organizational and departmental influences on crime rates, and the effect that different styles of law enforcement may exert on crime rates.

The next portion of the chapter detailed another more recent source of official statistics that was originally designed and developed to replace the UCR. Specifically, the National Incident-Based Reporting system (NIBRS), and its list of Group A and Group B offenses, was reviewed. The UCR and NIBRS were compared, highlighting the differences and improvements in the NIBRS system relative to the UCR system. The NIBRS system eliminated the hierarchy rule, provided demographic information on victim and offenders, changed the definitions of some crimes such as rape, and added a new category called "crimes against society" (Dunn & Zelenock, 1999). Limitations of NIBRS, particularly law enforcement reluctance to report, the potential for clerical error, the lack of resources, and potential inflation of the crime rate in NIBRS compared to UCR estimates, were also covered.

We also reviewed victimization surveys in detail with a specific focus on the National Crime Victimization Survey. The purpose of the NCVS was to shed light on the "dark figure" of unreported crime from the perspective of the victim. Victimization rates were reported using NCVS estimates, and specific limitations of this system, including underreporting, testing effects, and recall bias were detailed in comparison to the UCR. The NCVS also differs from the UCR in terms of the types of crimes measured, the crime definitions, and the crime rate comparisons (e.g., the different denominator of households compared to individual persons). The chapter concluded with a brief description of self-report offender surveys, including natural history of self-report data collection, the types of research topics that we use self-report surveys to assess, and some examples of well-known and frequently used self-report offender surveys.

KEY TERMS

Bounding interview A frequently used feature in the NCVS in which the interviewer reviews with a respondent a listing of events the respondent reported in previous interviews. This procedure was used with the NCVS to prevent duplicate reports from occurring.

Crime rate The ratio of total crimes in an area to the population of that area. This is expressed per 1,000 population (or 100,000) per year.

Dark figure of crime The term used by criminologists and sociologists, which refers to unreported and undiscovered crime. This figure calls into question the reliability of official crime statistics.

Hierarchy rule This states that only the highest rated (e.g., most severe crime) is marked and counted when multiple crimes are committed during one incident.

Household survey A survey conducted on a regular basis (this varies by survey type) that collects data by selecting and surveying all members of a household. In this chapter, household surveys typically refer to the NCVS as surveying households on crime victimization.

National Crime Victimization Survey (NCVS) Survey administered by the Bureau of Justice Statistics. It is a household-based survey conducted twice a year to measure the frequency of crime victimization and characteristics and consequences of victimization.

National Incident-Based Reporting System (NIBRS) Based on the occurrence of criminal incidents and is used by law enforcement agencies throughout the United States for collecting and reporting data on crimes.

Official statistics   Statistics of crime produced by governmental agencies to shed light on the prevalence of crime for the purpose of information and policy creation.

Part 1 crimes   The eight most severe crimes indexed within the UCR. Examples of Part 1 crimes include homicide, burglary, and motor vehicle theft.

Part 2 crimes   Another type of crime category contained with the UCR. Examples of Part 2 crimes include, fraud, gambling, drug offenses, and sex offenses.

Property crime index   A summative measure created from the Uniform Crime Report that adds up the following crimes: burglary, larceny theft, motor vehicle theft.

Recall problems   Inaccuracy or lapses in memory when reporting events.

Screening questions   Questions conducted prior to survey administration that determine participant eligibility to take part in a survey.

Self-report survey   A method of collecting data in which a research participant provides information about himself or herself via questionnaire or interview.

Series victimizations   According to the Bureau of Justice Statistics, *series victimizations* are types of crimes in which respondents report more than one type of event but cannot recall specific details relating to the event.

Supplemental Homicide Report (SHR)   A complementary/supplemental report to the UCR. Law enforcement agencies complete this form separately to gather more specific information about homicides.

Testing effects   When a respondent has been previously interviewed and is being interviewed again, they will remember the way they reported in the first interview. This is typically a problem in the NCVS.

Underreporting   Refers to individuals not reporting crimes to law enforcement. This occurs for a variety of reasons and biases official crime statistics.

Uniform Crime Reports (UCR)   Police-reported data on crime within the United States published by the FBI.

Victimization rate   The rate at which individuals are victimized in a given population. Depending on survey type and data source, it is reported differently.

Violent crime index   A summative measure created from the Uniform Crime Report that adds up the following crimes: murder and non-negligent manslaughter, forcible rape, robbery, and aggravated assault.

REVIEW QUESTIONS

1. Explain how the NCVS and UCR are similar. How are they different? Compare and contrast these two measures of crime.
2. According to the UCR, what are Part 1 crimes? What are Part 2 crimes? Provide an example of each.

3. What is the "dark figure" of crime? Why has this historically been a difficult concept in the official measurement of crime?
4. Please give an example of a self-report survey, as provided in the text. Generate a description of this survey. What does it measure?
5. What are testing effects? Describe how test effects might influence the results of a survey.

Useful Websites

www.fbi.gov/about-us/cjis/ucr/ucr. The official website of the Uniform Crime Report (UCR).

www.icpsr.umich.edu/icpsrweb/NACJD/NIBRS/. A resource guide for working with NIBRS.

http://ojjdp.gov/ojstatbb/ezashr/. Website providing access to the Supplementary Homicide Report.

www.icpsr.umich.edu/icpsrweb/NACJD/NCVS/. A resource guide related to the NCVS.

www.bls.gov/cps/. An example of a household survey from the Bureau of Labor Statistics.

References

Ansari, S., & He, N. (2012, in press). Convergence revisited: A multi-definition, multi-method analysis of the UCR and the NCVS crime series (1973–2008). *Justice Quarterly.* DOI:10.1080/07418825.2012.718355.

Braga, A. A., Piehl, A. M., & Kennedy, D. M. (1999). Youth homicide in Boston: An assessment of supplementary homicide report data. *Homicide Report Data, 3*(4), 277–299.

Chilton, R., & Jarvis, J. (1999).Victims and offenders in two statistics programs: A comparison of the national incident based reporting system (NIBRS), and the national crime victimization survey (NCVS). *Journal of Quantitative Criminology, 15,* 193–205.

Decker, S. H. (1977). Official crime rates and victim surveys: An empirical comparison. *Journal of Criminal Justice, 5*(1), 47–54.

Dunn, C. S., & Zelenock, T. J. (1999). NIBRS data available for secondary analysis. *Journal of Quantitative Criminology, 15*(2), 239–248.

Garofalo, J., Siegel, L., & Laub, J. (1987). School-related victimization among adolescents: An analysis of national crime survey (NCS) narratives. *Journal of Quantitative Criminology, 3*(4), 321–338.

Hashima, P. Y., & Finkelhor, D. (1999). Violent victimization of youth versus adults in the national crime victimization survey. *Journal of Interpersonal Violence, 14*(8), 799–820.

Hindelang, M. J., Hirschi, T., & Weis, J. G. (1979). Correlates of delinquency: The illusion of discrepancy between self-report and official measures. *American Sociological Review, 44,* 995–1014.

Krohn, M. D., Thornberry, T. P., Gibson, C. L., & Baldwin, J. M. (2010). The development and impact of self-report measures of crime and delinquency. *Journal of Quantitative Criminology, 26,* 509–525.

Meithe, T. D., & Meier, R. F. (1990). Opportunity, choice, and criminal victimization: A test of a theoretical model. *Journal of Research in Crime and Delinquency, 27*(3), 243–266.

Muehlenhard, C. L., Powch, I. G., Phelps, J. L., & Giusti, L. M. (1992). Definitions of rape: Scientific and political implications. *Journal of Social Issues, 48*(1), 23–44.

Myers, S. L. (1980). Why are crimes underreported? What is the crime rate? Does it really matter? *Social Science Quarterly, 61*(1), 23–43.

Nye, F. I. (1958). *Family relationships and delinquent behavior.* New York: Wiley.

Nye, F. I., Short J. F., & Olson V. J. (1958). Socioeconomic status and delinquent behavior. In: F. I. Nye (Ed.), *Family relationships and delinquent behavior* (pp. 23–33). New York: Wiley.

Porterfield, A. L. (1943). Delinquency and its outcome in court and college. *American Journal of Sociology*, 199-208.

Roberts, A. (2007). Predictors of homicide clearance by arrest: An event history analysis of NIBRS incidents. *Homicide Studies, 11*(2), 82–93.

Rosen, L. (1995). The creation of the Uniform Crime Report: The role of social science. *Social Science History, 19*(2), 215–238.

Short, J. F. (1957). Differential association and delinquency. *Social Problems*, 4, 233–239.

Skogan, W. (1977). The validity of official crime statistics: An empirical investigation. *Social Science Quarterly, 1*, 25–38.

Smith, T. W., Marsden, P. V., & Hout, M. (1972–2010). General Social Survey, 1972–2010 [Cumulative File]. ICPSR31521-v1. Storrs, CT: Roper Center for Public Opinion Research, University of Connecticut/Ann Arbor, MI: Inter-university Consortium for Political and Social Research [distributors], 2011-08-05. doi:10.3886/ICPSR31521.v1.

Thornberry T. P., & Krohn M. D. (2000). The self-report method for measuring delinquency and crime. In: D. Duffee, R. Crutchfield, S. Mastrofski, L. Mazerolle, & D. McDowall (Eds.), Criminal justice 2000 (vol. 4): *Measurement and analysis of crime and justice* (pp. 33–83). Washington: National Institute of Justice.

Widom, C. S., & Shepard, R. L. (1996). Accuracy of adult recollections of childhood victimization: Part 1. Childhood physical abuse. *Psychological Assessment, 8*(4), 412–421.

SURVEY RESEARCH AND QUESTIONNAIRE DEVELOPMENT

The most common method of collecting data in criminological research is by utilizing **surveys**, or standardized instruments that systematically collect data from a large number of research participants (Hagan, 1997). This chapter details the circumstances in which survey research is appropriate, the modes of survey administration, and survey development and construction more generally.

IS A SURVEY APPROPRIATE?

Suppose you want to study alcohol consumption at your university, and you believe that students who live off campus are more likely to use alcohol than those who live in residence halls. How would you go about finding this out? Although you could look at the number of alcohol-related violations filed with the university's disciplinary office, this is unlikely to give you a picture of how many students are actually using alcohol (Babor, Stephens, & Marlatt, 1987). In addition, use of records may bias your results toward those who live on campus (as those students may be more likely to be reported for alcohol violations), when this may have nothing to do with how much alcohol use is actually happening at your campus.

Clearly, the best way to answer your question about whether residential status is related to alcohol use is to directly ask students who live on and off campus about how much alcohol they consume. Assuming that your respondents tell you the truth, this will give a more accurate picture of alcohol consumption on your campus than any official record will be able to. The next step is to determine how you will collect the information from students. Will you use an e-mail survey? Or distribute a survey in classrooms? How will you choose which classrooms get selected? Which questions will you ask?

In the case above, a survey is probably the best way to gather information on the frequency and quantity of alcohol use among students at your university. However, there are several cases in which survey research may not be the most appropriate method for collecting data. For instance, if you are interested in whether arrest rates differ between those who live on and off campus, asking students whether they have been arrested may not be the most efficient or valid method of gathering this information. Some students may (or may not) consider a written arrest (or notice to appear) an arrest, or students may be hesitant to report this sensitive information for fear of retaliation by the university. In this case, the use of official arrest statistics from an administrative office or police department may be the better method for collecting accurate data. You must consider that the respondent is actively weighing the costs and benefits of telling you the truth about their behavior with the benefit of the research. In the event that there is no incentive for participating in your survey, the only potential outcomes for reporting illegal behavior could be negative for the student (e.g., the university finding out). Therefore, it is the job of the researcher to make sure that the respondent is confident in the anonymity (or confidentiality) of the survey when the only possible method for collecting data is by self-report (i.e., a survey in which respondents report their own behavior).

MODES OF SURVEY ADMINISTRATION

Now that you have identified that a survey is the method you will use to collect data, you will begin thinking about *how* you need to complete your survey. In our example, there are several viable options: you may choose to use e-mail, in-class surveys, or paper surveys mailed out to students on and off campus. The pros and cons of each method will be discussed in depth below.

Web or E-Mail Surveys

E-mail surveys are becoming the most convenient method of collecting a large amount of data rapidly from respondents who have access to the Internet (Dillman, Smyth, & Christian, 2008). This method is especially appropriate when you have access to the e-mail addresses of the entire sampling frame (the respondents from which you wish to draw the sample). In our example, the office of the university registrar would certainly have a list of the e-mail addresses for the entire student body. If you wish to generalize your findings to the entire student population at your university, you might randomly select a subsample of e-mail addresses from the registrar's list. Alternatively, if you attend a very small institution, you may be able to conduct a **census** (i.e., survey all students at the university about their alcohol use). In most cases, this is not feasible and a **sample**, or subset, of the population is surveyed. E-mail surveys are often developed using commercially available survey software (e.g., SurveyMonkey). In other cases, attachments may be included in an e-mail to distribute the survey.

In our study, we might wish to obtain a list of all students' e-mail addresses from the university registrar. We could cross-reference this list with a list from housing and residence life, which lists the e-mail addresses of all students who live on campus. We will assume that all students who are not listed as "on campus residents" by housing and residence life live off campus. Because we are interested in comparing those who live on and those who live off campus, we will **stratify** (or divide) our sample by residential status. We can then randomly select an equal number of students who live on and off campus to be surveyed. We would then e-mail a survey and wait for a response.

Despite their convenience, there are several limitations to using a Web-based survey design. E-mail surveys are notorious for having low **response rates**, or the ratio of the number of completed surveys to the total number of surveys sent out (around 30 to 36 percent is average; Sheehan, 2001). Also, the researchers will never know if the survey was refused or if the participant simply did not check their e-mail. Web surveys (particularly those with attachments) are often flagged as "spam" and never reviewed by the potential respondent. Finally, these surveys are only useful when your population of interest (in our case, students) has access to computers and e-mail. Therefore, this method is not suitable for low-income or elderly populations.

Mail- or Paper-Based Surveys

The classroom option for completing our study would be considered a mail- or paper-based survey, in which a researcher or graduate student would bring stacks of surveys into class on campus and all students in that particular classroom would be eligible to participate. In this case, we would have to ask students to self-report whether they are campus residents, and we would hope that we have a relatively equal division of on- and off-campus residents to make comparison. These classroom-based samples are generally known as **convenience samples**, because they are not selected in any systematic way. Instead, classrooms that are surveyed are done so because they are readily available to the researcher.

In nonclassroom settings, surveys are generally distributed via postal mail. Many private corporations sell mailing lists, and researchers and other agencies seeking to administer a mail-based survey often purchase these lists. Alternatively, you could obtain a list of mailing addresses from your university if you were wishing to conduct a mail-based survey of students. Response rates for mail-based surveys are comparable to e-mail surveys (Kaplowitz, Hadlock, & Levine, 2004), averaging around 33 percent. These low response rates may be the result of incorrect mailing/recipient information, perception of mail surveys as junk mail, or unwillingness of the respondent to participate. These surveys are expensive to administer, with costs conservatively amounting to $2 per unit, with total costs more than doubling the cost of administering a Web-based survey (Cobanoglu, Warde, & Moreo, 2001).

Prenotifications and Boosters

In both Web- and mail-based surveys, prenotifications and boosters are generally used to increase the response rate. **Prenotifications** are generally e-mails or letters that inform the respondent that they were selected to participate in a survey and they will be receiving the survey in the next few days or weeks. This alerts the participant to be on the lookout for the survey, and makes note of the incentive (if applicable) and the topic of the research. Studies have found that sending a preliminary notification can increase the response rate by about 15 percent (by mail) or 30 percent (if the prenotification was in the form of a phone call; Chiu & Brennan, 1990). Another reason for the prenotification letter or postcard is to determine whether the addresses obtained in the sampling frame are accurate. The researcher would send a postcard with the option "Address correction requested" to all selected participants. If a respondent did not leave a forwarding address (or the forwarding service by the post office has expired—generally 6 months to 1 year), the postcard will be returned to the researcher. This allows for a more accurate determination of who will receive the survey, and in some cases, replacement respondents may be selected and surveyed to replace those who cannot be contacted.

Boosters are postcards, letters, or text messages that are sent to remind the respondent of the survey and the associated incentive for completing it. These letters should include another copy of the survey instrument so that it is very easy for the respondent to return the survey. All surveys should also include a self-addressed, stamped envelope to return the survey, as the removal of more barriers (e.g., respondents are less likely to return a survey if they have to make a trip to the post office to purchase stamps) will increase the response rate. Follow-up letters (30 percent) and postcards (15 percent) have been shown to increase the follow-up rate of a survey. Beyond two follow-ups letters or postcards, however, the response rate will inflate at a much lower rate, making additional follow-ups not cost-effective (Chiu & Brennan, 1990).

Phone Surveys

Phone surveys are conducted from purchased lists of telephone numbers or **random digit dialing**, a systematic approach to sampling, which will be discussed in depth in Chapter 7. Using this method, researchers are able to randomly select households with a telephone line to participate in a survey. A system for each survey will be in place to select one member of the household to respond to the survey (rather than just interviewing the person who answers the phone, who is generally the female head of household). These surveys provide an immediate response and are inexpensive to administer.

The total costs of phone surveys extend far beyond the costs of administration, however. The response rate for phone surveys is at an unprecedented low, but they are generally better than mail-based surveys (Erhart, Wetzel, Krügel, & Ravens-Sieberer, 2009) and do not include cell-phone-only households (20 percent of all households; Hu, Balluz, Battaglia, & Frankel, 2011). Some large, national surveys, including the Behavioral Risk Factor Surveillance System, began using cell-phone-based samples in addition to traditional landline sampling (Hu et al., 2011), and the results suggest that households without landlines are substantially different on several risk factors and risk behaviors when compared to those who have landlines. Cell phone surveys have the added benefit of text message reminders about the survey and consent, which may increase the response rate.

Computer-assisted telephone interviewing (CATI) is commonly used in the social sciences to conduct telephone interviews, and it is of particular use when gathering data on sensitive topics such as criminal behavior. These methods vary drastically from the most simple method of using a computerized system to select random numbers and place the phone call, while the interview is conducted by a real person over the phone, to a completely computerized system in which the respondent is able to speak and provide responses to a computerized voice. The computer understands the respondent and is able to code and remember information from the interview. This more complex method is often called **interactive voice response (IVR)**.

In basic CATI, the computer places the call and flashes questions on the screen that the interviewer is prompted to ask the participant. The interviewer then records the response directly into the system, which is coded directly as data. The computer then prompts the interviewer as to which question to ask next, incorporating **skip patterns** into the survey. These skip patterns prevent the interviewer from asking questions that are clearly irrelevant based upon other questions asked in the survey. For instance, we do not need to ask how often someone uses alcohol if they reported not using alcohol at all in their lifetime. These skip patterns are more difficult to follow on paper-based surveys, so the method used by telephone survey software is a clear advantage that will increase the ease of administration.

As discussed above, there are many limitations to conducting telephone surveys. First, although these surveys are administered over the phone, they require a great deal of manpower. It may take several hours of constant calling to obtain one "complete" response. There may also be **bias** introduced into the results if cell phones are called (or systematically excluded) or dialed. However, the data collected from a telephone survey is also directly inputted into a computer for fast coding. This minimizes errors associated with data entry and coding. Compared to mail surveys, the cost per respondent is relatively low. These are also fast to administer and it is easy to conduct and manage a random digit dialing survey compared with a large mail-based survey. Each of these pros and cons must be considered when determining which design should be used for conducting your study.

Face-to-Face Interviewing

Interviewing includes face-to-face collection of data, in which a person will visit a location (often a respondent's home) and gather information. These interviews may be used to collect in-depth information that is difficult to gather on the phone or online (e.g., lengthy responses that require probes, or follow-up questions to increase the depth of the information collected).

These interviews may be structured, unstructured, or in-depth. **Structured interviews** are very similar to surveys, in that a set sequence of questions is asked of all respondents. These questions are generally straightforward and easy to answer. For our alcohol use survey, a structured interview might include questions such as, "In an average week, on how many days do you consume one or more alcoholic beverages?" An example of a commonly used structured interview in criminal justice, the National Crime Victimization Survey, is depicted in Figure 5.1. The **response options**, or closed-ended answers, are then read: "0 days, 1 day, 2 to 3 days, 4 to 5 days, or 6 to 7 days." During these structured interviews, the person administering the interview should avoid emotional or judgmental language, and should not deviate from the question as it is written on the survey.

In **unstructured interviews**, the purpose of the study dictates the form of the survey. In most cases, these interviews are comprised of open-ended questions to explore a topic in greater depth. In our survey of alcohol use, an example of an unstructured interview question may be, "What are the three main reasons that you use alcohol?" or "Why do you believe that students who

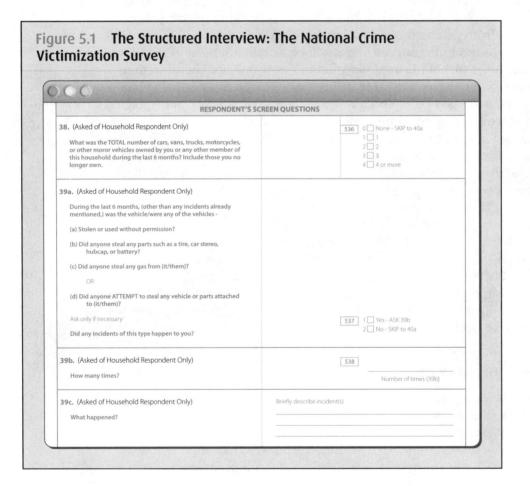

Figure 5.1 The Structured Interview: The National Crime Victimization Survey

RESPONDENT'S SCREEN QUESTIONS

38. (Asked of Household Respondent Only)

What was the TOTAL number of cars, vans, trucks, motorcycles, or other moror vehicles owned by you or any other member of this household during the last 6 months? Include those you no longer own.

536
0 ☐ None - SKIP to 40a
1 ☐ 1
2 ☐ 2
3 ☐ 3
4 ☐ 4 or more

39a. (Asked of Household Respondent Only)

During the last 6 months, (other than any incidents already mentioned,) was the vehicle/were any of the vehicles -

(a) Stolen or used without permission?

(b) Did anyone steal any parts such as a tire, car stereo, hubcap, or battery?

(c) Did anyone steal any gas from (it/them)?

OR

(d) Did anyone ATTEMPT to steal any vehicle or parts attached to (it/them)?

Ask only if necessary

Did any incidents of this type happen to you?

537
1 ☐ Yes - ASK 39b
2 ☐ No - SKIP to 40a

39b. (Asked of Household Respondent Only)

How many times?

538
_____
Number of times (39b)

39c. (Asked of Household Respondent Only)

What happened?

Briefly describe incident(s)

_____

_____

_____

live on campus are more likely to drink than those who live off campus?" There are no predetermined responses for these questions. Instead, the responses are exploratory and the researchers are looking for qualitative information.

Finally, **in-depth interviews** are a type of unstructured interview, and these surveys are generally much longer and have fewer respondents than most surveys. There are very few prescribed questions in these types of interviews; however, the researcher usually has a list of topics to cover during the interview. There is a great deal of discretion and flexibility in what is discussed. For this reason, this method is often used for case studies. In our example, we might conduct interviews with a small number of students to understand the reasons for their alcohol use. This may lead to a discussion of their friends' behavior, a fraternity or sorority, a desire to be accepted, or a perceived norm among students at their institution. Each interview will take its own course, and the researcher will have a diverse picture of why students use alcohol more or less often in the residence halls.

Each of these interview types is appropriate for a different type of research question (Opdenakker, 2006). Structured interviews are most common because they are the least expensive method of interviewing, and they are relatively easy to code and analyze. Unstructured interviews are used to understand more about a given topic for future research or program development. In-depth interviews are used when the researcher needs a great deal of information about a very specific topic. In other words, structured interviews provide the "width" of information (a large amount of information about a great deal of topics; however, we will know very little about each topic), while unstructured and in-depth interviews provide the "depth" (we know a great deal about one topic, but the one topic is very narrow).

Interviews are advantageous because they allow a rapport to be built between the researcher and the respondent. Fewer **break-offs**—that is, cases in which the respondent refuses to complete a survey before it is completed—are expected in interview settings compared to a telephone survey. Also, in the event that a respondent is confused about a particular question, a person is present to clarify the concept. This reduces **item nonresponse**, in which the respondent skips one or more questions. On the other hand, in some cases the presence of the interviewer may change the respondents' answers to questions, causing inaccurate reporting, known as the **interviewer effect**. Interviewers may also make mistakes and misread questions, which can present problems in the way the respondent answers the question.

An extension of mail-based surveys, **computer-assisted personal (or programmed) interviewing (CAPI)** integrates a paper-based survey with the ease of programmed skip patterns and self-coding data. In these cases, an interviewer will be present and administer an interview (generally structured) to a respondent. There are two variations on CAPI. In the first variation, the interviewer reads the question to the respondent and the respondent views the responses on a computer and marks the response. In the second, the respondent wears headphones and the question is read by the computer;

the respondent hears the question and marks the appropriate response on the computer (Baker, 1992). These two methods allow collection of sensitive data, such as heavy drug use or criminal behavior, without arousing fear in respondents that the interviewer will judge their behavior.

Factors Influencing Response Rates

As noted above, response rates are one of the greatest concerns when administering a survey. From a scientific perspective, the ideal situation would be if every person in your sample responded to your survey. However, this rarely happens in practice; therefore, a researcher is left to select the most appropriate mode of administrator given their population and research topic. The length of the survey, prenotification, follow-up, topic of the survey, and incentive all play a role in determining the response rate (Fox, Crask, & Kim, 1988; Sheehan, 2001).

The longer and more in-depth the survey is, the lower the response rate might be (Jepson, Asch, Hershey, & Ubel, 2005). This will be mitigated depending upon the amount of the incentive. For instance, you might be able to convince people to participate in your hour-long survey if you offer them $25 in cash, while they may not be willing to complete it for a lower price (less than $5). Different types of incentives also differentially affect the response rate (Church, 1993). Research suggests that lotteries are one of the least effective (and least convincing) methods of enticing respondents to complete your survey. The most effective method is enclosing cash (or a gift card, chocolate, or some other similar reward) in the envelope with the survey, even when the amount of cash is small. Guaranteeing a payment upon returning the survey has also proven to be effective in increasing response rate (Brennan & Charbonneau, 2009; James, Ziegenfuss, Tilburt, Harris, & Beebe, 2011).

There is some support for the notion that **personalization** may increase the likelihood that someone will respond to your survey (Houston & Jefferson, 1975). For instance, if you were to get a letter in the mail that was addressed to "Respondent" or "To whom it may concern," you may be inclined to throw the letter away. If the letter was addressed to you directly, however, you may begin to read it. Although this seems like a minor detail, some research suggests that it may increase the response rate of your survey (Fox et al., 1988). Therefore, researchers should attempt to include information about the person they are attempting to recruit whenever it is available.

What is an acceptable response rate varies substantially by discipline, mode, and topic (Sivo, Saunders, Chang, & Jiang, 2006). Ideally, every person who is selected to participate in your survey will complete the survey in its entirety. In practice, complete sample ascertainment is an extremely rare occurrence. Nonresponse matters because it can introduce serious bias into your findings, and increasing the response rate will maximize the likelihood that what you find is actually true (Etter & Perneger, 1997). In our hypothetical study, for example, assume we have a response rate of 35 percent, and we found that alcohol use is higher among students who live on campus. We also found, however, that most of the older respondents who live on campus did not complete the survey. Therefore, we may erroneously conclude that differences about alcohol use relate to residential status when the actual reason for the higher level of alcohol use among campus residents may be that they are younger, more likely to use alcohol, and more likely to complete our survey.

There are generally accepted rules of thumb for what is an acceptable response rate. In survey research, a response rate of 60 percent is considered minimally acceptable, while a rate of 70 percent or greater is ideal (Baruch & Holtom, 2008). When the response rate is lower, the results may be difficult to publish in academic journals, as the sample may not be valid or accurately represent a population. It is important to gain as much information about your participants at the onset of your study (e.g., age, gender, etc.) to determine whether those who responded to your survey were different on baseline demographic measures than those who did not respond. If there are no differences, you have a stronger argument that your sample that participated in your survey is representative of the sampling frame.

DEVELOPING THE SURVEY

Now that you have identified that a survey is the method you will use to collect data, you have to develop a list of questions to ask your respondents. Regardless of the mode (telephone, Web, or mail-based) of the survey, a questionnaire must be developed to gather the information that you need to answer your research question (Bradburn, Sudman, & Wasinik, 2004). In developing closed-ended questions, there are several guidelines to keep in mind:

1. Be sure the response options for every question are mutually exclusive. For instance, if you were to ask the question, "On how many days did you drink alcohol last week?" and provided the following options: "0 days," "1 to 2 days," "2 to 3 days," "3 to 4" days, and so on, it is possible that someone who drank on 2 days last week could be in two different groups. This practice should be avoided to reduce confusion of the respondent and introduction of bias.
2. Be sure the response options are exhaustive. When asking closed-ended questions, make sure that all possible responses are provided as response options. If you were to ask students, "What type of alcohol did you most recently consume?" and provided "beer," "wine," "liquor," and "mixed drinks" as response options, you leave those who drank malt beverages without a valid response. Be sure to brainstorm all possible response options or provide an "other" response option to reduce item nonresponse or inaccurate responses.
3. Be sure that questions and statements are clear. It may be necessary to provide a guideline sentence before a section of statements to guide the

respondent: "Please indicate how much you agree or disagree with each particular statement." Then provide a Likert scale of response options. If you abruptly switch between questions and statements without directions, the respondent may get confused.

4. Keep the questions/statements as brief as possible.

5. Avoid negatives. These add confusion and increase the risk that your question will be responded to inaccurately. Rewrite questions such as "How much do you dislike the negative effects of alcohol?" to read along the lines of "How do the effects of alcohol make you feel?"

6. Do not ask leading questions. The way questions are asked can influence responses. For example, the question, "Do you believe that semiautomatic weapons, like those that were responsible for large school shootings, should be regulated?" may be answered differently than the question, "Should semiautomatic weapons be controlled?" Also, using a name of a prestigious agency, such as the Supreme Court, may bias responses. Respondents are more likely to agree with the statement "Supreme Court decision to allow intrusive interrogation practices" rather than "intrusive interrogation practices."

7. Use neutral words. For example, asking respondents' attitude about "welfare" may provide a different response than asking about "assistance to the poor."

8. Use existing items whenever possible. This is arguably one of the most important tactics in developing a survey. A great deal of research time has been spent on measurement and instrumentation, and large-scale federal surveys (Behavioral Risk Factor Surveillance System, Monitoring the Future, NCVS) have been using the same questions for decades. This has a number of advantages; notably, you will be sure that your questions are measuring what they are intended to measure, and you will be able to compare the results of your survey with those from national sources. Following this guideline will positively influence the quality of your data.

DESIGNING THE QUESTIONNAIRE

Now that you have a list of the questions you would like to administer to your sample, you will have to organize them in some meaningful way. Improperly organizing your questions may be off-putting to some respondents and reduce the likelihood they will complete your survey (Passmore, Dobbie, Parchman, & Tysinger, 2002). Be certain that the survey looks neat on paper, organized into two vertical columns (or one, if you are using a grid or Likert scales). Be sure that the respondent knows which questions to answer first. Provide directions at the top of the page when there is any possibility for confusion. Do not make the font excessively small or squeeze in extra questions to reduce the page size; some respondents will be deterred from completing a difficult-to-read or cluttered survey. Do not use abbreviations without explaining them (if necessary to use them at all), and make sure that all skip patterns are clearly marked. In general, do not allow the respondent to find your survey unclear for any reason. An example of a real survey that has been used in the field is depicted in Figure 5.2 (this is from a police department survey in South Carolina).

Matrices, displayed in Figure 5.3, should have clear guidelines for completion and should stand alone on the page (Jarvenpaa & Dickson, 1988). Shading should be used to make large matrices easy to follow. All matrices should be read from left to right, with response options in the columns. The matrix design allows you to ask a large number of similar questions in a small amount of space, and these tables are easy for the respondent to follow and understand. In some instances, you may choose to remove the neutral "neither agree nor disagree" option to force respondents to have an opinion about each topic. If a respondent has no real feelings about a statement, however, the response may be left blank or answered inaccurately. For that reason, the neutral response option is traditionally left in the Likert scale (Matell & Jacoby, 1972).

Because some items are sensitive in nature, they are often administered at the end of the survey. This will allow time for the survey to build some informal "rapport" with the respondent. For instance, if you ask about respondents' illegal drug use immediately, they may refuse to complete your survey. If you first ask about them (demographic information), then about their household members, then about alcohol use, and only last about illegal drug use, the level

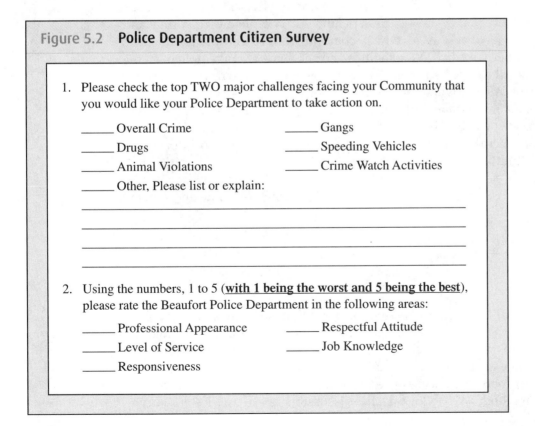

Figure 5.2 Police Department Citizen Survey

1. Please check the top TWO major challenges facing your Community that you would like your Police Department to take action on.

   _____ Overall Crime   _____ Gangs

   _____ Drugs   _____ Speeding Vehicles

   _____ Animal Violations   _____ Crime Watch Activities

   _____ Other, Please list or explain:

   _____

   _____

   _____

   _____

2. Using the numbers, 1 to 5 (**with 1 being the worst and 5 being the best**), please rate the Beaufort Police Department in the following areas:

   _____ Professional Appearance   _____ Respectful Attitude

   _____ Level of Service   _____ Job Knowledge

   _____ Responsiveness

Figure 5.3   **Survey Question Matrices Example**

	Strongly Disagree	Disagree	Neither Agree nor Disagree	Agree	Strongly Agree
The rules regarding alcohol use at my university are clear.	☐	☐	☐	☐	☐
The university enforces the alcohol policies.	☐	☐	☐	☐	☐
I will get in trouble with the university if I am caught using alcohol.	☐	☐	☐	☐	☐

of concern may have diminished to the extent that respondents are more likely to answer your more difficult questions.

Once you have drafted your survey, you should conduct a **pilot study**. This should include a small sample of people similar to those in your target population; however, it should not include any people who will directly participate in your study (Baker, 1994). These people will complete your survey and provide direct feedback as to which components are confusing, illogical, unclear, or underdescribed. You should instruct them to make notes when a response is not available for a closed-ended question (i.e., the response options are not exhaustive), or when they could answer a question in more than one way. After the pilot, a small, informal focus group may be conducted. During this session, you will discuss the survey and any problems encountered by those who participated in the pilot. The participants may also inform you on anything that is missing from the survey, whether the flow is disjointed, or if the sequence or language was not appropriate for the audience or could be improved. This will provide valuable feedback, saving both time and money, before you conduct a large-scale survey.

SUMMARY

This chapter looked at survey research methodology and questionnaire creation. We began this chapter by discussing whether it is appropriate to conduct a survey given your research question and sample. Next, we discussed differential modes of survey administration, including Web, e-mail, mail, phone, and in-person interviews, as well as the pros and cons associated with each method. We followed the discussion about modes of survey administration with "how to" information on instrument design. Some effective methods for designing questionnaires to increase participant response rates were discussed, and pilot testing and focus group feedback were discussed as preliminary methods for obtaining constructive feedback on the survey from the target population.

KEY TERMS

Bias Reflects the degree to which survey questions are answered inaccurately or not as they are intended to be answered. Several types of biases exist in survey research, including response bias and nonresponse bias.

Boosters Postcards, letters, or text messages that are sent to remind the respondent of the survey to complete the survey.

Break-off Occurs when respondents terminate the interview before answering all of the questions.

Census Method of systematically acquiring and recording information about all members of a given population. The term is most frequently used with the U.S. Census.

Computer-assisted personal interviewing (CAPI) An interviewing technique in which a respondent uses a computer to answer interview or survey questions. The interviewer is typically present as part of this process.

Computer-assisted telephone interviewing (CATI) A telephone surveying technique in which the interviewer follows a predetermined script provided by computer software. This structured system speeds up the collection and editing of survey data.

Convenience samples Types of nonprobability samples that involve drawing a sample from the most convenient/handy population, even if that population is not generalizable. This method is useful when populations are hard to reach.

In-depth interviews Longer types of unstructured interviews that typically have few survey respondents and few prescribed questions. These interviews are also used in exploratory research to gather a great deal of information about a very specific topic.

Interactive voice response (IVR) A computer-based technology that allows a computer to interact with humans through the use of voice input.

Interviewer effect Physical or personal characteristics of an interviewer (e.g., race, gender, overt friendliness) that influence how an interviewee completes or answers interview questions.

Item nonresponse Refers to when a survey participant skips a particular question in the course of completing a survey.

Personalization Includes minor details (e.g., including their name) added to survey communications to increase the participants' likelihood of responding.

Pilot study   A small-scale preliminary study that is conducted to evaluate the feasibility, cost, validation of data collection methodology, and so on, prior to full implementation.

Prenotifications   E-mails, postcards, or letters that inform potential survey respondents that they were selected to participate in a survey and that they will be receiving the survey in days or weeks to come. The purpose of this letter is to increase the response rate.

Random digit dialing   A sample selection method in which telephone numbers are generated at random for the purpose of selecting research participants.

Response options   Answers provided in a survey that a survey respondent may use to respond to each item.

Response rates   The number of people who answered a survey divided by the number of people who were selected to participate. Response rates are typically expressed as a percentage.

Sample   A subset of a population. It is usually not necessary to study an entire population; therefore, a representative sample of the population is used to make inferences about the entire population.

Skip patterns   Tools used in survey research to prevent respondents from answering questions that do not apply based on previous responses.

Stratify   A method used to sample subpopulations within a population. When your study requires a large number of people with one characteristic (and this characteristic is rare in the population), it is advantageous to sample from this group at a higher rate, or to *stratify*. The sampling frame is divided into groups based upon the characteristic of interest, and a (not necessarily equal) proportion of each group (strata) is selected into the sample.

Structured interviews   A quantitative research method used in survey research for the purpose of ensuring that each interview is composed of the exact same questions, in the exact same order. See also *unstructured interview*.

Surveys   Any measurement procedure that involves the investigator positing questions of research participants that require self-report responses.

Unstructured interviews   Interviews that can be adapted or changed to meet the needs of the interview respondent. They do not have predetermined questions or answers, and future questions are based on the responses from previous questions. These interviews are generally used for exploratory research. See also *structured interview*.

REVIEW QUESTIONS

1. What is an acceptable response rate in survey research? Explain the rationale behind this level of acceptability.
2. What are some important considerations one must be wary of when creating a survey questionnaire?

3. Explain the primary purpose of conducting a focus group when developing a survey instrument.
4. What is the primary purpose of the unstructured interview? How is this type of interview typically conducted?
5. What is the purpose of computer-assisted personal interviewing (CAPI)? Describe the differences between CAPI and the paper-based survey methods.

Useful Websites

www.unescap.org/stat/pop-it/pop-guide/capture_ch03.pdf. A helpful description of CAPI.
www.socialresearchmethods.net/kb/survwrit.php. Website discussing survey construction.
www.historylearningsite.co.uk/unstructured_interviews.htm. Information on creating unstructured interviews.
www.census.gov/. U.S. Census Bureau website; an example of a survey research.
www.surveymonkey.com. Popular Web-based survey creation resource.

References

Babor, T. F., Stephens, R. S., & Marlatt, G. A. (1987). Verbal report methods in clinical research on alcoholism: Response bias and its minimization. *Journal of Studies on Alcohol and Drugs, 48*, 410–423.

Baker, R. P. (1992). New technology in survey research: Computer-assisted personal interviewing (CAPI). *Social Science Computer Review, 10*(2), 145–157.

Baker, T. L. (1994). *Doing social research* (2d ed.). New York: McGraw-Hill.

Baruch, Y., & Holton, B. C. (2008). Survey response rate levels and trends in organizational research. *Human Relations, 61*(8), 1139–1160.

Bradburn, N. M., Sudman, S., & Wasnik, B. (2004). *Asking questions: The definitive guide to questionnaire design—for market research, political polls, and science and health questionnaires.* San Francisco: Wiley.

Brennan, M., & Charbonneau, J. (2009). Improving mail survey response rates using chocolate and replacement questionnaires. *Public Opinion Quarterly, 73*(2), 368–378.

Chiu, I., & Brennan, M. (1990). The effectiveness of some techniques for improving mail survey response rates: A meta-analysis. *Marketing Bulletin, 1*, 13–18.

Church, A. C. (1993). Estimating the effects of incentives on mail survey response rates: A meta-analysis. *Public Opinion Questionnaire, 57*(1), 62–79.

Cobanoglu, C., Warde, B., & Moreo, P. J. (2001). A comparison of mail, fax and web-based survey methods. *International Journal of Market Research, 43*(4), 441–452.

Dillman, D. A., Smyth, J. D., & Christian, L. M. (2008). *Internet, mail, and mixed- mode surveys: Tailored design method* (3d ed.). Hoboken, NJ: John Wiley and Sons.

Erhart, M., Wetzel, R. M., Krügel, A., & Ravens-Sieberer, U. (2009). Effects of phone versus mail survey methods on the measurement of health-related quality of life and emotional and behavioural problems in adolescents. *BMC Public Health, 9*(1), 491.

Etter, J., & Perneger, T. V. (1997). Analysis of non-response bias in a mailed health survey. *Journal of Clinical Epidemiology, 50*(10), 1123–1128.

Fox, R. J., Crask, M. R., & Kim, J. (1988). Mail survey response rate a meta-analysis of selected techniques for inducing response. *Public Opinion Quarterly, 52*(4), 467–491.

Hagan, F. E. (1997). *Research methods in criminal justice and criminology.* Needham Heights, MA: Allyn and Bacon.

Houston, M. J., & Jefferson, R. W. (1975). The negative effect of personalization on response patterns in mail surveys. *Journal of Marketing Research, 12*(1), 114–117.

Hu, S. S., Balluz, L., Battaglia, M. P., & Frankel, M. R. (2011). Improving public health surveillance using a dual-frame survey of landline and cell phone numbers. *American Journal of Epidemiology, 173*(6), 703–711.

James, K. M., Ziegenfuss, J. Y., Tilburt, J. C., Harris, A. M., & Beebe, T. J. (2011). Getting physicians to respond: The impact of incentive type and timing on physician survey response rates. *Health Services Research, 46*, 232–242.

Jarvenpaa, S. L., & Dickson, G. W. (1988). Graphics and managerial decision making: Research based guidelines. *Communications of the ACM, 31*(6), 764–774.

Jepson, C. J., Asch, D. A., Hershey, J. C., & Ubel, P. A. (2005). In a mailed physician survey, questionnaire length had a threshold effect on response rate. *Journal of Clinical Epidemiology, 58*(1), 103–105.

Kaplowitz, M. D., Hadlock, T. D., & Levine, R. (2004). A comparison of web and mail survey response rates. *Public Opinion Questionnaire, 68*(1), 94–101.

Matell, M. S., & Jacoby, J. J. (1972). Is there an optimal number of alternatives for Likert scale items? Effects of testing on time and scale properties. *Journal of Applied Psychology, 56*(6), 506–509.

Opdenakker, R. (2006). Advantages and disadvantages of four interview techniques in qualitative research. *Forum: Qualitative Social Research, 7*(4), 1–10.

Passmore, C., Dobbie, A., Parchman, M., & Tysinger, J. (2002). Guidelines for constructing a survey. *Family Medicine, 34*(4), 281–286.

Sheehan, K. B. (2001). E-mail survey response rates: A review. *Journal of Computer-Mediated Communication, 6:0.* doi: 10.1111/j.1083-6101.2001.tb00117.x.

Sivo, S. S., Saunders, C., Chang, Q., & Jiang, J. J. (2006). How low should you go? Low response rates and the validity of inference in IS questionnaire research. *Journal of the Association of Information Systems, 7*(6), 351–414.

SECONDARY DATA ANALYSIS

T his chapter describes and reviews examples of data available for secondary use, including the Uniform Crime Reports (UCR), the National Crime Victimization Survey (NCVS), the National Survey on Drug Use and Health (NSDUH), the Monitoring the Future (MTF) survey, the General Social Survey (GSS), the National Longitudinal Survey of Youth (NLSY), U.S. Census, content analysis, and meta-analysis. After a brief overview of the general types of secondary data and a direct comparison between official and self-report data as related to secondary data analysis, we will examine some of the more important of these sources for criminological research.

SECONDARY DATA

Secondary data refers to data that has been previously collected and reported on for some purpose other than your study. These data may also have been used in prior research, including prior use in data analysis and interpretation (Kleck, Tark, & Bellows, 2006). These sources provide data in two forms: public-use data and restricted-use data. **Public-use data** is freely available for use by individuals and researchers (Parmer, Torri, & Stewart, 1998). The number of home runs that individual baseball players have hit over the last two decades are public-use statistics. When each home run was hit, the fact that the hit occurred was primary data (i.e., recording home runs for calculating batting averages is the originally intended purpose of the data); however, once accumulated in the league record books and other repositories, it constitutes a published statistic, and its use would be secondary data (i.e., it is being used for purposes other than originally intended). You could take this publically available information and use it to perform a secondary data analysis—for example, identifying trends in home-run hitting for individual players or teams over time.

In contrast, **restricted-use data** refers to data that has been previously collected by individuals, departments, or agencies and not made readily available to the public for immediate access or use. Criminal justice agencies collect a lot of data on their personnel (police officers, correctional officers, treatment providers, etc.), their population of clients (inmates, patients), and their expenditures (salaries, benefits, operating costs), among other subjects. If you were interested in researching the disciplinary infractions of police officers or correctional officers, these agencies would not be likely to hand over their personnel files, as this information is often considered confidential. They may, however, agree to **de-identify data**—by removing any and all personal identifying information—and provide you with the de-identified data files for secondary use (Friedlin & McDonald, 2008). To provide another example, you may wish to investigate the nature of inmate disciplinary infraction while in prison. While the correctional administrators obviously keep a record of all of the occurrences, including which particular inmate committed an infraction/s and the type of infraction committed, the correctional administrators would likely be amenable to providing you with de-identified files on the inmate infractions for secondary use. These files are de-identified in that they will tell you about inmate infractions, but you will be unable to identify who perpetrated each specific behavior.

OFFICIAL DATA VERSUS SELF-REPORT DATA

Prior to reviewing more well-known and widely used criminology and criminal justice examples of sources of secondary data, it is important to recognize and learn the strengths and weaknesses in using either official or self-report data as sources for secondary data analysis. Historically, criminologists and criminal justice researchers have relied on **official data** to measure crime and delinquency. These official sources of data include police, court, prison records, and so on. Despite this long tradition of use as a main source of crime measurement, two central arguments have been made against their use, favoring instead using self-report data to measure crime and delinquency. The first argument addresses the so-called dark figure of crime (discussed in Chapter 4). Specifically, critics argue that a number of crimes go unreported to the police, thus making any estimates of crime or investigations into the patterns and trends of crime misleading because known crimes and trends derived from studying them represent the "tip of the iceberg." The second main argument against using official data addresses the bias in official records resulting from the disproportionate representation of minority and disadvantaged populations in official crime statistics.

In response to these criticisms, Edwin Sutherland (1949) provided the groundwork for **self-report data**—that is, data collected directly from individuals via a survey—in his research on crime and delinquency among white-collar criminals. Because of the widespread assumption at the time that white-collar workers did not engage in crime, official statistics focused on street crime rather than other forms of criminal behavior (such as white collar, or corporate, crime). Subsequent to Sutherland's observations, self-report studies were conducted over the course of the next several decades by scholars such as Porterfield (1943, 1946), who surveyed 200 men and 127 women from colleges in northern Texas; Wallerstein and Wylie (1947), who surveyed 1,698 adult women and men about their juvenile delinquency; and Short and Nye (1957, 1958), whose various publications presented their survey results from large samples of high school students who were asked 21 questions about their criminal and antisocial behavior. These early studies continue to spawn interest among researchers to apply the self-report method for a number of criminology and criminal justice–related topics and to test various criminological theories.

Despite the wealth of information gleaned from self-report crime and delinquency studies, they, like official data, are not without criticism. Hindelang, Hirschi, and Weis (1979) were among the first and most vocal critics of self-report data. By comparing self-report and official data, they demonstrated an apparent discrepancy between the two sources, which they attributed largely to the tendency of self-report surveys not to include many serious crimes resulting in arrest. Elliot and Ageton (1980) noted that most self-report studies limited the questions to whether the survey respondent engaged in the crime (yes/no) or limited the response options (0 times, 1 to 2 times, 3 or more times). They found that once they removed the fixed upper limits on questions about crimes, including serious crimes committed, the results from self-report data better resembled the results from official data. More recently, Thornberry and Krohn (2000) and Krohn, Thornberry, Gibson, and Baldwin (2010) outlined four specific recommendations for self-report studies and the items they use to measure crime and delinquency:

1. Self-report scales should include a wide range of delinquent acts so that the general domain of delinquency and its various subdomains are adequately represented.
2. The scale should include serious as well as minor acts.
3. A frequency scale should be used to record responses so that high-rate offenders can be isolated from low-rate offenders.
4. Extremely trivial, nonactionable acts that are reported should be identified and eliminated from the data.

Regardless of whether the data you use in a secondary data analysis is official or self-report, you need to be aware of its inherent limitations, which will directly affect what you can and cannot say with the data that you have. Proponents in both camps argue in favor of the superiority of their preferred date type, while other researchers believe in compromise and use both measures as appropriate and available to provide the best research results.

MAJOR SECONDARY SOURCES FOR CRIMINOLOGICAL RESEARCH

Uniform Crime Reports

As discussed in Chapter 4, the Uniform Crime Reports (UCR) is the most widely used official source of crime data currently available. The UCR data, originally collected by the local police agencies and jurisdictions, represents a primary source of data, but once these data are delivered to the FBI and published in the annual *Crime in the United States* report, it becomes publically available as a source for secondary data analysis. The FBI's website (www.fbi.gov) hosts these data by year and in a variety of user-friendly forms. For instance, you can go on the website and find the violent crime rates, property crime rates, clearance rates, and offense-specific information by region, state, or local agency. The site allows you to select as much and as detailed publicly available information as you like and will allow you to generate summary tables from it. In addition, user-friendly versions of the data can easily be exported into programs such as Microsoft Excel for use in secondary data analysis. Should you decide to use this source of data for secondary data analysis, you should recall the main limitations that previous researchers have summarized (Loftin & McDowall, 2010):

1. The procedures and definitions are not consistent across agencies.
2. Many crimes are not included because citizens do not report them to the police and the likelihood of citizen reporting varies in systematic ways.
3. The police are selective in reporting crime and this filtering process is biased (not constant across social groups or areas).
4. Some agencies do not report or report incompletely, and missing data are poorly documented.
5. The major data collections do not provide information on the characteristics of offenders (such as age, race, and gender), and these must be inferred from arrest data.
6. The UCR is not a statistical program in the usual sense of the term. Rather, it is a "house organ" of the police (Lejins, 1966) and reflects the organizational interests of agencies that may use the data to further those interests.

The UCR is the only source of official crime data providing estimates of total crimes, violent and property crimes, and specific crimes and rates over a long time period. Furthermore, UCR data has relied on the same definitions of crime since its inception (e.g., the UCR indicates that a stolen Xbox should be categorized as a "stolen VCR"), and it is the only nationally representative source of crime official data accounting for greater than 90 percent and 98 percent of residents in rural and urban areas, respectively.

National Crime Victimization Survey

The National Crime Victimization (NCVS) survey, also reviewed in detail in Chapter 4, is the most widely known source of victimization self-report data. Specifically, the NCVS was developed with the four following objectives:

1. To develop detailed information about the victims and consequences of crime
2. To estimate the number and types of crimes not reported to the police

3. To provide uniform measures of selected types of crimes
4. To permit comparisons over time and types of areas

The survey categorizes crimes as "personal" or "property." Personal crimes cover rape and sexual assault, robbery, aggravated and simple assault, and purse-snatching/pocket-picking, while property crimes cover burglary, theft, motor vehicle theft, and vandalism. The data from the NCVS survey are particularly useful for calculating crime rates, both aggregated and disaggregated, and for evaluating trends from year to year (see www.icpsr.umich.edu/icpsrweb/NACJD/NCVS/#About_NCVS). NCVS data is available for secondary analysis through the National Archive of Criminal Justice Data, which can be found online through the website of the **International Consortium for Political and Social Research (ICPSR)**. The ICPSR is a clearinghouse that provides extensive access to a wealth of publicly available, downloadable data for the purpose of secondary data analysis (see www.icpsr.umich.edu/icpsrweb/NACJD/NCVS).

As a researcher, you can actually perform secondary data analysis with these data online in an interactive platform. For instance, you can run frequencies of specific types of crime by state, compare crime rates, and examine relationships between certain variables and crime. Furthermore, you can select particular variables of interest and customize and carve out a smaller version of the data that you can quickly download and use for more customized secondary data analysis.

A word of caution is once again needed here when considering using the NCVS for secondary data analysis. Specifically, these data may suffer from recall problems (Waltermaurer, McNutt, & Mattingly, 2006), which arise when victims do not remember the victimization event accurately or vividly, and telescoping problems, which arise when respondents report a victimization occurring before the reference period targeted in the interview (e.g., reporting a victimization that occurred 2 years ago when the interviewer refers to the past year). Also, proxy interviews (interviews with someone other than the respondent) may be conducted in several cases, such as when the knowledgeable household members refuse to have members aged 12 or 13 years old directly interviewed; when parents/caretakers of a person who is physically and/or mentally incapable of responding to interview questions answer on their behalf; or when knowledgeable household members answer questions for persons who are away from the household during the entire interview period (Weir, Faul, & Langa, 2011). Finally, individuals may not report certain victimizations due to testing effects (having been interviewed previously and knowing that reporting crime lengthens the interview process) or fear or embarrassment.

National Survey on Drug Use and Health

The **National Survey on Drug Use and Health (NSDUH)** is an annual nationwide survey that is used to gather national and state-level estimates on the use of tobacco, alcohol, and drugs in the United States and mental health issues (Herman-Stahl, Krebs, Kroutil, & Heller, 2007). More specifically, the survey is conducted each year with funding provided by the Substance Abuse and Mental Health Services Administration (SAMHSA) in order to interview a random sample of approximately 70,000 individuals aged 12 and older. The original goals of the project are:

1. to provide accurate data on the level and patterns of alcohol, tobacco, and illegal substance use and abuse;
2. to track trends in the use of alcohol, tobacco, and other types of drugs;
3. to assess the consequences of substance use and abuse; and
4. to identify those groups at high risk for substance use and abuse (https://nsduhweb.rti.org).

Although the interviews are conducted in the privacy of the respondent's home, in an effort to ensure confidentiality, the participants' full names are never recorded and cannot be linked to their answers. The entire interview data file is also de-identified and each individual is identified only by a random number before electronic submission to Research Triangle Institute (RTI). RTI is then responsible for coding, cleaning, totaling, and disseminating national-level estimates that are publically available for use in secondary data analysis. The NSDUH is also available in a de-identified and downloadable format ready for use in secondary data analysis via ICPSR's online archive of publically available data (www.icpsr.umich.edu/icpsrweb/ICPSR/series/64).

Monitoring the Future

The **Monitoring the Future (MTF)** study was initiated in 1975 and targeted a nationally representative sample of approximately 16,000 high school seniors in over 130 public and private high schools (O'Malley & Wagenaar, 1991). In 1991, nationally representative samples of an equivalent number of eighth and tenth graders were added to the sampling strategy. Thus, the MTF surveys approximately 50,000 students in over 400 public and private high schools and secondary schools in the United States every year regarding a host of topics, including their beliefs, attitudes, and behaviors on various drug-related and risk behaviors. After the inaugural 1975 survey, the study design was amended to also collect follow-up data from a randomly selected sample from each senior class every 2 years after high school graduation in order to study changes in individuals' beliefs, attitudes, and behaviors as they age and enter adulthood. Specifically, if you were interested in using data from the MTF in a research project, you could investigate any of the following four different "kinds of change" in beliefs, attitudes, and behaviors (Thornton, 1989):

1. Changes in particular years reflected across all age groups (secular trends or "period effects")

2. Developmental changes that show up consistently for all panels ("age effects")

3. Consistent differences among class cohorts through the life cycle ("cohort effects")

4. Changes linked to different types of environments (high school, college, employment) or role transitions (leaving the parental home, marriage, parenthood, etc.) (http://monitoringthefuture.org/purpose.html).

As with the NCVS and the NSDUH, these data are also available in a de-identified and downloadable format ready for use in secondary data analysis via ICPSR's online archive of publically available data (www.icpsr.umich.edu/icpsrweb/SAMHDA/series/00035).

General Social Survey

The **General Social Survey (GSS)** is widely regarded as the best source for data on societal trends, including public perceptions of crime and crime-related issues (McPherson, Smith-Lovin, & Brashears, 2006). The GSS has been a data source since the early 1970s, and each survey (originally conducted annually) was administered to a representative sample of noninstitutionalized English-speaking persons in the United States aged 18 and older. Spanish speakers were added to the target sample in 2006. The cumulative data file from 1972 to 2010 includes more than 55,000 respondents and over 5,000 variables that measure a range of social, cultural, and political indicators (Smith, Marsden, & Hout, 1972–2010). The GSS has its own website hosted by the National Opinion Research Center (NORC) at the University of Chicago. You can go to their website (www3.norc.org/gss+website/) and perform your own analysis using their interactive secondary analysis tools. In addition, you can also carve out a smaller data set with only the variables you are interested in and perform your own analysis in another software program such as Microsoft Excel.

National Longitudinal Survey of Youth

The **National Longitudinal Survey of Youth (NLSY)** is a longitudinal and nationally representative survey of 12,686 young men and women conducted by the U.S. Department of Labor. These participants were first interviewed in 1979 when they were between the ages of 14 and 22 years old (Rodgers, 1994). These subjects were interviewed on an annual basis from 1979 up until 1994, and since 1994 they have been interviewed on a biennial basis. These data are rich and detailed, primarily due to the event history format in which the data are collected. As such, these data include information on the beginning and ending points of key life transitions, including labor force participation, marital status, fertility, and participation in government assistance programs. Of particular relevance to criminology and criminal justice, data are also available on educational attainment, training investments, income and assets, health conditions, workplace injuries, insurance coverage, alcohol and substance abuse, sexual activity, and criminal histories (www.bls.gov/nls/nlsy79.htm). Similar to the NCVS, the NSDUH, and the MTF study, these data are available in a de-identified and downloadable format ready for use in secondary data analysis via ICPSR's online archive of publically available data (www.icpsr.u-mich.edu/icpsrweb/ICPSR/series/129).

U.S. Census Bureau

The **United States Census Bureau**, which is part of the U.S. Department of Commerce, serves as the primary source of high-quality data about the U.S. population and the economy. Every 10 years, the U.S. Census counts every resident in the United States for the purpose of determining the number of seats that each state has in the U.S. House of Representatives and how to distribute federal funds across the country. Beyond this purpose, the decennial census serves as the richest source of data for consumers and researchers on a host of topics such as age, sex, race, ethnicity, income, education, poverty, homeownership, and population totals in urban and rural areas. These data are presented in a summary tabular format on the U.S. Census website for quick referencing of facts. You can also pick and choose certain variables that you want to study and can generate personalized tables or download personalized data sets for secondary analysis (www.census.gov/2010census/data/). For instance, if you wanted to study the relationship between poverty and crime rates in the United States' largest 100 cities, you could download the crime rates for the largest 100 cities at the FBI's UCR website and then download the poverty rates for these 100 cities along with other potentially relevant control variables such as the percent unemployed, the percent with a high school diploma, and the percent of minorities in each city from the U.S. Census' website (Shihadeh & Flynn, 1996). After downloading these data from these two sources, you could merge the files and conduct your secondary data analysis.

METHODS OF DEVISING SECONDARY DATA ANALYSIS RESOURCES FOR CRIMINOLOGICAL RESEARCH

Content Analysis

A **content analysis** represents another source for secondary data analysis that involves selecting contents from mass communication sources and classifying this data in a systematic way (Elo & Kyngas, 2008). Two sources are commonly used for such studies: popular media (e.g., newspaper, Internet, and television news reports) and academic journals.

To research, for example, how crime had been portrayed in the your hometown's media over the last two decades, the best method would be a content analysis. You could do this by accessing, either online or via microfilm, all of the front page crime stories of your local hometown newspaper for the period, systematically coding the information in the articles such as characteristics of the presumed offender, the victim, the type of crime, the site of the crime, and so on. After coding the relevant data into a spreadsheet, you can analyze the data for common themes. For instance, you may find that the majority of the crime-related stories report violent crimes by male offenders against female victims that take place at night in economically disadvantaged areas. As a side note, this may or may not accurately reflect *actual* crime; instead, only high-profile cases or those of perceived interest to the public may be reported by the media.

The second application of content analysis as a method of secondary analysis involves studying the topical coverage of research published in a particular academic journal or set of journals. For example, Copes, Brown, and Tewksbury (2011) examined the percentages of published articles in the top 15 criminology and criminal justice journals that involved ethnographic or qualitative methods in their research. After reviewing, coding, and classifying the content from each article published in journals, Copes et al.'s results demonstrated that only 4 percent of articles published in these top journals involved ethnographic research, and the typical ethnographic articles involved interviews with 46 participants who were not paid for their involvement, were either offenders or professionals, and were not of a particular race or gender. Similar types of content analysis have been performed on the coverage of women (Baro & Eigenberg, 1993) and minorities (Greene & Gabbidon, 2003) in criminology and criminal justice textbooks.

Meta-Analysis

A **meta-analysis** gathers secondary data to quantitatively synthesize the results of multiple studies by systematically searching the literature for research on a particular topic with specific inclusion/exclusion criteria (Glass, 1979). This technique allows us to summarize the body of research findings into one number that represents the overall effect of the relationship you are interested in. Consider your last research paper for a class assignment. Before you began to write, you had to search the literature for articles on your research paper topic and then try to tie these findings from the several sources that you found into a quality research paper. This is exactly the purpose of a meta-analysis, but done on a much larger scale and in a more systematic fashion. Consider the following example.

Your professor asks you to assist with a meta-analysis on the effect of video games on violence, similar to the one conducted by Anderson (2004). A series of steps must be followed. First, you must develop a clearly indicated search strategy to determine eligibility. You devise a set of criteria for the studies you will include: studies focused on video games and violence; studies of individuals who self-reported playing video games; studies that directly measure violence; studies that calculate an effect size for video game playing on violence; studies published in the previous 10 years; and studies published in English. After you determine your eligibility criteria, you search the literature for relevant studies using a variety of methods, including performing a key word search across several online abstract databases, searching the reference lists of relevant articles, doing hand searches through leading journals in the field, reviewing government and agency websites, and perhaps even contacting experts in the field to ask if they are aware of any studies you may have missed in your search.

Once you have identified and gathered the potentially relevant studies on video game playing and violence, you would then read each study carefully to make sure it meets all of your eligibility criteria. Next, you would take all of the studies that meet your eligibility criteria and code the data you want into a spreadsheet. For instance, you would separately code the rates of violence for video-game-playing individuals in each study and for the non-game-playing individuals. Once all data are coded, you are ready to perform your secondary data analysis, or meta-analysis.

The differences in the rates of violence between those who played video games and those who did not would generate what is referred to as an effect size for each study. Each study has a specific effect size for this relationship, and the purpose of the meta-analysis is to pool the overall studies to create one cumulate effect size for the relationship between game playing and violence, known as the *overall mean effect size* (Antman, Lau, Kupelnick, Mosteller, & Chalmers, 1992). This mean effect size would tell you whether there is a statistically significant effect for playing video games on committing violence and the magnitude of this effect. The most common effect size measure is **Cohen's *d*** (Cohen, 1992). A Cohen's *d* of 0.2 is considered a small effect, 0.5 a moderate effect, and 0.8 a large effect. Ultimately, meta-analyses are widely respected and well received by consumers and researchers, as they provide systematic and rigorous compilations of material on a particular topic that can answer whether the literature points toward a lack of an effect of a variable of interest on an outcome or whether there is an effect and how large that effect may be.

SUMMARY

We began this chapter with a discussion of different types of data that are available for secondary analysis, defined as the differences between public use and restricted use data sources. We then showed how official and self-report data differ in scope. Official data are collected by the government for informational and policy-related purposes (in the case of this section, this typically relates to crime statistics), while self-report data are collected directly from individuals about their personal behaviors, opinions, attitudes, and beliefs. The history of both self-report and official data in this context was also briefly reviewed.

We then covered crime records versus self-report by providing examples of popular data sources in the field of criminal justice: the Uniform Crime Reports, Monitoring the Future, the National Longitudinal Survey of Youth, and the General Social Survey. A brief review of the ICPSR, a center at the University of Michigan that houses, organizes, and provides assistance with secondary data, was also discussed as a user-friendly tool available to researchers who wish to conduct secondary analyses. We concluded with a brief overview of the content analysis methodology, a mostly qualitative method that is used to analyze historical records, and meta-analysis, a method in which previously published (or in some cases, unpublished) studies are aggregated to generate a single effect size for a given relationship.

KEY TERMS

Cohen's *d*   The most common effect size measure. A Cohen's *d* of 0.2 is considered a small effect, 0.5 a moderate effect, and 0.8 a large effect.

Content analysis   A method in the social sciences frequently used to study mass communication. More specifically, content analysis may include the study of recorded human communications, books, websites, paintings, and laws.

De-identified data   Refers to the removal of identifiable markers from data sets to preserve anonymity and to allow data to be reused by the public.

General Social Survey (GSS)   A sociological survey used to collect data on demographic characteristics and attitudes of residents in the United States. The survey is conducted via face-to-face interviews by researchers at the University of Chicago.

International Consortium for Political and Social Research (ICPSR)   An entity housed at the University of Michigan that maintains and provides access to an archive of social science data for research and instructional use. ICPSR also offers training in quantitative methods to increase the efficacy of data use.

Meta-analysis   A technique in which identical outcomes from different studies are pooled for the purpose of obtaining one effect size to describe the strength of a relationship (e.g., pooling the literature that evaluates the effect of drink specials at a bar on impaired driving).

Monitoring the Future (MTF)   A long-term epidemiological study that surveys high school students on both their licit and illicit drug use. Other risk behaviors, attitudes, and opinions about the substance use are also measured in this study.

National Longitudinal Survey of Youth (NLSY)   A series of surveys conducted by the U.S. Department of Labor Statistics for the purpose of gathering information on multiple time points on significant life events of several population samples of U.S. citizens, specifically labor market activities.

National Survey on Drug Use and Health (NSDUH) A survey conducted by the National Institute on Drug Abuse (NIDA) that collects data annually on the prevalence of drug usage and abuse.

Official data Data collected by government agencies or other public research agencies for use in policy and practice.

Public use data Any information readily available for use by researchers and available to the public for consumption.

Restricted use data Any information that has previously been collected by researchers, the government, and so on, that is not available to the public for usage.

Secondary data Data used for statistical analysis that has previously been collected by someone other than the researcher for some other purpose.

Self-report data Data collected by survey, questionnaire, or poll, in which respondents read a question and select the most appropriate response option reflecting their own behavior, without researcher assistance or interference.

United States Census Bureau The governmental organization responsible for the U.S. Census. The bureau also collects demographic and economic data.

REVIEW QUESTIONS

1. What is official data? Describe some of the drawbacks of this type of data.
2. What are self-report surveys? What are some of the limitations/drawbacks of this type of methodology?
3. What is the purpose of a meta-analysis? Find one example of meta-analysis in criminological research, and discuss.
4. What is a content analysis? Explain how you could use it to measure exposure to crime.
5. Describe the steps for conducting a meta-analysis.

Useful Websites

www.fbi.gov/about-us/cjis/ucr/ucr. The official website of the Uniform Crime Report.

www.monitoringthefuture.org. The official website of the Monitoring the Future study.

www.icpsr.umich.edu/icpsrweb/NACJD/NCVS/. NCVS resource guide from ISCPSR.

www.bls.gov/nls/. Official website of NLSY.

www.icpsr.umich.edu/icpsrweb/landing.jsp. The official website of ICPSR.

References

Anderson, C. A. (2004). An update on the effects of playing violent video games. *Journal of Adolescence, 27*, 113–122.

Antman, E. M., Lau, J., Kupelnick, Mosteller, F., & Chalmers, T. C. (1992). A comparison of results of meta-analyses of randomized control trials and recommendations of clinical experts: Treatments for myocardial infarctions. *Journal of the American Medical Association, 268*(2), 240–248.

Baro, A., & Eigenberg, H. (1993). Images of gender: A content analysis of photographs in criminology and criminal justice textbooks. *Women & Criminal Justice, 5*, 3–36.

Cohen, J. (1992). A power primer. *Psychological Bulletin, 112*(1), 155–159.

Copes, H., Brown, & Tewksbury, R. (2011). A content analysis of ethnographic research published in top criminology and criminal justice journals from 2000–2009. *Journal of Criminal Justice Education, 22*, 341–359.

Elliott, D. S., & Ageton, S. S. (1980). Reconciling race and class differences in self-reported and official estimates of delinquency. *American Sociological Review, 45*, 95–110.

Elo, S., & Kyngas, H. (2008). The qualitative content analysis process. *Journal of Advanced Nursing, 62*(1), 107–115.

Friedlin, J. F., & McDonald, C. J. (2008). A software tool for removing patient identifying information from clinical documents. *Journal of the American Medical Information Association, 15*(5), 601–610.

Glass, G. V. (1979). Integrating findings: The meta analysis of research. *Review of Research in Education, 5*, 351–358.

Greene, H., & Gabbidon, S. L. (2003). African American scholarship in criminological research published in the 1990s: A content analysis. *Journal of Criminal Justice Education, 14*(1), 1–15.

Herman-Stahl, M. A., Krebs, C. P., Kroutil, L. A., & Heller, D. C. (2007). Risk and protective factors for methamphetamine use and nonmedical use of prescription stimulants among young adults aged 18 to 25. *Addicted Behaviors, 32*(5), 1003–1015.

Hindelang, M. J., Hirschi, T., & Weis, J. G. (1979). Correlates of delinquency: The illusion of discrepancy between self-report and official measures. *American Sociological Review, 44*, 995–1014.

Kleck, G., Tark, J., & Bellows, J. J. (2006). What methods are most frequently used in research in criminology and criminal justice? *Journal of Criminal Justice, 34*(2), 147–152.

Krohn, M. D., Thornberry, T. P., Gibson, C. L., & Baldwin, J. M. (2010). The development and impact of self-report measures of crime and delinquency. *Journal of Quantitative Criminology, 26*, 509–525.

Lejins, P. P. (1966). Uniform crime reports. *Mi Law Rev, 64*, 1011–1030.

Loftin, C., & McDowall, D. (2010). The use of official records to measure crime and delinquency. *Journal of Quantitative Criminology, 26*, 527–532.

McPherson, M., Smith-Lovin, L., & Brashears, M. E. (2006). Social isolation in America: Changes in core discussion networks over two decades. *American Sociological Review, 71*(3), 353–375.

O'Malley, P. M., & Wagenaar, A. C. (1991). Effects of minimum drinking age laws on alcohol used, related behaviors, and traffic crash involvement among American youth: 1976–1987. *Journal of Studies on Alcohol, 52*(5), 478–491.

Parmer, M. K. B., Torri, V., & Stewart, L. (1998). Extracting summary statistics to perform meta-analyses of the published literature of survival endpoints. *Statistics in Medicine, 17*(24), 2815–2834.

Porterfield, Austin L. (1943). Delinquency and outcome in court and college. *American Journal of Sociology, 49,* 199–208.

_____. (1946). *Youth in trouble.* Fort Worth: Leo Potishman Foundation.

Rodgers, J. L. (1994). DF analysis of NLSY IQ/achievement data: Nonshared environmental influences. *Intelligence, 19*(2), 157–177.

Shihadeh, E. S., & Flynn, N. (1996). Segregation and crime: The effect of black social isolation on the rates of black urban violence. *Social Forces, 74*(4), 1325–1352.

Short, J. F., Jr., & Nye, F. I. (1957). Reported behavior as a criterion of deviant behavior. *Social Problems, 5,* 207–213.

_____. (1958). Extent of unrecorded juvenile delinquency: Tentative conclusions. *Journal of Criminal Law and Criminology, 49,* 296–302.

Smith, T. W., Marsden, P. V., & Hout, M., General Social Survey, 1972–2010 [Cumulative File]. ICPSR31521-v1. Storrs, CT: Roper Center for Public Opinion Research, University of Connecticut/Ann Arbor, MI: Inter-university Consortium for Political and Social Research [distributors], 2011-08-05. doi:10.3886/ICPSR31521.v1.

Sutherland, E. H. (1949). *White-collar crime.* New York: Holt, Rinehart and Winston.

Thornberry T. P., & Krohn, M. D. (2000). The self-report method for measuring delinquency and crime. In D. Duffee, R. Crutchfield, S. Mastrofski, L. Mazerolle, & D. McDowall (Eds.), *Criminal justice 2000* (vol. 4): *Measurement and analysis of crime and justice* (pp. 33–83). Washington: National Institute of Justice.

Thornton, A. (1989). Changing attitudes toward family issues in the United States. *Journal of Marriage and Family, 51*(4), 1103–1116.

Wallerstein, J. S., & Wylie, C. J. (1947). Our law-abiding law-breakers. *Probation, 25,* 107–112.

Waltermaurer, E., McNutt, L. A., & Mattingly, M. J. (2006). Examining the effects of residential change on intimate partner violence. *Journal of Epidemiology and Community Health, 60*(11), 923–927.

Weir, D. R., Faul, J. R., & Langa, K. M. (2011). Proxy interviews and bias in cognition measures due to non-response in longitudinal studies: A comparison of HRS and ELSA. *Longitudinal and Life Course Studies, 2*(2), 184–201.

Chapter 7

SAMPLING

Consider the following scenario: You are interested in collecting data to evaluate whether the presence of school resource officers (SRO) in high schools reduces crime and violence. To your knowledge, no secondary data sources are available to answer this research question. This leaves one option: collect your own data. Because the quality of your findings will be directly related to the quality of your sample, sample selection is especially important. For example, a survey of only rural public-school SROs will yield data particular to similar schools and officers and will not be relevant for understanding the role and effect of SROs in urban or suburban schools.

SAMPLING IN GENERAL

Sampling, or selecting respondents for your research, is necessary because it is usually impossible to include the entire population of interest in your research survey. In the hypothetical study described above, surveying all high schools in the United States (our population of interest) would clearly be cost-prohibitive and logistically impossible; therefore, we must select a subsection (or sample) and **generalize**, or extrapolate, our findings to the entire population (Radhak-rishna, & Doamekpor, 2008). In addition, conducting a census of schools is not statistically necessary to answer your research question. In other words, when a representative sample gets large enough, it statistically approximates (or represents) the entire population. Adding additional participants at that point becomes analytically unnecessary and simply increases the time and monetary commitment.

The "gold standard" method of sample selection is **probability sampling**, in which the entire population eligible for participation in the study has an equal probability of being selected to participate. These types of samples utilize some form of random sampling, in which participant selection is entirely **random** and not based on any particular characteristic or behavior. Several types of probability (and nonprobability) sampling will be discussed in this chapter and applications of each type will be covered.

PROBABILITY SAMPLING

The principal strength of using a probability sampling method is your ability to attribute your findings to the general population, beyond those who participated in your study. Probability sampling allows us to use a subset of a population to make inferences about the population as a whole (Crum, Anthony, Bassett, & Folstein, 1993). Therefore, if we were interested in understanding how students at a school feel about the impact of the school resource officer, we could select a random sample of students at that school. If the sample was truly random, we could infer that these responses reflect the range of opinions held by the entire study body.

In probability sampling, each member of a population has a known and equal probability of being selected. For instance, if you need to study 10 percent of a population consisting of 1,000 people, each person has a 1 in 100 probability of being selected. If the population is homogeneous demographically, behaviorally, or on any other study-related variable, random selection is not necessary for generalization. Unfortunately, this is a rare instance, as very few populations meet these criteria; therefore, the scientific community generally considers random samples necessary for generalization.

A **sampling frame**, introduced in Chapter 5, includes a list of *all* members of a target population of interest. The **population** includes all persons who you have been identified as exposed to your independent (exposure) or dependent variable (outcome)—such as arrest, prison, and violent behavior. In the example study here, you may include as your population everyone in enrolled in a U.S. high school (some with exposure to an SRO and some students without such exposure), to evaluate whether the SRO had an impact on crime or perceptions of crime. Ideally, the sampling frame should include the entire population eligible for participation in your study. For studies of individual people, lists may be obtained from driver's licenses or voter registration lists. When studying schools or organizations, complete lists of enrollees are generally obtained directly from the organization or school. Note, however, that these lists are not always accurate. For instance, anyone without access to or need for a car may never have obtained a driver's license, thus biasing that sample toward the wealthier segment of the population. Also, school district enrollee lists (particularly in large, transient, urban school districts) are not necessarily updated and complete. Therefore, it is always important that the list serving as the sampling frame be as accurate as possible, and limitations or exclusions from the sampling frame should be noted.

There are several types of probability sampling, each of which serves a different purpose and is practical for a different situation. These methods include simple random sampling, systematic random sampling, stratified random sampling, disproportionate stratified sampling, and multistage cluster sampling.

Simple Random Sampling

Simple random sampling (SRS) is the most basic and intuitive method of random sampling (Avadhani & Sukhatme, 1968). When using this method, a researcher begins with a list of the sampling frame (e.g., a list of all enrollees in a high school). A random number table is often used (Fig. 7.1), or statistical software may generate a random list of numbers. Each participant in the sampling frame is assigned a number from this table, in order. To use the random number table, participant 1 will be assigned number "10460" from the table. Participant 2 will be assigned "15011," and participant 3 will be assigned "02011." Complete this sequence until your entire list has been assigned a number. Then, sort your respondents so that they appear with the smallest random value first and the largest random value last. Then, you may use the first 100 (or your desired sample) even numbers or odd numbers. It is irrelevant whether even or odd numbers are used; either will ensure random sampling as long as selection is consistent. If you have electronic access to the sampling frame, simple random samples can be automatically selected to generate a specified sample size using Microsoft Excel or SPSS. All inferential statistics and probability theory are based on the premise of simple random sampling.

Systematic Random Sampling

Systematic random samples are drawn by applying a predetermined interval to a sampling frame. For instance, we decide that, given the total number of people listed in our sampling frame (400), we need 100 participants in our study. Therefore, we select every fourth person listed on the sampling frame in the sample. It has been argued that these samples are not random in many cases due to the clustering of ethnic family names (e.g., Rodriguez, Ramirez), or when the list is ordered in some meaningful way. For instance, this sample may not be representative if our sampling frame included a list of disciplinary records listed in order of number of days in detention. Optimally, the list will be organized randomly (if not possible, alphabetical organization can result in a random sample as well).

To begin using this sampling method, a **random start** number is chosen. This number may be selected from a random number table or other list of random numbers. After all members of the sampling frame have been numbered, the randomization will begin with the number randomly selected, and every fourth person (or other interval determined) will be selected and sampled. Upon reaching the end of the list, continue with the first participant on the list until the total number of sampled individuals you needed at the onset of the study is reached. For example, if we are selecting every fourth person on our sampling frame and we randomly select a start value of six, we would include respondents 6, 10, 14, 18, 22, 26, and 30, continued until we reach 100 participants drawn.

Figure 7.1   Random Number Table

Col. Line	(1)	(2)	(3)	(4)	(5)	(6)	(7)	(8)	(9)	(10)	(11)	(12)	(13)	(14)
1	10460	15011	01536	02011	81647	91646	69179	14194	62590	36207	20969	99570	91291	90700
2	22368	46573	25595	85393	30995	89198	27982	53402	93965	34095	52666	19174	39615	99505
3	24130	48360	22527	97265	76393	64809	15179	24830	49340	32081	30680	19655	63348	58629
4	42167	93093	06243	61680	07856	16376	39440	53537	71341	57004	00849	74917	97758	16379
5	37570	39975	81837	16656	06121	91782	60468	81305	49684	60672	14110	06927	01263	54613
6	77921	06907	11008	42751	27756	53498	18602	70659	90655	15053	21916	81825	44394	42880
7	99562	72905	56420	69994	98872	31016	71194	18738	44013	48840	63213	21069	10634	12952
8	96301	91977	05463	07972	18876	20922	94595	56869	69014	60045	18425	84903	42508	32307
9	89579	14342	63661	10281	17453	18103	57740	84378	25331	12566	58678	44947	05585	56941
10	85475	36857	53342	53988	53060	59533	38867	62300	08158	17983	16439	11458	18593	64952
11	28918	69578	88231	33276	70997	79936	56865	05859	90106	31595	01547	85590	91610	78188
12	63553	40961	48235	03427	49626	69445	18663	72695	52180	20847	12234	90511	33703	90322
13	09429	93969	52636	92737	88974	33488	36320	17617	30015	08272	84115	27156	30613	74952
14	10365	61129	87529	85689	48237	52267	67689	93394	01511	26358	85104	20285	29975	89868
15	07119	97336	71048	08178	77233	13916	47564	81056	97735	85677	29372	74461	28551	90707
16	51085	12765	51821	51259	77452	16308	60756	92144	49442	53900	70960	63990	75601	40719
17	02368	21382	62404	60268	89368	19885	55322	44819	01188	65255	64835	44919	05944	55157
18	01011	54092	33362	94904	31273	04146	18594	29852	71585	85030	51132	01915	92747	64951
19	52162	53916	46369	58586	23216	14513	83149	98736	23495	64350	94738	17752	35156	35749
20	07056	97628	33787	09998	42698	06691	76988	13602	51851	46104	88916	19509	25625	58104
21	48663	91245	85826	14346	09172	30168	90229	04734	59193	22178	30421	61666	99904	32812
22	54164	58492	00421	74103	47070	25306	76468	26384	58151	06646	21524	15227	96909	44592
23	32639	32363	05597	24200	13363	38005	94342	28728	35806	06912	17012	64161	18296	22851
24	29334	27001	87637	87308	58731	00256	45834	15398	46557	41135	10367	07684	36188	18510
25	02488	33062	28834	07351	19731	92420	60952	61280	50001	67658	32586	86679	50720	94953
26	81525	72295	04839	96423	24878	82651	66566	14778	76797	14780	13300	87074	79666	95725
27	29676	20591	68086	26432	46901	20849	89768	81536	86645	12659	92259	57102	80428	25280
28	00742	57392	39064	66432	84673	40027	32832	61362	98947	96067	64760	64584	96096	98253
29	05366	04213	25669	26422	44407	44048	37937	63904	45766	66134	75470	66520	34693	90449
30	91921	26418	64117	94305	26776	25940	39972	22209	71500	64568	91402	42416	07844	69618
31	00582	04711	87917	77341	42206	35126	74087	99547	81817	42607	43808	76655	62028	76630
32	00725	69884	62797	56170	86324	88072	76222	36086	84637	93161	76038	65855	77919	88006
33	69011	65795	95876	55293	18988	27354	26575	08625	40801	59920	29841	80150	12777	48501
34	25976	57948	29888	88604	67917	48708	18912	82271	65424	69774	33611	54262	85963	03547
35	09763	83473	73577	12908	30883	18317	28290	35797	05998	41688	34952	37888	38917	88050
36	91567	42595	27958	30134	04024	86385	29880	99730	00036	84855	29080	09250	79656	73211
37	17955	56349	90999	49127	20044	59931	06115	20542	18059	02008	73708	83517	36103	42791
38	46503	18584	18845	49618	02304	51038	20655	58727	28168	15475	56942	53389	20562	87338
39	92157	89634	94824	78171	84610	82834	09922	25417	44137	48413	25555	21246	35509	20468
40	14577	62765	35605	81263	39667	47358	56873	56307	61607	45918	89686	20103	77490	18062
41	98427	07523	00062	64270	01638	92477	66969	98420	04880	45585	46565	04102	46880	45709
42	34914	63976	88720	82765	34476	17032	87589	40836	32427	70002	70663	88863	77775	69348
43	70060	28277	39475	46473	23219	53416	94970	25832	69975	94884	19661	72828	00102	66794
44	53976	54914	06990	67245	68350	82948	11398	42878	80287	88267	47363	46634	06541	97809
45	76072	29515	40980	07391	58745	25774	00987	80059	39911	96189	41151	14222	60697	59583
46	90725	52210	83974	29992	65831	38857	50490	83765	55657	14361	31720	57375	56228	41546
47	64364	67412	33339	31926	14883	24413	59744	92351	97473	89286	35931	04110	23726	51900
48	08962	00358	31662	25388	61642	34072	81249	35648	56891	69352	48373	45578	78547	81788
49	95012	68379	93526	70765	10592	04542	76463	54328	02349	17247	28865	14777	62730	92277
50	15664	10493	20492	38391	91132	21999	59516	81652	27195	48223	46751	22923	32261	85653

Stratified Random Sampling

Stratified random sampling requires knowledge of important characteristics of the study population before the sample can be selected. It will be important to notice the demographic characteristics, including age, gender, race, ethnicity, and income, as well as other characteristics that are related specifically to your research question. For instance, in our study of SROs, it is relevant to know the proportion of the sample that is enrolled in college prep or advanced placement courses, truancy in the school, or criminal behavior of the population at each school before a sample can be systematically selected. To use this type of sampling, a researcher would group the population into several homogeneous strata (e.g., one group of white, upper-class females who are enrolled in college prep course; another group of white, lower-class females who are enrolled in college prep courses, etc.).

Once participants are grouped, participants will be selected by using either **proportionate** or **disproportionate sampling**, depending upon the decision made by the researcher. To sample proportionately, you would select a proportion from each group to mirror their representation in the actual population. Using this method, if the population was 30 percent black, lower class, advanced placement youth, you would randomly select 30 percent from that stratum. Alternatively, disproportionate sampling, also known as *oversampling*, is conducted when you include a larger proportion of a given strata in your sample than occurs in the original population. This may be done when you are interested in learning more about a group that is only a small portion of the population (e.g., Native Americans, Asians, those with a history of incarceration, etc.). In these cases, because of the small sample sizes that proportionate sampling would yield, we would need to generate more cases to conduct a meaningful analysis of this subpopulation.

When oversamples are used, **weighting** is a technique that allows us to readjust the sample to be representative of the population. When oversamples are used, the population no longer represents the aggregated population; instead, it is biased in favor of the oversamples. Using weighting, those who were oversampled are weighted down (e.g., counted as less than one person), while those who were undersampled are weighted up (e.g., counted more than once in the sample) to reflect the composition of the original population.

Cluster Sampling

Cluster sampling is typically conducted for logistical purposes in large-scale studies that require in-person interviewing. Specifically, **cluster sampling** identifies a population of interest divided into clusters, such as school districts, counties, census tracts, or block groups (a division of a census tract). These clusters can be identified randomly or nonrandomly. More commonly, clusters are identified and then participants are randomly selected for a sample within the cluster (Zelin & Stubbs, 2005). This is referred to as **multistage cluster sampling**. It combines multiple methods of sampling, spanning cluster sampling, stratified sampling, and simple random sample methodologies (Milligan, Njie, & Bennett, 2004). First, a large geographic area is generally divided into large, meaningful units. Within each unit or region, **clusters** are selected randomly. Within clusters, simple random samples of each cluster will be selected for participation in the study. In our study of SROs, we may be interested in all school districts within a state. Because the state has both urban and rural regions, we divide the state into four quadrants (north, south, east, and west), drawing an equal number of school districts randomly from each quadrant. Within school districts, we may use random sampling to select classrooms (in which all students will be surveyed) or students. Each of these methods will result in a random sample of students from the state to which we wish to generalize, or **extrapolate**.

ALTERNATIVE METHODS: NONPROBABILITY SAMPLING

Any sampling method in which the probability of each individual being selected to participate in any study cannot be calculated is considered a nonprobability sample (Feild, Pruchno, Bewley, Lemay, & Levinsky, 2006). These methods are limited in their generalizability; however, they are appropriate and useful in several settings. These methods include convenience sampling, quota sampling, purposive sampling, and snowball sampling.

Convenience/Available Subjects Sampling

Convenience samples are compiled when a researcher includes in their research study any participant who is readily available (Kam, Wilking, & Zechmeister, 2007). These samples are particularly common in psychology labs at universities, where undergraduate students are given extra credit to participate in research opportunities. In addition, a faculty member may survey all students in a section of their large introductory lecture class. This method is very common because it is a relatively easy and inexpensive way to collect a large amount of data. Unfortunately, the practical usefulness and external validity of these data are extremely limited. For example, it is a stretch to believe that the responses from your introductory criminal justice class of 50 students are representative of the entire population at your university. Therefore, the merit of this method pales in comparison to probability-based methods of sample selection.

Given these limitations, convenience sampling can nonetheless be used in innovative, useful ways. If you are interested in, say, assessing whether motorists care about a new enforcement policy that tickets drivers who do not stop for pedestrians in a crosswalk, you might select a few popular crosswalks in town. You might pay some students to walk back and forth on the crosswalk, counting how many people stop for them out of the total number of cars that pass. This would be an application of reliance upon available motorists; however, the practical implications of these findings are meaningful for policy. Therefore, use of a convenient sample can be meaningful; however, a solid argument as to the representative nature of the population sampled must be made.

Quota Sampling

Quota sampling begins with some knowledge of the population of interest, similar to stratified sampling (Owen, McNeill, & Callum, 1998). Before setting out to collect data, the researcher will stratify the population into meaningful groups, generally demographics. Then, a "quota," or maximum number of participants per strata, will be determined based upon the composition of the population. Data will be collected from any and all individuals possible within the population until the quota within that segment is reached. This method is commonly used among marketing companies when doing product evaluation. Specifically, a large survey will be administered to thousands of people. Once the ideal number of African American females ages 25 to 30 is reached, no more will be invited to participate in the survey. Therefore, these methods require a "first come, first serve" mentality. Data is collected in an ongoing matter until all quotas for all demographic groups are filled.

Purposive Sampling

Purposive sampling is utilized when the researcher has a clear and specific idea about which participants need to be included in a given study (Barbour, 2001). The most well-known application of purposive sampling is the ability of election forecasters to predict the results of an election several hours in advance of poll closure. Based upon the results of previous election polls, television networks select voting precincts that have results that are representative of the entire region. Based upon groups of these purposely selected regions, forecasters are able to predict to which party the votes for a particular state will go. Purposive sampling methods are conducted for consumer product reviews (e.g., only wish to survey users of one particular brand of shampoo) or for developing movie ratings.

Snowball Samples

Snowball samples are commonly used in criminological research because they are easy to conduct and suitable for obtaining samples that cannot be obtained through random sampling methods (Biernacki & Waldorf, 1981). For instance, if a researcher was interested in surveying drug users about whether they believe needle-exchange programs reduce sharing of dirty needles, where could they obtain a sampling frame? It would be easier to locate one drug user, survey and gain the trust of that person, and then ask for a referral to other users, tracking those people down through information provided by the first subject. This approach can be a feasible method of collecting data among hard-to-reach populations.

These samples are referred to as *snowball samples* because research participants are obtained one at a time, and through referrals, the sample tends to snowball. These studies are generally exploratory in nature and have been used to study gang members (Toy, 1992) and undercover police (Solomey, 1979). The first participants are generally found at social services or neighborhood agencies (such as a needle-exchange or methadone clinics). Depending on the population of interest, regional parks, homeless shelters, or soup kitchens may provide some initial participants. As an incentive for referrals, the referring participant is generally offered cash, clothing, or other incentive. This method requires strong, knowledgeable field research staff able to convince skeptical individuals to participate in research. Therefore, data collection using the convenience sample method is an art and a science.

SAMPLING BIAS

The illustrations above suggest that sampling is fairly straightforward and there is little opportunity to introduce bias. However, consider the situation in which you send an undergraduate research assistant to interview drug users at a methadone maintenance clinic. You ask her to interview every third person that walks in the door; however, she is intimidated by a few men, and the idea of speaking with them at length about their drug use makes her feel uncomfortable. Therefore, she decides to skip those who intimidate her and elects to interview the next person who walks in the door. Although this seems like a minor deviation from the protocol, bias has been introduced into the sample. Because these men were excluded, the sample is no longer representative of the population from which it was drawn. By extension, we might believe that a voter's registration list or a selective service registration list is representative of the population (or the population of age to register for the draft). However, we know that some people will never register, and these people may be less educated or otherwise different from the rest of the population. This influences the external validity (or generalizability) of the findings. We thought we could generalize our findings to the whole population; instead, we can only apply our findings to the population who is registered to vote. Although this distinction may be minor in many cases, this mistake commonly has the potential to misrepresent the sampling pool and misapply the findings.

SAMPLING DISTRIBUTION AND ERRORS

Everything that we know about generalization and probability of selection is derived from probability theory. Probability theory teaches us that the only method of using a sample to approximate a population is by using truly random selection techniques (Levin, 1974). The purpose of random selection is to use a **statistic** (value of a variable in a sample) to approximate a **population parameter**, or the true value of the variable you are measuring in the entire population (Teddlie & Yu, 2007). Although there is no way to confirm that your findings from a sample will be applicable to the population, the use of a sound random sampling design will make the likelihood of this inference more reasonable. True random selection does not introduce any form of bias, whether conscious or unconscious on the part of the research staff (Wilkinson, 1999).

A normal sampling distribution follows a bell curve, with most people concentrated around the average (**mean**) value, as shown in Figure 7.2. Let's say that we asked everyone in a one-hundred-student classroom about their grades (in numeric values) last semester. For instance, let's say that the average overall grade was 85, and average grades ranged from 70 to 100. Based upon the normal distribution, the majority (68 percent) of grades will be between +/- 1 **standard deviation** from the average (85). Further, 96 percent of grades will be between 2 standard deviations from the average, and nearly all will be within 3 standard deviations. Assuming the distribution is perfectly normal, 96 percent of grades will fall between 75 and 95, and all grades will fall between 70 and 100 (which we know, based upon the data collected). Theoretically, however, this will not always be the case.

It is important to understand the basics of the sampling distribution in order to understand how samples are generalized. The following sections will discuss how confidence intervals are calculated, which allow us to make generalizations about the parameters based upon observed statistics.

Confidence Intervals

Confidence intervals are probabilities that a true population parameter lies within a given range of values derived from an observed statistic (Curran-Everett, 2009).

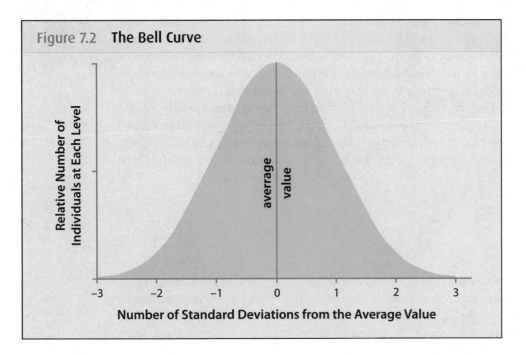

Figure 7.2 **The Bell Curve**

Relative Number of Individuals at Each Level

averrage value

-3   -2   -1   0   1   2   3

Number of Standard Deviations from the Average Value

Using our sample, we are able to calculate the effect of the SRO on attitudes of criminal behavior in a school, compared with attitudes on criminal behavior from schools that do not have an SRO. We may find that 56 percent of students in our sample believe that the SRO is helpful in preventing criminal and delinquent behavior in their school. Based upon this statistic and the distribution of attitudinal scores, we will calculate a confidence interval in which we believe the true parameter lies (if we had sampled the entire population).

Confidence Levels

Confidence interval calculations are based upon an a priori (or predesignated) **confidence level**, or the probability that the true parameter is within this confidence interval. For instance, we might specify a 90 percent, 95 percent, or 99 percent confidence level. For a 95 percent confidence level, we might say, "We are 95 percent confident that between 50 and 62 percent of students believe that the SRO decreases delinquency in this school." Using a 99 percent confidence interval, we would say, "We are 99 percent confident that between 46 and 66 percent of students believe that the SRO decreases delinquency in this school." As you may have noticed, the greater the confidence level, the larger the confidence interval will be. As we seek to become more confident about our findings, we have less tolerance for being wrong. Therefore, the interval in which the parameter lies must become greater.

Power Calculation

The concept of the sampling distribution and confidence levels provide the foundation for a **power** calculation, or the method for determining how large your sample should be (Hoenig & Heisey, 2001). Although a discussion of statistical power is beyond the scope of this text, there are several calculators available online or in statistical software programs that will assist researchers in determining how large their sample should be. However, it should be clear that the foundation for sound scientific findings lies in the quality of the research design. Any statistics performed using a biased sample will be biased and will not reflect the true population. Therefore, the development of a sound, appropriate research design given the research question is the most salient topic discussed in a text on research methods in criminal justice.

SUMMARY

This chapter focused on sampling and the wide variety of sampling techniques that can be applied in social science research. We began this chapter with a discussion of the role of sampling in research and how sampling is used to make generalizations about a population without including the entire population in our study. We discussed probability sampling, the gold standard method of sampling from a population due to the property of generalization of findings. We also discussed each specific method of probability sampling, including simple random sampling, systematic random sampling, and stratified random sampling.

Following the discussion on probability sampling was a discussion of non-probability sampling methods, or manners of sampling in which the probability of an individual being selected to participate in a research study cannot be directly calculated. Different types of probability sampling were discussed, including quota sampling, snowball sampling, and purposive sampling. Finally, we closed this chapter by covering sampling bias, or the effect of systematic exclusion of members of a population from a sample. Statistical assumptions and how they change based upon the sampling procedure was also detailed.

KEY TERMS

Cluster   In statistics, a *cluster* is a grouping of individuals or units that is used for sampling purposes.

Cluster sampling   A sampling technique that involves dividing a natural but homogenous group of a population, and then selecting these groups using simple random methods.

Confidence interval   A type of interval estimate of the population parameter used for the purpose of indicating the reliability of an estimate. Confidence intervals include ranges of values that act as estimates of unknown population parameters.

Confidence level   A value set by the researcher that indicates the degree of confidence the researcher has that the observed relationship with the population is a true relationship and is not due to chance alone. The *confidence level* is inversely related to the confidence interval.

Convenience sampling   A nonprobability sampling technique in which subjects are selected based on their accessibility or convenience to the researcher.

Disproportionate sampling   A type of stratified sampling. Within this process, the sizes of different groups vary and do not represent the percentage of the group with a larger population. This type of sampling is used when one or more subgroups are very small compared to other groups, and the researcher is specifically interested in small subgroups.

Extrapolation   The generalization of findings in research study beyond those who participated in the actual study.

Generalize   In statistics, *generalize* is the process of extrapolating findings from a sample to make inferences or conclusions about an entire population.

Mean   The arithmetic or statistical average for a given population or sample.

Multistage cluster sampling   A more complex form of cluster sampling. The researcher randomly selects elements from each cluster instead of using all elements contained within the constructed clusters (e.g., randomly selecting classrooms within schools).

Population   A set of entities (individuals, institutions, etc.) from which statistics inferences may be drawn.

Population parameter   A quantity or a statistical measure for a given population.

Power   The probability that a statistical test will reject the null hypothesis when the null hypothesis is false. Generally, power is a function of possible distributions, typically determined by a parameter based on alternative hypotheses. This calculation is beyond the scope of this text, but it is often used when planning a study to determine how many participants should be included in the study.

Probability sampling   Any method of selecting a sample that utilizes a form of random selection of study participants, when all members of the population have a known an equal probability of being selected to participate in the study.

Proportionate sampling   A sampling strategy used when a population consists of several subgroups that differ in their proportion of the population. The number of participants drawn from each subgroup is determined by the proportion they comprise in the entire population.

Purposive sampling   A sample based on the knowledge of the population and purpose of the study, and subjects are selected because of some characteristic. Also sometimes called *judgmental* or *judgment sampling*.

Quota sampling   The population is selected into mutually exclusive subgroups similar to stratified sampling. Subjects are then selected from each group based on specific proportions.

Random   Selecting participants without basing their characteristics on any particular trait.

Random start   Occurs when selecting a systematic sample at an interval. In this process, the first random number for selection within a survey is generated by drawing or finger-point.

Sampling   The process of selecting a subset of individuals from a population for the purpose of estimating characteristics of the whole population.

Sampling frame   A list of the population from which a sample can be drawn. The sampling frame lists individuals, households, or institutions.

Simple random sample (SRS)   A subset of individuals from a larger population. In this type of sample, each individual is selecting randomly or entirely by chance. This is often done using a random number table.

Snowball sample   A type of nonprobability sampling typically used by researchers to identify subjects that are hard to locate. The researcher gains access to an initial subject and from there/through that subject gets access to subsequent subjects.

Standard deviation   The measure of how much variety or dispersion exists from the average in a given population or sample.

Statistic   A single measure of some attribute of a sample.

Stratified random sampling   A sampling process in which the population is divided into smaller subgroups called *strata* (could be a census block, school, or wing of a prison). Strata are created based on members' shared attributes or characteristics. A random sample is then taken from each stratum in a proportional number to the size of the strata comparable to the population.

Systematic random sample   A type of random sample in which a researcher begins by randomly selecting the first participant from the sampling frame, and thereafter selects each (nth) subject from the sampling frame.

Weighting   A process used in sampling when the sampling design used a stratified or proportionate multilevel sampling method. Each participant in the sample is weighted so that the sample is equivalent (based upon the variables that the researcher is interested in—generally demographics) to the characteristics of the population. Weighting is also frequently used in dealing with nonresponse, as participants who are demographically or behaviorally similar to those who were lost to follow up may be counted more heavily.

REVIEW QUESTIONS

1. When would a researcher use a snowball sample? Think of a population in criminological research in which a snowball sample would be useful.
2. What is the difference between a probability sample and a nonprobability sample?
3. List each method of sampling discussed in this chapter, along with one key strength and one limitation of each method.
4. What is sampling bias? List some reasons why sampling bias might occur.
5. As a researcher, when would you want to use a convenience sample? In criminological research, what type of population would you want to study using a convenience sample?

Useful Websites

www.socialresearchmethods.net/kb/sampling.php. Information on sampling from the Web center on social research.

www.statpac.com/surveys/sampling.htm. A guide relating to different sampling methods.

www.monitoringthefuture.org. Link to the Monitoring the Future website; provides information on sampling procedures used within the study.

www.fort.usgs.gov/landsatsurvey/SnowballSampling.asp. Information on snowball sampling from the United States Geological Survey.

http://painconsortium.nih.gov/symptomresearch/chapter_20/sec21/cabs21pg1.html1 An example of a stratified cluster sampling design.

References

Avadhani, M. S., & Sukhatme, B. V. (1968). Simplified procedures for designing controlled simple random sampling. *Australian Journal of Statistics, 10*(1), 1–7.

Barbour, R. (2001). Checklists for improving rigour in qualitative research: A case of the tail wagging the dog? *BMJ, 322*(1794), 1115–1117.

Biernacki, P., & Waldorf, D. (1981). Snowball sampling: Problems and techniques of chain referral sampling. *Sociological Methods and Research, 10*(2), 141–163.

Crum, R. M., Anthony, J. C., Bassett, S. S., & Folstein, M. F. (1993). Population-based norms for the mini mental state examination by age and education level. *JAMA, 269*(18), 2386–2391.

Curran-Everett, D. (2009). Explorations in statistics: Confidence intervals. *Advances in Physiology Education, 33*(2), 87–90.

Feild, L., Pruchno, R. A., Bewley, J., Lemay Jr., E. P., & Levinsky, N. G. (2006). Using probability vs. nonprobability sampling to identify hard to access participants for health related research costs and contrasts. *Journal of Aging Health, 18*(4), 565–583.

Hoenig, J. M., & Heisey, D. M. (2001). The abuse of power: The pervasive fallacy of power calculations for data analysis. *The American Statistician, 55*(1), 1–6.

Kam, C. D., Wilking, J. R., & Zechmeister, E. J. (2007). Beyond the "narrow data base": Another convenience sample for experimental research. *Political Behavior, 29,* 415–440.

Levin, L. A. (1974). Laws of information (nongrowth) and aspects of the foundation of probability theory. *Probability Peredachi Information, 10*(3), 30–35.

Milligan, P., Njie, A., & Bennett, S. (2004). Comparison of two cluster sampling methods for health surveys in developing countries. *International Journal of Epidemiology, 33*(3), 469–476.

Owen, L., McNeill, A., & Callum, C. (1998). Trends in smoking during pregnancy in England, 1992–7: Quota sampling survey. *BMJ, 317*(7160), 728–730.

Radhakrishna, R., & Doamekpor, P. (2008). Strategies for generalizing findings in survey research. *Journal of Extension, 46*(2).

Solomey, J. (1979). The glory boys: Notes on the police underground. Senior Thesis, Mercyhurst College.

Teddlie, C., & Yu, F. (2007). Mixed methods sampling: A typology with examples. *Journal of Mixed Methods Research, 1,* 77–100.

Toy, C. (1992). A short history of Asian gangs in San Francisco. *Justice Quarterly, 9,* 647–665.

Wilkinson, L. (1999). Statistical methods in psychology journals: Guidelines and explanations. *American Psychologist, 54*(8), 594–604.

Zelin, A., & Stubbs, R. (2005). Cluster sampling: A false economy? *International Journal of Market Research, 47*(5).

8

EXPERIMENTAL AND QUASI-EXPERIMENTAL DESIGNS

E xperimental designs are rarely applied in criminological research, despite the opportunity they present for the sound advancement of knowledge on the causes of criminal behavior. **Experiments** are the most scientifically sound research design available to researchers because they rule out many threats to validity simply by following the structure of the design. Minimizing threats to validity allows for **causal inference**, or an understanding of which cause precipitates a given effect (Chapin, 1949). Unfortunately, it is difficult to randomize people to a risky exposure, such as hanging out with delinquent friends (to assess the extent to which one's peer group influences crime) or having parents who use drugs. However, these designs are ideal in evaluating prevention and/or intervention programming, such as those used in correctional settings. Therefore, we will use program evaluation as our example illustrating the implementation of experimental and quasi-experimental designs.

This chapter will look at the effectiveness of Drug Abuse Resistance Education (DARE) in schools in one U.S. city. This city contains one major school district with eight high schools, 10 middle schools, and 12 elementary schools. The program aims to teach students from young ages to "say no to drugs," with the hope that this program will reduce drug and alcohol use as students age. How can we test this hypothesis using the strongest possible research design? By conducting an experiment!

AN INTRODUCTION TO THE EXPERIMENTAL DESIGN

When designing an experiment, it is important to consider your **unit of analysis**, the nature of the independent and dependent variables, your sample, and how the exposure will be manipulated. As discussed in earlier chapters, a scientific study is defined by evaluating the influence of an independent variable on a dependent variable. In this case, we would be interested in assessing whether the independent variable (enrollment in the DARE program) caused a change in the dependent variable (e.g., drug use in high school). An experiment may only be conducted when the **exposure** (or independent variable in an experiment) can be manipulated. In this case, we will randomly assign people to be exposed to the DARE curriculum, hence manipulating the exposure variable. In most criminological research (and social science research for that matter), exposure cannot be manipulated.

Randomization is necessary for a true experimental design to ensure that the **experimental groups** and **control groups** are equivalent (Vickers, 2006). In our study, the experimental group will be administered the DARE curriculum in its entirety. The control groups serve as a comparison group that is similar to the experimental group *in all respects*, with the exception of being exposed to the curriculum. This will allow us to examine the specific effect of the DARE curriculum on drug use in high school.

Another trademark of the experimental design is the use of multiple testing to evaluate change over time. For instance, before we administered the curriculum to students randomly assigned to the experimental group, we would conduct a **pretest** of all students involved in our trial (not just the experimental group). The purpose of this pretest is to examine baseline measures of drug use, alcohol use, and other outcomes of interest; to obtain demographic information; and to measure possible **confounding variables**. Confounding variables may include having parents or friends who use drugs or alcohol, access to alcohol in the home, and/or having friends who use drugs. These confounders introduce a threat to the validity of the experiment (which will be discussed later); however, this threat is manageable as long as we measure these variables (Schwartz & Coull, 2003). For instance, we can statistically adjust for prior alcohol use if we know that it exists, but we might inaccurately conclude that DARE decreases alcohol use when in fact, the difference is due to unmeasured differences in alcohol use at baseline. This would be referred to as a *spurious* conclusion, as the results are not due to the program; rather, the results are attributable to differences in alcohol use. Therefore, our conclusion is not correct.

Pretests should be exhaustive and measure as many variables that are related (or potentially related) to either the independent or dependent variables. These pretest measures will also allow us to evaluate how comparable the experimental and control groups are after randomization has taken place. Our outcomes measures will be obtained using the identical questionnaire after administration of the DARE curriculum. This would be referred to as the **posttest**. There could be one or multiple posttests.

Steps to Conducting an Experiment

To conduct our experiment, we must first identify the experimental and control groups. In the case of our schools, we would randomly assign classrooms to either the DARE condition or the **treatment as usual** condition (in this case, this is no curriculum). Treatment as usual may be the generic drug education used by the school district, or no treatment at all. This will serve as the reference group when we interpret our results. For instance, we may say that the DARE curriculum was more effective in preventing drug use than the curriculum used in the school or that the DARE curriculum is more effective than no treatment at all, depending upon the treatment received by the control group.

Once the two groups are prepared, you are ready to administer a pretest to, first, ensure the groups are comparable and randomization was effective in producing equal groups, and, second, to identify baseline levels of outcome measures (e.g., drug use, alcohol use) and confounders and to describe the sample demographically. This pretest should be administered to every student who is participating in the experiment, regardless of which group they are in. Whenever possible, the person administering the pretest and collecting all data should be unaware of the group to which each classroom is assigned (known as a **single-blind experiment**). It is ideal for the person physically collecting the data and the person conducting the analysis to be completely unable to identify which group is receiving the intervention and which group is not (**double-blind experiment**) to avoid unknowingly introducing any bias. This is important for several reasons. First, the person administering the pretest may unintentionally introduce the purpose of the study differently to classrooms assigned to the experimental and control groups. The way the study and its purposes are described must be consistent to avoid any effect even slight differences might cause in the way participants in the various classrooms and groups respond to the pretest. In addition, the investigator or others performing the statistical analysis of the results should also be unaware of the classroom assignments to avoid consciously or unconsciously "looking for" an effect.

For instance, we think that the DARE program will decrease drug use; however, it is possible that those who participated in the DARE program are more likely to use one or more drugs in high school. If we analyze the data as we originally intended and the investigator finds results inconsistent with the hypothesis, there may be some incentive to tweak the model or to conduct additional unplanned analyses. Therefore, to maintain the integrity of the scientific process, it is important that the analyst be unaware of how participants are categorized (e.g., the coding of the randomization variable).

After the pretest has been administered, the intervention may be conducted in the experimental group. The intervention may be as short as a few minutes (known as **brief interventions**) or as long as multiple years in length. In our case, a "dose" of the program is administered weekly by a police officer in each of the experimental group fifth-grade classrooms. The control fifth-grade classrooms do not receive any prevention program. After the intervention has been fully administered, one or more posttests are given to all students (both experimental and control) to evaluate the success of the program. The first posttest is generally administered on the last day of the program. In some cases, posttests are often given at regular intervals after the program to evaluate whether the lessons learned or effects of the intervention are sustained over time. For instance, we might administer a posttest the day the program ends and at

1-month intervals for 6 months to a year afterward. This will allow us to answer three questions:

1. Immediately after the intervention was completed, how do the drug-related attitudes and behaviors of the intervention youth differ from those in the control group?
2. Are these differences sustained after the intervention is completed?
3. At what point do the intervention effects (if any) diminish? If the effects diminish at 3 months, for example, this would indicate the need for a **booster session**, or brief program reinforcing the principal components of the original program.

The Experimental Intervention

In some cases, the effects of an intervention may not present immediately. Alternatively, the intervention may have an influence of behaviors that were not measured (e.g., if you only measured behavior, the program might have influenced attitudes toward that particular behavior). These attitudes might influence behavior over a longer period of time than you originally set out to measure. This is referred to as a **lagged effect** and is the reason behind longer-term follow-ups than seem appropriate. For example, DARE is implemented in fifth grade, and we would expect to see the greatest differences in behavior in fifth to sixth grades. However, it is possible that a lagged effect of the program might present in high school. Therefore, some researchers choose to collect data for a very long time, even after the intervention and several booster sessions have ceased.

The steps to collecting data using an experimental design are depicted in Figure 8.1. In this diagram, the O refers to an observation of the intervention, meaning a DARE officer came and administered the program. An X indicates data collection or that a pretest or posttest is collected at that time. Although this standardized notation may be confusing, it accurately depicts the process of program administration and evaluation most efficiently. As shown, the experimental group receives a pretest (X), the DARE program (O), and a posttest (X). In comparison, the control group only receives a pretest (X) and a posttest (X). There is no intervention (O) in the control group.

Figure 8.1   Steps to Conducting an Experimental Evaluation of DARE

Randomization (Experimental Group):	**X O X**	
Randomization (Control Group):	**X X**	

EXPERIMENTS AND CAUSAL INFERENCE

The purpose of an experiment is to move one step closer to understanding a cause-and-effect relationship. Because experiments are more controlled than nonrandomized observational designs, we are able to state more confidently that we believe that differences in the outcome of interest between the experimental and control groups are due to differential exposure (as in our DARE experiment). This design works by minimizing several threats to the **internal validity** of the findings, or processes that could make our conclusions invalid (e.g., we thought the DARE program reduced drug use, when in fact drug use declined for some other reason). The threats to internal validity, and the way they are minimized by the experimental design, are discussed below.

History

An event of historical importance related to your program or outcome may differentially affect your findings. For example, if there is widespread negative publicity about the police in your city while you are implementing a police-based DARE program, it is possible that the students will have less trust in the DARE officer, mitigating your results. Although this is highly unlikely, this could introduce bias into the findings of your study. A more likely historical event is the highly publicized drug-related arrest or suicide of a professional football player. This may influence drug-related attitudes among your participants; however, as long as the influence is equal across both experimental and control conditions, excess bias is not a problem. The presence of a comparison group allows for the measurement of historical events unrelated to the exposure (DARE).

Maturation

People evolve daily, both in their attitudes and behavior. We know that drug and alcohol use increase with age through adolescence and then decrease when a person reaches early adulthood (Clark, Thatcher, & Tapert, 2008). Because we know that this behavior changes with age, we could expect to see that drug/alcohol use increases over time, even during the DARE program. However, we would expect that the *gains* in substance use in the experimental group are smaller than the gains in the control group. This would indicate that DARE slowed the growth of substance use. We are able to measure changes in maturation by including the control group, as these persons are maturing age-appropriately without the influence of the intervention.

Test

A test effect may be defined as the effect of taking a test, participating in an intervention, or taking a survey on a person's responses on the assessment.

For instance, on our last day of the DARE program, we may receive responses to our posttest that suggest that those in the DARE program believe that drug use is less favorable and they are less likely to use drugs or alcohol than the control group. However, because the experimental group just received the intervention, they understand that the purpose of DARE is to reduce drug use, and they have caught on to the negative attitudes associated with drug and alcohol use. Respondents may also be concerned that a police officer is nearby, and they do not wish to admit drug use. Regardless, the results of the posttest will be biased because of some variable related to the test or having the test closely tied with the program. A way around this bias is to administer the posttest entirely independent of the program, such as the following week after the last DARE session without a police officer present.

Instrumentation

Changing a questionnaire in the middle of a study may have drastic effects on the outcomes, introducing measurement bias. For instance, if we decide to change the wording of our outcome variable from "drug" to "substance," we may get different answers from participants. Also, if we change the time frame from "past week drug use" to "past month drug use," there may be differences in participants' ability to accurately recall drug use during each time period. The best method for minimizing instrumentation threats to validity is by maintaining the same questionnaire throughout the study period. All questions, responses, and the order of the questions should be identical across all pre- and posttests. Something as seemingly harmless as adding a question could introduce bias into your results.

Statistical Regression to the Mean

It is possible to initiate your study with a group of participants who are at behavioral extremes (Barnett, Van der Pols, & Dobson, 2005). For instance, if we were to conduct our DARE trial in urban Chicago, where gun violence and felony crime is abundant, it is very likely that youth would be using drugs and alcohol very often. Therefore, because the "average" (or mean) level of drug use is so high, there is nowhere to go but down. Similarly, it would not benefit us to conduct our trial in fifth-grade classrooms in which nobody uses drugs or alcohol, as we will not be able to see a reduced effect in behavior (assuming that behavior is our goal) because the average level of drug use is zero. Instead, we may look for a change in that more negative drug-related attitudes are evident among the experimental group. Therefore, when current behavior is at the extremes (particularly high or particularly low), it is difficult to attribute changes in behavior to your program. Instead, the behaviors naturally tend toward more normative (or average level) values without the help of your program, resulting in the misinterpretation of this change in behavior being caused by your program. You will be able to detect these extreme values by thoroughly examining pretest and posttest scores for unexpected results.

Selection Bias

Selection bias is introduced by the differential selection of certain groups of people into your study. For instance, in our study, we would likely send home informed consent letters to potential participants' parents (both experimental and control). It is possible that the students who are most likely to use drugs and alcohol also have parents who are not involved in their lives or who refuse to sign the informed consent. Alternatively, these children may not wish to be included in the program and so do not take the letter home. This makes our sample biased in favor of students who are less involved in risk behavior. However, the use of a control group, and the randomization to the experimental and control groups, minimizes the likelihood that selection bias will occur in our study. Specifically, we would expect that at-risk students are randomly assigned to both groups, and these students will not participate in the study equally across groups.

Attrition

Attrition, or loss to follow-up, occurs when participants who complete the pretest do not complete the intervention posttest. Similar to the example above, assume that all participants in both groups sign the informed consent to participate in our study and complete the pretest. Now, assume that some students end up in school-based detention, were expelled from school, or were placed in juvenile detention. These students are probably more likely than those who completed the program to use drugs and alcohol. So, we will probably find that drug and alcohol use declined during our intervention; however, we conclude this because we lost the drug and alcohol users from our sample (they did not complete the posttest). If the rate of attrition in the experimental group is different from that in the control group, the findings from our study may not be valid. However, the assumption of equal attrition may be tested when you have pretest information on the participants who dropped out of your study.

Temporal Ordering

The final major threat to internal validity is the establishment of the ordering of cause and effect. In criminal justice, it is often difficult to deal with the "chicken and the egg" problem of which behavior came first. For instance, were uninvolved parents and lack of supervision causing the child to act out, or was the child acting out and the parents, as a result, became disassociated? In the case of our experiment, we are able to manipulate the exposure (DARE). Therefore, we are certain that exposure to the program came first, and then the reduction in drug and alcohol use followed suit. The use of the pretest measures baseline behavior, and we are able to see if the DARE program changed individuals' drug use attitudes and behaviors after the program has been completed. The only possible explanation for these differences is the program.

Other Factors Affecting Experimental Results

There are other concerns that must be considered when designing an experiment. First, we must understand that some students will not attend all DARE programming; in fact, they may only be present for one or two sessions. What do we do with these students? We could exclude them from our study, but then we run the risk of excluding at-risk students and introducing bias. Instead, many researchers choose to conduct an **intent-to-treat** analysis, in which all students are included in the pretest and all posttests, regardless of how many intervention sessions they went to (Hollis & Campbell, 1999). Although this may reduce the intervention effect size (or make the intervention seem like it was less effective than it actually was), it ensures that there will be no differential attrition between the experimental and control groups.

Second, we must also consider **contamination** effects across the experimental and control groups. This may occur when some experimental group students share their intervention materials with those in the control group, or the control group sees the police officer in the school and this changes their alcohol and drug-related attitudes and behaviors (Torgerson, 2000). Fortunately, contamination will serve to reduce the apparent effectiveness of the intervention (making the intervention seem less effective in the experimental group compared to controls) rather than introducing any systematic bias.

CRITERIA FOR EVALUATING CAUSATION

If you wish to assess whether your study can draw conclusions of causation, there are three criteria that must be met (Weed, 1997). First, there must be a strong and significant correlation between your cause and your effect. This is the simplest criteria to meet, as we may be able to show that the DARE program was significantly associated with a reduction in drug use 6 months later. Because this was an experiment, we are confident that the findings are true and reflective of actual behavioral change.

Second, we must show that the cause preceded the effect. Although this is more difficult, our use of a pretest demonstrates behavior before the intervention, and the multiple posttests details the change in behavior that occurred after the program. If we are able to show that, in the control group, the pretest and posttest scores were similar on drug and alcohol use, we can deduce that there was no change in this group. Then, in assessing change in the experimental group, we may see that there is a reduction in reported drug and alcohol use during the time of the intervention. Because these groups are randomly assigned and comparable on drug/alcohol use and demographics at baseline, we have a strong argument in favor of DARE's effect on drug and alcohol use.

And third, the most difficult criteria to deduce causation is the elimination of all other potential explanations for the reduction in drug and alcohol use in the experimental group. We must be able to show that no bias was introduced, no historical event differentially influenced the intervention group, and no test effect or other change in the school environment led to the observed result. We must be able to confidently say that we are certain that *no other factor* explains the observed findings. When these three criteria are met, we may say that an exposure caused a given effect.

MULTILEVEL RANDOMIZATION

In our example, we selected classrooms within a school district to participate in our intervention study. This design was chosen for several reasons. First, the program is administered in the classroom setting. Second, using several classrooms within one school district means the students within the school are similar to one another, both demographically and in terms of their drug use. Third, this design makes data collection and **quality assurance** (e.g., the researchers' ability to be certain that the program is being administered as we would expect) logistically simple.

In our case, we chose to administer the program in classrooms because we could have a police officer administer the intervention during classroom time. If we chose to have an after-school administration of the program, we could have randomly selected students from all fifth graders in the school. Nevertheless, our study is relatively small, consisting of a handful of fifth-grade students. However, many studies are much larger and require a more complex sampling structure to meet the needs of the study. For instance, if we wanted to measure whether the "no refusal" weekends (a program that requires a suspected intoxicated driver to take a Breathalyzer test or provide a blood sample to police) influenced impaired driving rates on New Year's Eve, we would need to first obtain a list of all departments or jurisdictions that enact this policy on New Year's Eve. Because this list will likely be extensive, it is impossible for us to survey all people in all jurisdictions; therefore, we may choose to randomly select jurisdictions. Within these jurisdictions, we could obtain a list of people who live within these jurisdictions, and randomly select individual people for a telephone and/or mail survey about their attitudes and behaviors regarding "no refusal" weekend. Due to the properties of randomization, this multilevel sample (two stages of randomization) provides an example that is representative of the entire original population (e.g., all people in all jurisdictions who implement "no refusal" weekend).

QUASI-EXPERIMENTAL DESIGNS

In many cases, randomization to an exposure condition is not ethical, practical, or possible (Edwards, Braunholtz, Lilford, & Stevens, 1999). When randomization cannot occur, a **quasi-experiment** is the next best option for testing a hypothesis (McCleary, Hay, Meidinger, & McDowall, 1980). These designs are similar to experiments, without the property of randomization. Unfortunately, the primary strength of the experimental design lies in the randomization of people (or groups) to experimental conditions, which rules out several threats to internal validity. According to the seminal work on experimental and quasi-experimental designs, Shadish, Cook, and Campbell (2002) explained that there are two distinct types of quasi-experiments: **nonequivalent groups designs** and **time-series designs**. These will be discussed in more depth below.

Nonequivalent Groups Designs

As discussed above, a quasi-experimental design is similar to an experimental design in every way, with the exception of comparable groups obtained through randomization. Therefore, a nonequivalent groups design occurs when experimental conditions are utilized in the absence of randomization (Bryk & Weisberg, 1977). In other words, we would use an experimental and control condition; however, classrooms would not be randomized to receive DARE (or not). This might occur if only some teachers were willing to devote classroom time to a drug prevention program. In this case, only those classrooms in which the teacher was willing to participate would be administered the curriculum. The other classrooms would comprise the control group. This could also occur if we had a natural experiment in which one school district did not use DARE and another implemented the program. In this case, all fifth-grade classrooms in the one district would get the program, while those in another would not. Clearly, this introduces some potential problems in terms of internal validity. We must assume that the two schools are comparable before the program is administered. This means that the students should be as demographically and behaviorally similar as possible. We would not want to compare a private school with a public school or a suburban school with an urban school of a different size. Several variables cannot be measured; the anti-drug environment of the school, the commitment to the DARE program of school faculty and administrators, or major drug- or alcohol-related historical events at the school may influence the effect of the program.

In many cases, matching experimental and comparison individuals are used to minimize the shortcomings associated with nonequivalent group designs (Kenny, 1975). In our example, matching is difficult to achieve because we are implementing the program at the classroom level. If the intervention was being administered to individuals, we could ensure that our experimental and *comparison* (rather than *control*, to reflect the inequality of the groups) conditions were similar by matching one experimental and one comparison individual based on race, ethnicity, gender, academic achievement, previous drug use, and so on. This would allow for some degree of investigator control over group equality when randomization is not possible.

Time-Series Designs

Time-series designs are generally used for policy evaluations, or intensive longitudinal data—a study with many measures of the same behavior over time (Roussas, Tran, & Ioannides, 1992). This design is not appropriate for evaluating our DARE program because we only have one pretest and seven posttests, and the intervals between these evaluations are not equal. A simple example of an appropriate time-series design is evaluating the effect of alcohol taxes on alcohol-related traffic mortality (from impaired driving). For instance, public records provide measures of the number of people who died in car accidents every month of every year since the mid-1970s. Assume that we could determine from these records how many people had alcohol in their system at the time of the crash. Now, tax law dictates the rate (and date) of increases in alcohol taxes, and for which type of alcohol they apply (e.g., liquor, wine, beer). Using this information, we can use a time-series model to evaluate whether the taxes had an impact on impaired driving mortality.

This method is depicted in Figure 8.2. The large number of pretest measures (O) allows us to establish a baseline trend, and the large number of posttest measures (O) allows us to determine whether the trend was interrupted (or changed significantly) by the tax policy (X).

These designs become more complex as comparison groups are added. To the simple interrupted time-series design, we might add a comparison group of another state that had a tax policy change; however, the policy changed in a different year (Fig. 8.3). We know that the comparison group is not selected randomly and is not equal to the first group. Therefore, we would call this comparison group a nonequivalent comparison group. If we were assessing the effect of alcohol taxes in Kentucky on alcohol-related traffic accidents, we might use Ohio as the comparison group, assuming that they had no tax changes around the same time. This is a stronger design than the simple time-series evaluation, as it rules out any large-scale effects (e.g., historical events or related confounding variables) that may be responsible for the decrease in alcohol-related mortality.

Figure 8.2   **Steps to Conducting a Time-Series Policy Evaluation, Simple Interrupted Time-Series Design**

O   O   O   O   O   X   O   O   O   O   O

Figure 8.3 Steps to Conducting a Time-Series Policy Evaluation, Interrupted Time-Series Design with Non-Equivalent Comparison Group

Kentucky: O O O O O X O O O O O

Ohio: O O O O O   O O O O O

The third and final type of time-series design, which provides the most protections against threats to internal validity, is the interrupted time-series design with removed treatment, using a comparison group (Wagner, Soumerai, & Ross-Degnan, 2002). This design is appropriate when you have one state (Kentucky) that increased alcohol taxes and then, several months or years later, decreased their alcohol taxes. If alcohol taxes were related to traffic mortality, we would expect to see a decrease in fatal traffic accidents when taxes were increased and an increase in accidents when taxes were decreased. If we compare these rates to those in Ohio (which had no changes), we have an exceptionally strong case that taxes are related to impaired driving.

Every day, we hear about new studies on the news that conflict with other studies, or with a concept that we always thought was true. These differences in empirical findings are due to different sampling populations, differences in the quality of the experimental design, and threats to internal (and external) validity. When you are evaluating which findings you truly believe, use the concepts discussed in this chapter to evaluate the quality of the research that you use in your daily life.

SUMMARY

This chapter expands on the design and theory behind experimental and quasi-experimental research designs. We used the DARE program to show how experimental research might be conducted in a criminological, real-world setting. We dissected an experimental design, randomization, multi-level random sample selection, pretesting, posttesting, and blinding.

The relationship between experiments and the process of making causal inferences was covered, as causal inference is the ultimate goal of the research enterprise. We discussed how the experimental (and quasi-experimental) designs remedy some common threats to validity that might preclude causal inference. We also discussed how the experimental design helps to meet the three criteria for causal inference (consistent statistical relationship between the proposed cause and effect, temporal ordering, nonspuriousness of the find-ings). Finally, the manner in which quasi-experimental designs differ from regular experiments was discussed within this section of the chapter, and we concluded with examples of the two types of quasi-experimental designs: the nonequivalent group design and the time-series design.

KEY TERMS

Booster sessions Elements of experiments that are reintroduced some point later in the course of experimental research to reinforce treatment effects that may have atrophied over time.

Brief interventions Experimental trials that are often as short as a few minutes in duration.

Causal inference The attribution of one variable as the cause of another.

Confounding variables These variables are related to both the exposure and the outcome of interest. This variable may be established as the "cause" of the outcome; however, it is only associated with the outcome because of its relationship with the other exposure measured. Potential confounds make it difficult to determine cause-and-effect relationships between variables.

Contamination This occurs when the control group is inadvertently exposed to some of the treatment. This might occur due to error, members of the experimental group sharing information or aspects of the treatment with the control group, or by some other manner.

Control group The group used as a standard for comparison in a control experiment, which receives no treatment, lesser treatment, or treatment for an unrelated problem.

Double-blind experiment An experiment conducted on human subjects, in which neither the individuals participating in the experiments nor the researchers conducting the experiment know who belongs to the control group or who belongs to the treatment group. This reduces bias in experiments.

Experiment A type of research design conducted under controlled conditions for the purpose of demonstrating a known truth, examining the validity of a hypothesis, or determining the efficacy of something previously untried.

Experimental group A group of subjects that are exposed to the treatment condition of an experiment.

Exposure The condition of being subject to some effect or influence.

Intent-to-treat An analysis that includes all students receiving a treatment or participants in an experiment in both the pretest and posttest regardless of how much of an intervention they may have been exposed to. This is a conservative method for evaluating the outcome of an experiment.

Internal validity The degree to which the results of a study are actually true (e.g., no systematic bias or confounding is introduced into the study). A strong research design and a valid and reliable questionnaire increase the likelihood that the findings from the study are correct.

Lagged effects Effects of a treatment intervention or experimental condition that come about well after the fact, often after measurement and the official experiment has ceased.

Nonequivalent groups design The most frequently used design in social research. This design is similar to a pretest, posttest randomized experiment but lacks the feature of randomization.

Posttest A survey or other data-collection method administered to research participants after completion of a treatment to determine change in behavior and effect of the treatment. This is used in conjunction with a pretest.

Pretest A preliminary test administered to determine baseline behaviors and characteristics prior to treatment.

Quality assurance The researchers' ability to be certain that the program is being administered as expected.

Quasi-experiment An empirical study similar to an experiment in all manners with the exception of lacking the element of random assignment of participants.

Single-blind experiment An experiment where information that could reduce bias or otherwise skew the result is withheld from the participants but is completely known to the experimenter.

Time-series design A quasi-experimental research design in which periodic measurements are made on groups or individuals both before and after the implementation of an intervention or policy.

Treatment as usual The treatment received by the control group within an experiment. "Treatment as usual" may be no treatment at all, another unrelated program, or a bare-bones version of the experimental condition treatment program.

Unit of analysis The entity that you are studying in research. Units of analysis can be individuals, groups, artifacts (books, newspapers), geographical areas (towns, states, countries), or social interactions (marriages, divorces).

REVIEW QUESTIONS

1. What is the primary difference between an experimental design and a quasi-experimental design?
2. Why is an experiment considered the "gold standard" research design?
3. List two threats to internal validity and discuss how the experimental design remedies these threats. If you do not believe that the design adequately addresses the issues, state your reasons for doubt.
4. What are the steps/criteria for determining causation?
5. What is the difference between a double- and single-blind experiment? Please define the two terms and compare the two methods.

Useful Websites

www.dare.com/home/default.asp. Official website of DARE.

www.encyclopedia.com/doc/1G2-3403000080.html. Discussion of criminology and criminal justice research methods in criminology; focuses on experimental designs within the field.

http://srmo.sagepub.com/view/the-sage-dictionary-of-social-research-methods/n208.xml. Discussion of time series research designs from SAGE.

www.cdc.gov/nchs/fastats/druguse.htm. Statistics on illegal drug usage from the Centers for Disease Control.

www.psychmet.com/id12.html. A website looking at threats to internal validity.

References

Barnett, A. G., Van der Pols, J. C., & Dobson, A. J. (2005). Regression to the mean: What it is and how to deal with it. *International Journal of Epidemiology, 34*(1), 215–220.

Bryk, A. S., & Weisberg, H. I. (1977). Use of the nonequivalent control group design when subjects are growing. *Psychological Bulletin, 84*(5), 950–962.

Chapin, F. S. (1949). Experimental designs in sociological research. *Journal of the American Statistical Association, 44*(247), 460–462.

Clark, D. B., Thatcher, D. L., & Tapert, S. F. (2008). Alcohol, psychological dysregulation, and adolescent brain development. *Alcoholism: Clinical and Experimental Research, 32*(3), 375–385.

Edwards, S. L., Braunholtz, D. A., Lilford, R. J., & Stevens, A. J. (1999). Ethical issues in the design and conduct of cluster randomized trials. *BMJ, 318*(7195), 1407–1409.

Hollis, S., & Campbell, F. (1999). What is meant by intention to treat analysis? Survey of published randomized control trials. *BMJ, 319*–670.

Kenny, D. A. (1975). A quasi-experimental approach to assessing treatment effects in the nonequivalent control group design. *Psychological Bulletin, 82*(3), 345–362.

McCleary, R., Hay, R. A., Meidinger, E. E., & McDowall, D. (1980). *Applied time series analysis for the social sciences.* Thousand Oaks, California: Sage.

Roussas, G. G., Tran, L. T., & Ioannides, D. A. (1992). Fixed design regression for time series: Asymptotic abnormality. *Journal of Multivariate Analysis, 40*(2), 262–291.

Schwartz, J., & Coull, B. C. (2003). Control for confounding in the presence of measurement error in hierarchical models. *Biostatistics, 4*(4), 539–553.

Shadish, W. R., Cook, T. D., & Campbell, D. T. (2002). *Experimental and quasi-experimental designs for generalized causal inference.* Boston, MA: Houghton Mifflin.

Torgerson, D. J. (2000). Contamination in trials: Is cluster randomization the answer? *BMJ, 322*–355.

Vickers, A. J. (2006). How to randomize. *Journal of Social Integrated Oncology, 4*(4), 194–198.

Wagner, A. K., Soumerai, S. B., & Ross-Degnan, D. (2002). Segmented regression analysis of interrupted time series studies in medication use research. *Journal of Clinical Pharmacy and Therapeutics, 27*(4), 299–309.

Weed, D. L. (1997). On the use of casual criteria. *International Journal of Epidemiology, 26*(6), 1137–1141.

LONGITUDINAL DESIGNS

I magine yourself in the following situation: You are a recent graduate with a degree in criminology/criminal justice recently hired as a program evaluator at the local police department. The department recently implemented a new violence-monitoring program intended to track serious violent offenders closely while they are on probation and parole. As a part of this program, you are responsible for contacting program participants each week to ensure they have maintained employment and housing and have refrained from crime. Every week until they have completed probation or parole, you call each participant and record their answers to a series of questions. At the end of their term, you potentially have hundreds of records that measure the continuity of employment, housing, and association with deviant friends and family members during the respondents' time in the correctional system. This is an example of a longitudinal research design. This chapter reviews the circumstances in which longitudinal designs are applicable, the types of longitudinal research designs, and issues faced with employing longitudinal designs.

WHY USE A LONGITUDINAL DESIGN?

Longitudinal research designs provide important information beyond the one-time, cross-sectional designs that were discussed in previous chapters (Ployhart & Vandenberg, 2010). For example, a one-time phone call would only capture the participants' housing, employment, and peer and family associations at one time during their community supervision; in other words, it would be only a "snapshot" of the relevant information. Parole or probation typically lasts several years, so the participants' housing and employment information, as well as their list of friends and acquaintances, may change.

As a program evaluator, using a cross-sectional design could lead you to the conclusion that participants were refraining from hanging out with old friends, had jobs, and had secured permanent housing. However, what you might not find out is that 1 month after your follow-up calls, the participants quit their jobs, were evicted from their apartments, and moved back into their old neighborhoods with old roommates involved in drug dealing. If you had tracked these individuals on a weekly basis, you would come across this information when you called their places of employment and apartment complexes. Without regular check-ins, the re-arrest of these participants would surprise you, since your snapshot did not indicate any identifiable risk for recidivism.

As illustrated in this example, **longitudinal designs**—following people over a period of time—provide more information than one-time snapshots of individuals' behavior (Berk & Rossi, 1998). This is because most behaviors vary over time. For example, think about how your circle of friends changed from when you were in high school to when you enrolled as a freshman in college. It is likely that you kept in touch with some friends from high school, but you hang out more often with those who are in your classes or reside closer to where you currently live.

This example illustrates a couple of important concepts in longitudinal research designs. First, the more measurements we have, the more confident we can be that our findings are correct (e.g., that the probationer you were responsible for monitoring did, in fact, have a job during the entire duration of their probation) (Harrison, 1997). This enhances the internal validity, or the likelihood that our findings are accurate, of our program evaluation (Leonard-Barton, 1990). Second, the example highlights the potential for loss-to-follow-up, a case in which you lose touch with some participants that you were supposed to contact weekly. This is especially concerning among mobile and transient populations, such as former felons. This loss, also known as sample **attrition**, may impact the findings of your evaluation if those who you lose touch with are more likely to recidivate than those you maintain contact with (Ellickson, 1989; Grimes & Schulz, 2002).

Instrumentation

In order to evaluate change over time, the questions you ask each participant in your program should stay consistent each time you make contact (Grimes & Schulz, 2002). Because the order of the questions, the tone in which they are asked, and the response options all play a role in how the question is answered, these should remain constant across all follow-up periods. This means that questions should not be regularly added or removed from the questionnaire between follow-ups without pilot testing (Schulz et al., 2005). Pilot testing an instrument for data collection will allow you to identify differential patterns in responses when you change the ordering of questions, add or delete items, or change response options. This pilot testing should be done on a group of people who are similar to the population in your evaluation (Mackey & Gass, 2005); however, your study population should never respond to the pilot questionnaire in the event that you notice changes in responses to certain items based upon changes that you made to the instrument (Schulz et al., 2005).

Retaining Your Sample Over Time

Because it is so important to retain all of your probationers and parolees in your evaluation to make sure that your conclusions regarding the program evaluation are correct, a number of techniques could be used to encourage them to be responsive to you and to maintain contact during the several years of their required community supervision. Incentives, generally in the form of gift cards, cash, or vouchers, are commonly used to encourage participation in research studies and evaluations (Laurie & Lynn, 2009). Participants are notified at the beginning of the evaluation (when they provide informed consent) that they will be remunerated at specific intervals (e.g., at each time of contact). The investigator should also inform the participant as to whether the incentive would be cash, a gift card, or some other form of payment, and whether questionnaire completion is required in order to receive the incentive (Nyden, 2003).

The amount of the incentive is based upon the level of commitment needed from the respondent, the number of follow-ups, and the knowledge of the population (Collins, Ellickson, Hays, & Mccaffrey, 2000). In your situation, for example, it may make sense to offer a monthly incentive or a gift card to a chain store (e.g., Walmart, Target) or a prepaid credit card. This decision would be made based upon the length of the questionnaire (in your situation, less than 10 items) and frequency of responses (weekly participation is required). Because respondents may find this frequent correspondence to be a mild burden, remuneration would encourage them to maintain participation in your study (Laurie & Lynn, 2009; Robinson, Dennison, Wayman, Pronovost, & Needham, 2007).

TYPES OF LONGITUDINAL DESIGNS

The most basic longitudinal design uses only two measurements: a pretest and a posttest (White & Arzi, 2005). The first measurement, often called the *pretest*, is intended to measure behavior as soon as possible (Kumar, 2005) after the individual is released on probation or parole. This *pretest* will identify the level of risk upon release, and any change from that risk level will be identified at the second follow-up, the *posttest*. At a minimum, this will provide information as to whether your participants had a job, housing, and so on, when they were released from incarceration and at the end of their probation or parole term. However, you will not be able to identify whether each individual was consistently employed, moved constantly, or was participating in other risk behaviors between follow-ups. Because it provides more information than a simple cross-section, this rudimentary longitudinal design should be preferred over "snapshot" evaluation designs whenever possible (White & Arzi, 2005).

Although you are conducting weekly follow-ups as a part of your program evaluation, this is not necessarily the appropriate frequency for all studies and evaluations. The distance between your phone calls (or mailings, or home visits) depends primarily upon how often you expect changes in the variables you are measuring to occur (Jackson & Mare, 2007). For example, if you were conducting an entirely different study to investigate the recidivism rate in your city, you might only need to do annual record checks to identify re-arrest or reconviction rates within your sample (Kurlycheck, Brame, & Bushway, 2006). Alternatively, if you are looking at behaviors that change frequently, such as drug and alcohol use, school attendance, or community service completion, follow-up surveys may be conducted at more frequent intervals (Greenfield & Kerr, 2008).

Repeated Cross-Sectional versus Longitudinal Designs

An important feature of these longitudinal designs is the ability to evaluate **intra-individual**, or within a person, change in employment, housing, and peer associations over time (Lynn, 2009). This feature differentiates longitudinal methods from less sophisticated **repeated cross-sectional designs** (Menard & Elliott, 1990). To illustrate this distinction, your longitudinal evaluation is following the same group of recent parolees and probationers over a period of several months to years (Piquero, Blumstein, Brame, Mulvey, & Nagin, 2001), or using a **panel design**. To conduct a similar study using a repeated cross-sectional design, you would draw a new sample of recent parolees and probationers each week (Asher et al., 2006) and administer your questionnaire to that particular sample only once (Kravitz, Cavanaugh, & Rigsbee, 2002). Each week, a new sample is drawn and a new set of responses is obtained. Although this provides you with information on the prevalence of job ascertainment, housing, and deviant family and peer associations, you will not administer a questionnaire to that same participant again. Therefore, you cannot track how their responses change over the course of their probation or parole term. Relatedly, **cohort designs** are longitudinal designs where you follow a group of individuals over time who share a common characteristic such as year of birth. For example, you may select a cohort of probationers born in 1980 and then reconstruct their criminal histories from 1980 until the current date.

Intensive Longitudinal Designs

A more complex type of longitudinal design, called **intensive longitudinal designs**, are often used when secondary sources have a large number of follow-ups (Hamilton, 2002; Land, Teske, & Zheng, 2009). These designs are often used by large databases with frequent measurement (monthly or annual measurements for many years), such as the Uniform Crime Reports (UCR) or the Fatal Alcohol Reporting System (Federal Bureau of Investigation, 2010; National Highway Traffic Safety Administration, 2010). By nature, these databases are repeated cross-sections of crime and fatal alcohol crashes, as they measure the frequency of crime incidents or traffic fatalities in the United

States (Baker, Brady, Rebok, & Li, 2011). These designs are especially useful for evaluating the impact of a recent policy change (Wagenaar, Maldonado-Molina, Ma, Tobler, & Komro, 2007); in fact, the time-series design discussed in the previous chapter is an example of an intensive longitudinal design. As an example, let's say you wanted to know whether the introduction of sex offender registration policies reduced the number of arrests for sex offenses. In this case, you would have UCR measures of sex offense arrests for decades prior to the legislation and for several years afterwards (Prescott & Rockoff, 2011). This type of design would allow you to investigate whether the introduction of the community registration policy caused a significant change in the number of arrests for sex offenses, while considering the trends before the policy. Also, this design will provide information on lagged effects (i.e., the policy did not have an immediate impact but 1 year later, sex offense arrests declined drastically) and **rebound effects** (i.e., the policy reduced arrests at first, but the number of arrests increased again after a few years) (Land et al., 2009).

Retrospective Longitudinal Design

A final type of longitudinal design is not really a longitudinal design at all. Instead, the **retrospective longitudinal design** is an attempt to remedy some of the flaws of a cross-sectional design to gather more detailed information about changes within an individual over the course of several months or years, or even a lifetime (Henry, Moffitt, Caspi, Langley, & Silva, 1994; Menard & Elliott, 1990).

For example, let's get back to your program evaluation. Your supervisor is impatient and wants to know whether the consistency of housing and employment are related to recidivism among the parolees and probationers. Because you do not have time to follow a new sample over the course of several months or years, you decide to select a group of probationers and parolees who were released from correctional supervision 5 years ago. You find that many of them are reincarcerated, while others are not. When you interview each of them, you ask questions about the time they spent on parole or probation since their last offense. You may ask questions like, "While you were on parole for your last offense, did you have a job within the first month after release?" You might also ask, "How long did you remain at that job?" and "Did you have a job consistently during your parole?" This information will give you an idea as to the consistency of employment during the time of parole. However, you must consider that their memory may not be perfect and some information that they provide may be inaccurate.

In this example, it is important to identify yourself as conducting a research evaluation (Hawkins, Catalano, & Miller, 1992), and this research will not be linked to their eligibility to maintain parole or probation (Elger & Spaulding, 2010; Morselli & Tremblay, 2010). This distinction is extremely important when working with vulnerable populations, and the integrity of your findings as an evaluator is at stake. Consider yourself as the participant in this situation. If you are currently on probation or parole, how likely are you to report that you are moving back in with your old roommate, who was recently released from serving a long sentence for drug trafficking? If the information that you provide will be placed in your supervision file, it is unlikely that you will truthfully report this information. However, if you are assured that this information is separate and will be used for evaluation purposes only, then the parolee or probationer may be more inclined to tell the truth (Morselli & Tremblay, 2010). Although there is possibly an element of distrust regardless of the evaluator's reassurance, the likelihood that the respondent will provide you with accurate information is more likely when it will not be used against them.

WHEN ARE LONGITUDINAL DESIGNS APPROPRIATE?

Although longitudinal designs provide rich information about someone's behavior, these designs are not always practical or necessary (Menard & Elliott, 1990). As briefly described above, you may need to find an answer to a research question within a month, when a longitudinal design would take you several years or even decades to gather the data that you need (Farrington, 1979; Piquero, Farrington, Shepherd, & Auty, 2011). In this case, you would need to conduct a study using secondary data, or collect data using the retrospective method described above. Also, a longitudinal design is often not appropriate when your outcome variable is rare (Grimes & Schulz, 2002). Fortunately for you, recidivism is not a rare outcome, as nearly two-thirds of those released from state prison reoffend within 3 years of release (Beck & Shipley, 1989; Langan & Levin, 2002). However, if your outcome of interest was death from homicide, a longitudinal design would not be appropriate (Flynn, Shaw, & Abel, 2007). This is because your sample will ultimately have so few people who die from homicide deaths (if you have any), that you will not be able to identify how job and housing continuity are related to homicide deaths (Grimes & Schulz, 2002). When your outcome is rare, you may choose to use cross-sectional or case-control research designs, as discussed in their respective chapters.

An additional element of the longitudinal design that must be briefly discussed is the time, effort, and cost involved in the process (Berger, 1986). In our example, you are tracking parolees and probationers (n = 500 for simplicity) for several years after incarceration. You may be providing incentives (a $25 gift card) to reduce attrition (Grant & Sugarman, 2004). These incentives add up to $300 per person, per year (e.g., 12 interviews x $25). If you measured every person in your study every month, this would amount to $150,000.

Some of these participants are fairly easy to track and maintain, as they provide you with new phone numbers, physical addresses, and employment information. However, the majority of these participants will not be easy to track (Faden et al., 2004). Some may move out of state, change residences without being listed on a lease or title, or have "off the books" employment. You will never hear from them, and they are not interested in being a part of your evaluation. These individuals will require the most of your time. You will constantly be contacting relatives, friends, former colleagues, and so on, to gather information on these individuals. You will also need to record this information directly into a database, which would hold a large amount of confidential information. This information must be backed up and stored on a secure server, adding up to several hundred dollars each year. In the end, your entire salary of $40,000 is dedicated to this project. This excludes the phone bills, long-distance charges associated with tracking these participants, administrative fees at your agency, gas and transportation for interviews, and computer maintenance and Internet access. Over 1 year, collecting longitudinal data can easily amount to several hundred thousand dollars.

SUMMARY

Overall, it is important to consider the questions that you are trying to answer when deciding which type of longitudinal design to use. Although these designs can provide a great deal of information about a group of people, it is not always appropriate or feasible, depending on the research question that you are interested in answering and the resources that are available to you. These designs also require substantial effort from the researcher to maintain contact with a large number of respondents over a long period of time. Nevertheless, these designs are scientifically worthwhile and exceptionally valid when conducted properly and when they may suitably address the research question of interest.

KEY TERMS

Attrition The loss of participants in a study from the original sample, also known as *loss to follow-up*.

Cohort Designs A type of longitudinal design where a group of people are followed over time who share a similar experience or characteristic such as birth year, generation, survivors of Hurricane Katrina, and so on.

Intensive longitudinal designs A useful method when large databases include frequent measurements of the same participants or sampling unit over time. These designs have multiple measurements (often 10 or more, as a rule of thumb) before and after an intervention, behavior change, or policy change. They are more powerful analytically than other types of longitudinal designs.

Intra-individual Being or occurring within an individual. This often relates to individual characteristics or performances on surveys or cognitive tasks.

Longitudinal design A research design in which participants, processes, or systems are studied over time. Data are collected at multiple time points or intervals. A study must have at least two measurements to be considered longitudinal.

Panel design A type of longitudinal design where the same individuals are followed over time.

Rebound effects The disappearance of a short-term effect of a policy, law, or intervention. In other words, the program had a short-term effect, and the participants rebounded back to normal levels of violence 1 month later.

Repeated cross-sectional designs Cross-sectional surveys that are repeated at regular or irregular time intervals for the purpose of estimating change at the aggregate or population levels.

Retrospective longitudinal design An attempt made to remedy flaws that occur with cross-sectional research by collecting data about individual behavior using recall methods several years after the behavior of interest occurred.

REVIEW QUESTIONS

1. What are some of the benefits of longitudinal designs? What are some of the drawbacks?
2. Why are longitudinal research designs not appropriate with rare outcome variables?
3. What are some of the different types of longitudinal research designs? Explain the different types and provide an example of each.
4. Can you think of some situations where cross-sectional research designs are more appropriate than longitudinal research designs? Elaborate on why or why not.
5. What is a retrospective longitudinal research design? When is this type of research design appropriate?

Useful Websites

www.neiu.edu/~wenjogu/design.htm. Information about research designs from Northeastern Illinois University.

www.mpicc.de/ww/en/pub/forschung/forschungsarbeit/kriminologie/cohortstudy .htm. Link to the Frieburg Cohort Study, a criminological cohort study.

http://blog.surveymonkey.com/blog/2011/04/12/academic-research-on-incentives/. Interesting site looking at the use of research incentives in academia.

www.academia.edu/1373705/._DATA_SOURCES_FOR_CRIMINOLOGICAL_ RESEARCH. Link to file listing secondary data sources in criminological research.

References

Asher, M. A., Montefort, S., Bjorksten, B., Lai, C. K. W., Strachan, D. P, Weiland, S. K., & Williams, H. (2006). Worldwide time trends in the prevalence of symptoms of asthma, allergic rhinoconjuncivitis, and eczema in childhood: Isaac phases one and three repeat multicountry cross-sectional surveys. *Lancet, 368,* 733–743.

Baker, S. P., Brady, J. E., Rebok, G., & Li, G. (2011). Alcohol in fatal crashes involving Mexican and Canadian drivers in the USA. *Injury Prevention, 17,* 304–308.

Beck, A. J., & Shipley, B. E. (1989). *Recidivism of prisoners released in 1983.* Washington, DC: Bureau of Justice Statistics, U.S. Department of Justice.

Berger, M. P. F. (1986). A comparison of efficiencies of longitudinal, mixed longitudinal, and cross-sectional designs. *Journal of Educational and Behavioral Statistics, 11,* 171–181.

Berk, R. A., & Rossi, P. H. (1998). *Thinking about program evaluation 2.* Thousand Oaks, California: Sage.

Collins, R. L., Ellickson, P. L., Hays, R. D., & Mccaffrey, D. F. (2000). Effects of incentive size and timing on response rates to a follow-up wave of a longitudinal mailed survey. *Evaluation Review, 24,* 347–363.

Elger, B. S., & Spaulding, A. (2010). Research on prisoners—A comparison between the IOM committee recommendations (2006) and European regulations. *Bioethics, 24,* 1–13.

Ellickson, P. A. (1989). Limiting nonresponse in longitudinal research: Three strategies for school-based studies. *The RAND Corporation.*

Faden, V. B., Day, N. L., Windle, M., Windle, M., Grube, J. W., Molina, B. G. S., . . . & Sher, K. J. (2004). Collecting longitudinal data through childhood, adolescence, and young adulthood: Methodological challenges. *Alcoholism: Clinical & Experimental Research, 28,* 330–340.

Farrington, D. P. (1979). Longitudinal research on crime and delinquency. *Crime & Justice, 1,* 289–348.

Federal Bureau of Investigation. (2010). Uniform Crime Reports. Retrieved from www.fbi.gov/about-us/cjis/ucr/ucr.

Flynn, S. M., Shaw, J. J., & Abel, K. M. (2007). Homicide of infants: A cross sectional study. *Journal of Clinical Psychiatry, 68*(10), 1501–1509.

Grant, R. W., & Sugarman, J. (2004). Ethics in human subject research: Do incentives matter? *Journal of Medicine and Philosophy, 29*(6), 717–738.

Greenfield, T. K., & Kerr, W. C. (2008). Alcohol measurement methodology in epidemiology: Recent advances and opportunities. *Addiction, 103*(7), 1082–1099.

Grimes, D. A., & Schulz, K. F. (2002). Cohort studies: Marching towards outcomes. *Lancet, 359,* 341–345.

Hamilton, J. (2002). *Time Series Analysis.* Princeton: Princeton University Press.

Harrison, L. (1997). The validity of self-reported drug use in survey research: An overview and critique of the research methods. *NIDA Research Monograph,* available at http://archives.drugabuse.gov/pdf/monographs/monograph167/017-036_Harrison.pdf.

Hawkins, D. J., Catalano, R. F., & Miller, J. Y. (1992). Risk and protective factors for alcohol and other drug problems in adolescence and early adulthood implications for substance abuse prevention. *Psychological Bulletin, 112*(1), 64–105.

Henry, B., Moffitt, T. E., Caspi, A., Langley, J., & Silva, P. A. (1994). On the "remembrance of things past": A longitudinal evaluation of the retrospective method. *Psychological Assessment, 6,* 92–101.

Jackson, M. I., & Mare, R. D. (2007). Cross-sectional and longitudinal measurements of neighborhood experience and their effects on children. *Social Science Research, 36,* 590–610.

Kravitz, H. M., Cavanaugh, J. L., & Rigsbee, S. S. (2002). A cross sectional study of psychosocial and criminal factors associated with mentally ill female detainees. *Journal of American Academy of Psychiatry and Law, 30,* 380–390.

Kumar, R. (2005). *Research methodology: A step by step guide for beginners.* Thousand Oaks, California: Sage.

Kurlycheck, M. C., Brame, R., & Bushway, S. D. (2006). Scarlet letters and recidivism: Does an old criminal record predict future offending? *Crime and Justice: An Annual Review of Research*, 187–220.

Land, K. C., Teske, R. H. C., & Zheng, H. (2009). The short-term effects of executions on homicides: Deterrence, displacement, or both? *Criminology, 47*, 1009–1043.

Langan, P. A., & Levin, D. J. (2002). *Recidivism of prisoners released in 1994.* Washington, DC: Bureau of Justice Statistics, U.S. Department of Justice.

Laurie, H., & Lynn, P. (2009). The use of respondent incentives on longitudinal surveys. In P. Lynn (Ed.), *Methodology of longitudinal Surveys.* Chichester, UK: Wiley.

Leonard-Barton, D. (1990). A dual methodology for case studies: Synergistic use of a longitudinal single site with replicated multiple sites. *Organization Science, 1*(3), 248–266.

Lynn, P. (2009). Methods for longitudinal surveys. In P. Lynn (Ed.), Methodology of longitudinal surveys. Chichester, UK: Wiley.

Mackey, A., & Gass, S. M. (2005). *Second language research: Methodology and design.* Mahwah, NJ: Taylor and Francis.

Menard, S., & Elliott, D. S. (1990). Longitudinal and cross-sectional data collection and analysis in the study of crime and delinquency. *Justice Quarterly, 7*, 11–55.

Morselli, C., & Tremblay, P. (2010). Interviewing and validity issues in self-report research with incarcerated offenders: The Quebec inmate survey. In W. Bernasco (Ed.), *From offenders on offending: Learning about crime from criminals* (pp. 68–83). Portland, OR: Willan.

National Highway Traffic Safety Administration. (2010). *Fatality Analysis Reporting System (FARS).* Available at www.nhtsa.gov/FARS.

Nyden, P. (2003). Academic incentives for faculty preparation in community-based participatory research. *Journal of General Internal Medicine, 18*(7), 576–585.

Piquero, A. R., Blumstein, A., Brame R., Mulvey, E. P., & Nagin, D. S. (2001). Assessing the impact of exposure time on incapacitation on longitudinal trajectories of criminal offending. *Journal of Adolescent Research, 16*(1), 54–74.

Piquero, A. R., Farrington, D. P., Shepherd, J. P., & Auty, K. (2011). Offending and early death in the Cambridge study in delinquent development. *Justice Quarterly*, 1–28.

Ployhart, R. E., & Vandenburg, R. J. (2010). Longitudinal research: The theory, design, and analysis of change. *Journal of Management, 36*(1), 94–120.

Prescott, J. J., & Rockoff, J. E. (2011). Do sex offender registration and notification laws affect criminal behavior? *Journal of Law and Economics, 54*, 161–206.

Robinson, K. A., Dennison, C. R., Wayman, D. M., Pronovost, P. J., & Needham, D. M. (2007). Systematic review identifies number of strategies important for retaining study participants. *Journal of Clinical Epidemiology, 60*, 757–765.

Schulz, A. J., Zenk, S. N., Kannan, S., Israel, B. A., Koch, M. A., & Stokes, C. A. (2005). Selected new and revised items included in the HEP survey after input from the steering committee or survey subcommittee, focus group themes, or pilot testing of existing items. In B. Israel, E. Eng, A. J. Shulz, & E. Parker (Eds.), *Methods in community-based participatory research for health.* San Francisco, CA: Wiley.

Wagenaar, A. C., Maldonado-Molina, M. M., Ma, L., Tobler, A. L., & Komro, K. A. (2007). Effects of legal BAC limits on fatal crash involvement: Analyses of 28 states from 1976 through 2002. *Journal of Safety Research, 38*, 493–499.

White, R. T., & Arzi, H. J. (2005). Longitudinal studies: designs, validity, practicality, and value. *Research in Science Education, 35*, 137–149.

Chapter 10 CASE-CONTROL DESIGNS

For this chapter, we will use the example that a researcher is using data from a large, maximum-security prison. She is interested in what makes someone commit homicide compared to other violent offenses. This is a difficult question to answer using other research designs. For instance, we cannot conduct an experiment because we cannot randomly assign the risk factor (if we knew what we were looking for) and see if someone becomes a murderer or a rapist. This is both practically and ethically impossible. It is also impractical to use a nonequivalent group design, because we would need to have a master list of all people who had the potential for becoming a murderer or rapist. We would have to follow them prospectively, record their exposure to the risk factor of interest, and then assign people to an experimental and comparison group based upon their exposure to the risk factor. Then we would have to wait until they became a murderer or a rapist in order to conduct our statistical analysis. Clearly, this could take decades, and very few people will become murderers. Therefore, it makes sense for us to find a list of murderers, rapists, and other violent offenders and look back at their lives to see if they had been exposed to our theoretically hypothesized risk factor(s). This is a time-efficient method of learning what predicts homicide, and it provides us a large enough sample size for us to statistically evaluate whether the risk factor is a *significant* predictor of homicide. The specifics on conducting a case-control design in a criminological setting are discussed in detail in this chapter.

CASE-CONTROL DESIGN

A **case-control research design** is a method that selects participants for a research study based upon having (or not having) the outcome of interest (e.g., crime) and looking backward in time to explore which exposures best predict the outcome (e.g., gender, environment, neighborhood, delinquent friends). Although there is an abundance of data collected in the criminal justice system, very few researchers are trained in the case-control method. These designs require backward thinking when compared to some of the other methods discussed in this text such as longitudinal or experimental studies.

Although this may seem confusing at first, this design is appropriate when a researcher seeks to collect data in a correctional setting or other justice institution (Schulz & Grimes, 2002). The primary strength of this design is that it allows a researcher to evaluate risk factors, or predictors, of an outcome that is unusually rare. Fortunately, crime (particularly heinous crimes such as rape or homicide) is a rare event (Harper & Voigt, 2007).

SUBJECT SELECTION

The primary difference between case-control designs and other research designs are that research participants are selected based upon the outcome (incarcerated for homicide or violent assault) rather than the exposure (e.g., drug use, alcohol use, previous violence, previous record of delinquency or incarceration for nonviolent offenses, etc.) (Kopec & Esdaile, 1990). These studies select participants who have committed homicide (**cases**) and a comparison group of similar people who have not committed homicide (**controls**) (Brent, Perper, Moritz, Baugher, Schweers, & Roth, 1993). All other types of studies will select either a sample of the general population to follow them and observe their violent behavior over time, or they will select an experimental and control/comparison group, in which the exposure can be manipulated over time. Because of this key difference, case-control designs are often called **retrospective designs.**

Case-control studies are frequently used in medical research, when we have no idea what is causing a particular disease (Hess, 2004). We would use patients who have been diagnosed with the disease of interest and then match those patients with other patients (diagnosed with other nonrelated diseases) who were hospitalized on the same day for a different condition. Then, we would ask them all about their food intake, behavior, activities, and so on, to evaluate the cause of disease. There should be a trend in that the cases will have a consistent exposure to some lifestyle activity of behavior that controls do not. This applies directly to our example of convicted murderers: We aren't sure what makes them different from offenders who committed rape or a more minor assault; however, we expect that there will be some difference. So, we will ask them a wide variety of questions to try to assess what specific behavior is predicting homicidal behavior.

To select our sample, we must first obtain our sampling frame. For our study, we need a sample of convicted murderers from the prison (cases) and a sample of rapists, violent batterers, and others in the same prison serving sentences for violent crime (controls). We are specifically interested in what makes homicide offenders different from other violent offenders. Because there are usually a small amount of homicide offenders incarcerated in any given prison, we select all of the homicide offenders to serve as our cases in our study. This would be verified using records maintained by the court. It is especially important that all cases are verified to be true cases (to have the "disease"—in this case, perpetrated homicide). A very specific **case definition** should be developed that is detailed enough to allow a third party to conduct your study without question (Lewallen & Courtright, 1998). The case definition requires that you specifically define the outcome that you are selecting cases by (e.g., record of a court-convicted homicide) and a statement of eligibility criteria.

The eligibility criterion applies to both cases and controls. Specifically, we want to include participants in our study only if they have some risk of being exposed to the risk factors that we believe predict homicide. In other words, if we think that having a gun at home predicts homicide, we would need to select cases (people who have had access to a gun who were convicted of homicide) and controls (people who have access to a gun who were convicted of a non-homicide violent offense). This does not mean that they need to have ever touched a gun or used a gun; however, they must have had access at some point. For instance, a screening question might be used such as, "How easy is it for you to obtain a firearm?" If a respondent says, "Difficult to impossible," they are not a good candidate for your study given your hypothesis.

Selection of controls becomes more complicated. It would be ideal for controls to have exactly the same life experiences (and potential for exposure, in this case, to guns) as the control group, with a different outcome. This would allow you to pinpoint one specific difference between cases and controls, and you would have a strong argument for causality. Although there is no perfect way to select controls, there are several methods that have been proposed (Robinson, 2007). First, controls should be selected from the same population as the cases. Therefore, because our cases came from the maximum-security prison, the controls could also come from that prison. This method of selection is referred to as **hospitalized controls** (in our case, we might call them *institutionalized controls*) (Rothbaum, Weisz, & Snyder, 1982). Alternatively, we might select controls from the community or geographic area in which the cases (homicide offenders) came from. This may be difficult, given that most states have very few maximum-security prisons, and offenders are generally shipped relatively far from their home communities to be placed in these institutions. These controls are referred to as **community (or population) controls** (Jackson, Nelson, Weiss, Neuzil, Barlow, & Jackson, 2008). These types of participants may also be selected using random-digit dialing or other probabilistic method of sample selection discussed in Chapter 7.

A third and final method that may be appropriate given our population is the use of a convenience sample of controls (Teddlie & Yu, 2007). We could ask our cases to provide the contact information for friends, siblings, or other family members, associates, or colleagues to serve as their control. We would ask the offender to nominate people "of similar circumstance" to themselves. Although each of these methods has their strengths and weaknesses, they have been used successfully in biomedical and behavioral research (see Table 10.1).

Table 10.1	List of Strengths and Weaknesses for Common Sources of Controls		
	Hospital Controls	**Community/Population Controls**	**Convenience Controls**
Strengths	The researcher has access to all of their court, police, and correctional records, limiting recall bias	Accessible and easy to obtain	Accessible and easy to obtain, inexpensive
	Easy to obtain these controls in large numbers	Come from the same population as the cases	Likely to share a similar demographic and behavioral background with the case
	May be demographically and behaviorally similar to your cases	Will allow you to generalize your findings to the entire population if selection was random	Relative controls are useful when you believe there is a genetic risk factor that could explain the behavior
Weaknesses	Institutionalized controls may come from a different population than the cases (e.g., if your institution is the only one in the state to house homicide offenders)	Random sampling of the population is often impossible	Not randomly selected, limited generalizability
		Less convenient than using controls from the same institution or place as the cases	Increased risk of inaccurate reporting to provide socially desirable responses or to help the friend
		Recall bias	May be too similar to the case, causing an overmatch
		Population controls may be less likely to participate in your study than institutionalized or convenience controls	Case may not be willing to provide friend/relative contact information

MATCHING CASES AND CONTROLS

Matching a case with one or more controls is an important part of the case-control study design (Bloom, Schisterman, & Hediger, 2007). Depending on the information available, you will seek to match your cases and controls on the *strongest confounders* available. For example, in our sample of homicide offenders, we might match one homicide offender with a rapist based upon age, race, gender, and prior offending history. These variables are strongly associated with violent perpetration (and likely, with the risk factor that we will identify as the cause of homicide). The matching process takes these variables out of consideration; in other words, the cases and controls are equal in terms of age, gender, race, and offending history. This will allow us to isolate the effect of the risk factor of interest (e.g., guns) on homicide.

It is generally acceptable to match one case with one control (and up to four) to maximize statistical power (Breslow, 1982). Additional controls matched to one case add a negligible amount of statistical power, making this addition unnecessary and generally not cost-efficient. Adding more than four controls is generally done in two instances: You have these controls readily accessible in a database and no further data collection is necessary, or you do not have enough cases to detect an effect for the risk factor. In either situation, additional controls may be added to help you answer your research question. Matching more than one control per case is generally denoted as 1:1, 1:2 (two controls per case), 1:3, 1:4, or 1:k. The latter notation is used when statistical programs match as many controls as are available in the data set to one case. Therefore, one case may have 10 matches, while another may have two.

It is possible to **overmatch**, or to match on too many variables (Fisher & Mazur, 1997). For instance, we want to identify guns as a risk factor for homicide perpetration. If we match on whether or not a gun was used (or other related measures), we will not find an association between access to guns and homicide because we have taken this variable out of the equation. Therefore, we should plan and be especially careful to match only on variables that are confounders but that do not measure the exposure (or risk factor) of interest in our study. This matched design removes bias in the design and increases the efficiency of the study (making it especially appropriate when the outcome—homicide—is rare). Matching is the primary hallmark of the case-control design.

METHODS OF ANALYSIS AND INTERPRETATION

There are several methods to proceed in analyzing the results of a case-control study (Thompson, 1994). The most simplistic method is using a **2X2 table**. Although this method is too simple for complex matched studies, it may be used in our sample of homicide offender cases and violent controls (as long as we did not match). The 2X2 table will allow us to compute an **odds-ratio**, or an effect size that will tell us the magnitude of the relationship between the exposure and our outcome. The basis for the odds-ratio is 1.00, indicating no relationship between the exposure (guns) and the outcome (homicide conviction). The larger the odds-ratio, the stronger the relationship. For instance, an odds-ratio of 2.5 will be interpreted to mean that those who have ready access to guns are 2.5 times more likely than those without access to guns to be convicted as a homicide offender than of other violent crimes. An example of an unmatched 2X2 table is depicted in Table 10.2.

To calculate an odds-ratio from this table, you would use the following formula: $a*d/c*b$. An example is provided in Table 10.3.

Table 10.2   A 2X2 Depiction of the Relationship Between the Exposure (Guns) and the Outcome of Interest (Homicide Conviction)

	Cases (Homicide Offenders)	Controls (Violent Non-Homicide Offenders)
Had easy access to a gun (exposed)	a	b
Did not have easy access to a gun (unexposed)	c	d

Table 10.3   An Example of the Relationship Between Exposure (Guns) and the Outcome (Homicide Conviction)

	Cases (Homicide Offenders)	Controls (Violent Non-Homicide Offenders)
Had easy access to a gun (exposed)	100	50
Did not have easy access to a gun (unexposed)	50	100

Using our calculation to produce an odds-ratio, we would compute (100*100)/(50*50), which reduces to 10,000/2,500. This produces an odds-ratio of 4, indicating that those who had easy access to guns were four times (or 400 percent) more likely than those who did not have easy access to guns to be homicide offenders.

Although this 2X2 table is a straightforward method of deriving an effect size, this calculation becomes much more complicated when participants are matched. These calculations are rarely done by hand; instead, statistical packages employing the **conditional logistic regression** command are often used (Heinze & Schemper, 2002). The packages use an algorithm to identify an odds-ratio for a risk factor while conditioning (incorporating) the matched variables into the model.

STRENGTHS AND WEAKNESSES OF THE CASE-CONTROL METHOD

As noted above, the case-control design is not appropriate to assess every research question; however, it provides several distinct advantages over other methods:

1. The case-control design is an efficient way to describe and predict rare outcomes (homicide, child abuse, homicide victimization).

2. It is relatively quick to conduct, given the reliance on official/record data that already exists.
3. Case-control studies are inexpensive if data is secondary or prerecorded.
4. The design is powerful enough statistically so that it requires a smaller number of participants when compared to other methods.
5. There is no risk to participants, as additional data collection is generally not necessary.
6. We can evaluate multiple predictors for one single (rare) outcome when we are unsure of what to look for.

Despite these strengths, several weaknesses must also be considered:

1. The data are often based on recall, which may not be accurate.
2. It is difficult to show that the information provided by the respondent or participant is correct.
3. A cause may not be identified accurately if it is not included in the list of questions asked to participants.
4. "Controls" may be difficult to identify, and weaknesses are associated with each type of control selection (detailed in the table above).
5. The identified "controls" may have the outcome of interest but may hide it from researchers (e.g., they may be murderers themselves, although in jail for simple assault).
6. The case-control method may determine a risk factor, but the reason it predicts the outcome may remain unknown. The researcher can only speculate as to why the risk factor predicts the outcome.

SUMMARY

This chapter discussed an underutilized research design that can be of great utility in the field of criminological research. We discussed the practicality of the case-control method to research in criminal justice, as violence and crime are inherently a rare outcome in the general population and are best studied using this retrospective method. Case and control selection, matching, and the unique analytical requirements of this design are also covered in depth. Because the bread-and-butter of the case-control design lies in the selection of research participants, a great deal of time is spent deconstructing the strengths and weaknesses of each method of case and control selection. Overall, given the availability and accessibility of public records, the case-control design should be integrated into research on crime.

KEY TERMS

2X2 table The simplest method available for analyzing data in case-control studies; however, this method is not always applicable when more complex (e.g., matched) designs are utilized.

Case The group of participants that has experienced the outcome of interest (e.g., the offenders). They are contrasted to controls. For example, if a researcher was studying homicide, cases would be those who had committed homicide.

Case-control research design A type of observational study in which two existing groups differing by the outcome measure are identified and compared on the basis of some supposed predictor or risk factor (often called a *retrospective study*). Case-control studies are often used to identify factors that may contribute to a medical condition by comparing subjects who have that condition/disease (the cases) with patients who do not have the condition/disease but are otherwise similar (the controls).

Case definition A method used by researchers to select which participants are included as cases in the study.

Community (or population) controls Selecting control groups from the same community or geographic location that cases were obtained from.

Conditional logistic regression A statistical command that uses an algorithm to identify the odds-ratio for a risk factor, while simultaneously incorporating matched variables into a model.

Controls Research participants from the same population as cases; however, they do not have the outcome of interest (e.g., they were not offenders). In the homicide example, controls have not committed homicide.

Hospitalized controls The same as institutional controls. The idea behind hospitalized controls is that if cases come from a population, controls for the purposes of comparison should come from the same population (incarcerated inmates, hospitalized patients, etc.).

Matching The process in which cases are paired with one or more controls based upon the strongest hypothesized confounders.

Odds-ratio An effect size that represents the magnitude of the relationship between the exposure and the outcome in question. The larger the odds-ratio (greater than 1), the stronger the relationship between the exposure and the outcome.

Overmatching Matching too many control variables, preventing associations between the variables of interest from being made.

Retrospective designs A type of study design in which a search is conducted for a relationship between an outcome that occurred more recently than the exposure. In other words, we are "looking backward" in time to identify causes and correlates of our outcome of interest.

REVIEW QUESTIONS

1. How does the case-control research design differ from some other types of research designs? Cross-sectional? Longitudinal?
2. What is the function of the 2X2 table? What type of research design(s) is it appropriate to use with?
3. What are some of the risks associated with overmatching variables?

4. How are research participants selected in case-control studies?
5. Why are case-control designs called *retrospective designs*?

Useful Websites

www.gwumc.edu/library/tutorials/studydesign101/casecontrols.html. A primer on case-control studies.

www.icpsr.umich.edu/icpsrweb/content/NACJD/guides/homicide.html. From International Consortium for Political and Social Research; provides linkages to homicide research data.

www.research.uci.edu/ora/hrpp/subjectselection.htm. Guide to research subject selection from University of California at Irvine.

http://bjs.ojp.usdoj.gov/index.cfm?ty=tp&tid=317. Rape and sexual assault data, from Bureau of Justice Statistics.

http://support.sas.com/rnd/app/da/new/daexactlogistic.html. Link to conditional logistic regression software from Statistical Analysis Software (SAS).

References

Bloom, M. S., Schisterman, E. F., & Hediger, M. L. (2007). The use and misuse of matching in case-control studies: The example of the PCOS. *Fertility Sterilization, 88*(3), 707–710.

Brent, D. A., Perper, J. A., Moritz, G., Baugher, M., Schweers, J., & Roth, C. (1993). Firearms and adolescent suicide: A community case control study, *American Journal of Disabled Child, 147*(10), 1066–1071.

Breslow, N. (1982). Design and analysis of case control studies. *Annual Review of Public Health, 3*, 29–54.

Fisher, W. W., & Mazur, J. E. (1997). Basic and applied research on choice responding. *Journal of Applied Behavioral Analysis, 30*(3), 387–410.

Harper, D. W., & Voigt, L. (2007). Homicide followed by suicide: An integrated theoretical perspective. *Homicide Studies, 11*(4), 295–318.

Heinze, G., & Schemper, M. (2002). A solution to the problem of separation in logistic regression. *Stats in Medicine, 21*, 2409–2419.

Hess, D. R. (2004). Retrospective studies and chart reviews. *Respiratory Care, 49*(10), 1171–1174.

Jackson, M. L., Nelson, J. C., Weiss, N. S., Neuzil, K. M., Barlow, W., & Jackson, L. J. (2008). Influenza vaccination and risk of community-acquired pneumonia in incompetent elderly people: A population-based, nested case control study. *Lancet, 372*(9636), 398–405.

Kopec, J. A., & Esdaile, J. M. (1990). Bias in case-control studies. A review. *Journal of Epidemiology Community Health, 44*(3), 179–186.

Lewallen, S., & Courtright, P. (1998). Epidemiology in practice: Case-control studies. *Community Eye Health, 11*(28), 57–58.

Robinson, S. (2007). A statistical process control approach to selecting a warm-up period for a discrete-event simulation. *European Journal of Operational Research, 176*(1), 332–346.

Rothbaum, F., Weisz, J. R., & Snyder, S. S. (1982). Changing the world and changing the self: A two-process model of perceived control. *Journal of Personality and Social Psychology, 42*(1), 5–37.

Schulz, K. F., & Grimes, D. A. (2002). Case-control studies: Research in reverse. *Lancet, 359*(9304), 431–440.

Teddlie, C., & Yu, F. (2007). Mixed methods sampling: A typology with examples. *Journal of Mixed Methods Research, 1*, 77–100.

Thompson, W. D. (1994). Statistical analysis of case-control studies. *Epidemiological Review, 16*(1), 33–50.

Chapter 11

QUALITATIVE DESIGNS

W hile the bulk of information you have read in this textbook thus far has mainly been geared toward quantitative research, this is not meant to devalue the importance of information provided by qualitative research. Recognizing this contribution, this chapter begins with a brief review of the relative prominence of qualitative research in criminology and criminal justice before focusing more specifically on qualitative research and its dimensions and decision-making processes. These processes include the role of the observer (researcher) and how they choose to portray their role. The chapter concludes by identifying potential validity, reliability, and generalizability concerns in qualitative research.

QUALITATIVE RESEARCH IN CRIMINOLOGY AND CRIMINAL JUSTICE

Qualitative research generally refers to research conducted in the field with a focus on narratives and themes (Shaw et al., 2004). **Quantitative research** typically involves analysis of numerical data collected, available for secondary use, or gathered from survey questionnaires. From a historical perspective, qualitative research was important in creating criminology as a discipline. In the 1920s, Robert Park and Ernest Burgess, professors in sociology at the University of Chicago (often colloquially considered the birthplace of criminology), encouraged their students to get out of the classroom and walk around the city's streets to observe people and places in real time. The goal was to better understand elusive concepts such as crime, disorganization, and social ecology difficult to grasp from books and classroom discussions.

These experiences led to their development of the concentric zone theory, depicted in Figure 11.1, which posited that cities could be mapped in concentric rings starting from areas of social disorganization and crime in the city's center and moving outward toward more stable, prosperous, and low-crime areas near the city's limits. Although Park and Burgess (1921) championed this revolutionary qualitative approach, quantitative research soon became (and continues to be) the dominant mode of criminological and criminal justice research.

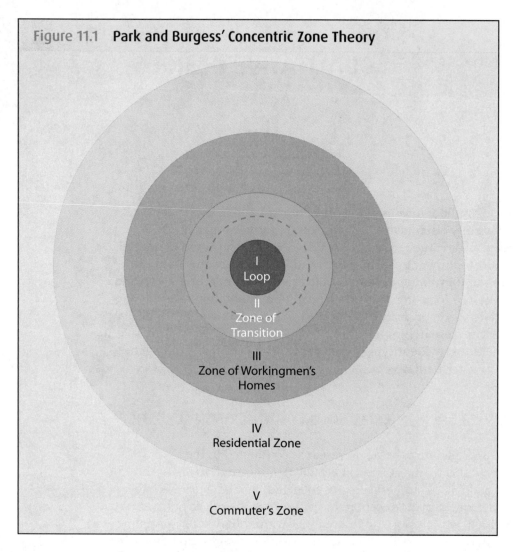

Figure 11.1 **Park and Burgess' Concentric Zone Theory**

The lack of criminological research conducted using qualitative methods was the subject of a research project by Tewksbury, Dabney, and Copes (2010), published in the *Journal of Criminal Justice Education*. Using a content analysis (itself a type of qualitative method involving selecting contents from mass communication sources and classifying the data systematically) of all articles published in 2004 through 2008 in the top criminology and criminal justice journals listed below, they identified only 120 articles—just 5.74 percent, or one in every 100—that applied a qualitative design and analysis plan:

Deviant Behavior
Theoretical Criminology
Law & Society Review
Journal of Criminal Law & Criminology
Journal of Interpersonal Violence
Criminology

Crime & Delinquency
Journal of Criminal Justice
Journal of Research in Crime/Delinquency
Justice Quarterly
Criminology & Public Policy
Law & Human Behavior
Criminal Justice & Behavior

ROLE OF THE OBSERVER

When researchers conduct qualitative research in the field, one of the main issues they have to consider is what their role as an observer is going to entail. This role can operate on a continuum, with one end representing a complete outsider and the other end being a full participant. Taking an **outsider** role involves the researcher acting as a true outsider to the group and the phenomenon that they are interested in studying (Maxwell, 1992). For example, a researcher interested in studying the interactions between exotic dancers and their patrons might choose to be an outsider and stand in the corner of the room and take **field notes** (brief narratives and notes jotted down in the field to aid the researcher's memory when writing up findings later; Wolfinger, 2002). Comparatively, if the researcher decides to be a **full participant** in the dancer/patron interaction, he deliberately becomes fully immersed in the group being studied. Researchers who choose full participation do so at the risk of **going native** and becoming a member of the group under study (Hayano, 1979).

The researcher must choose a stance toward the study group but must also determine whether or how to present that role. Numerous factors come into play (Rossman & Rallis, 2012), including the researcher's safety and not inhibiting or threatening the group. For instance, to study why gang members graffiti buildings and what this graffiti (or *tagging*) represents to them, you should avoid acting as a **covert observer**, hiding in the bushes and taking field notes. The gang members will have no idea of your intentions and may feel threatened, taking you for the police, an informer for the police, or even a rival gang member. The role of **overt observer**, in which you identify yourself as a researcher, would make more sense (Maykut & Morehouse, 1994).

Various approaches are possible to revealing the purpose of the research as well, ranging from full, to partial, to no disclosure, to a false explanation of the real purpose of the study. These decisions are largely based on what is likely to yield the best real-world narratives without risking the safety of the group or the researcher. Full disclosure would seem the best option if a researcher wanted to study a gang's rituals for "beating in" new members, as the researcher's safety would surely be compromised by trying to secretly observe this event. Partial explanation may be necessary if disclosing your true purpose might inhibit or alter the behavior you are interested in studying. For example, you might conceal your purpose of studying how well prostitutes look out for one another's well-being by stating your intention to study how they approach potential clients. Not offering an explanation can be risky, especially if those being studied suddenly learn and disapprove of your purpose, but it can be a way of gaining access to the private information you are interested in studying.

At times, an alternative explanation is necessary to ensure access to the phenomenon that you are studying while protecting your own safety. For instance, to study drug trafficking among outlaw motorcycle gang members, you may decide to approach the leader and members and tell them you are interested in studying the gang's history, the patches and tattoos, and overall lifestyle. With their support to research these aspects of gang life, you may develop **rapport** with the group and have the opportunity to gather information about any drug trafficking you observe (Patton, 1990).

A final decision when undertaking this type of study is how long your observation period needs to be to get the desired information. In some cases, a one-hour **focus group** may be sufficient, and in other cases multiple observations may be necessary to untangle more complex subcultures and power and influence structures. Some studies may conceivably require years spent "underground" in a secretive, militant organization before sufficient rapport can be developed to obtain the rich and detailed information otherwise unobtainable from one or a few encounters.

VALIDITY AND RELIABILITY ISSUES

Validity and reliability issues arise in the context of reviewing or conducting qualitative research. A major threat to validity is the **social desirability bias**, where people generally want to "look good" when they are being observed, which can lead them to behave a particular way to be seen in the best possible light (King & Bruner, 2000). The **Hawthorne effect** describes the similar tendency individuals have to work harder and perform better when they are being observed (Adair, 1984). This effect was first identified by a group of Harvard researchers conducting a study of worker productivity and the work environment. Their experiment involved increasing or decreasing the amount of light in Western Electric's Hawthorne Works plant to test the effect of lighting on worker productivity. They concluded that observed increases in productivity were unrelated to lighting levels but were directly attributable to the mere presence of the research team! Another issue is subjects trying to determine what the researcher is looking for and behaving accordingly. All of these scenarios can affect the validity of the research findings from a qualitative design.

Reliability concerns in qualitative research can be summarized into four general categories: credibility, transferability, dependability, and confirmability. **Credibility** centers on whether the reporting and research findings about the group you are studying constitute an accurate portrayal. The only way to demonstrate the credibility of qualitative research is to have the observed group members themselves review and judge it. If you spent 2 months with a number of gang members, it would be important to have the gang members read or listen to what you wrote about them and their lifestyle. Although qualitative researchers are supposed to be unbiased observers, hidden biases may come through when reporting results.

Transferability refers to whether qualitative research and its results apply to other groups in similar situations or contexts (Krefting, 1991). This concept is related to the **generalizability** of qualitative research—that is, whether the results presented in the research can be observed in other samples, places, or over time (Marshall, 1996). Consider, for example, a researcher who spent 3 months observing 10 prostitutes working a particular block in their city and then reported a series of themes based on the observations and field notes gathered over that time: the prostitutes citing money as their main reason for prostituting, generally working every night for 4 hours at a time, and expressing little regret or guilt. These themes have transferability if they would be identifiable and expressed by a different group of prostitutes in a different area of the city or in another city. One method researchers use to enhance the transferability of their research is to describe and detail thoroughly the context in which they conducted their research, outlining all of the assumptions behind their central research questions and the reasons they chose the particular group and phenomenon they qualitatively investigated.

Dependability in qualitative research refers to the degree to which consumers can trust the integrity of the researcher and the unbiased nature of the results (Golafshani, 2003). For instance, a qualitative researcher interested in studying the quality of marriage relationships among aboriginal people may begin by taking field notes as a completely unbiased observer; after observing the regular verbal abuse of the men on their spouses, however, the same researcher may unknowingly start to empathize with the spouses and to hold strong negative feelings against the abusers. Once researchers have allowed study phenomena to affect them personally, their documentation and interactions with the study group may change and reflect bias. Qualitative researchers work to preserve the dependability of their results by documenting any changes in the setting (e.g., a hurricane, suicide, etc.) and how these changes may or may not have affected the researchers' approach to the study throughout the duration of their observations. Full disclosure on the part of a qualitative researcher of foreseen and unforeseen circumstances is always necessary.

The last general reliability issue arising in qualitative research is its demonstrated confirmability. **Confirmability** focuses on whether the narrative and related findings can be verified. This can be done by minimizing errors and including quality control measures during the data collection to ensure that you can find the same results again. This gives the researcher confidence that the findings were not simply artifactual or found by chance (Morrow, 2005). Qualitative researchers must make a concerted effort at all stages of data collection to check and recheck their data. A **data audit** can also be performed on their data (Rodgers & Cowles, 1993), during which the qualitative researcher shares all of her materials (e.g., field notes, audio- and videotape recordings, etc.) with another qualitative researcher with no conflict of interest regarding the study or its findings. This outsider reviews all of the material as a purely independent observer, uncovering any inconsistencies or inaccuracies, detecting potential bias, and engaging the original researcher as a devil's advocate to search out any issues that might affect the reliability of the results.

SUMMARY

This chapter focused on qualitative research methods in criminology and criminal justice. We described qualitative research and how it is distinct from quantitative research. Qualitative research is a derivative from the historical roots of criminology, as a sociological domain of inquiry. These methods are used to answer questions from a different perspective; in many cases, self-report data is insufficient to explain the mechanisms by which theoretical processes operate. The strengths and limitations of this method were highlighted and examples of how qualitative methods apply in criminal justice research were described.

KEY TERMS

Data audit A quality assurance process in which a qualitative researcher shares all of her materials (e.g., field notes, audio- and videotape recordings, etc.) with another qualitative researcher with no conflict of interest regarding the study or its findings to ensure the conclusions are valid.

Confirmability How the results of qualitative research can be verified to minimize errors, or whether there were quality controls in place during the data collection process.

Covert observer Someone who is observing participants covertly (i.e., not letting participants know they are being observed). This at times involves the researcher participating in whatever activity he or she is observing.

Credibility The degree to which a researcher can trust or believe in the truthfulness of the information they are being given by research participants.

Dependability The degree to which consumers of qualitative research can trust they are getting unreliable and unbiased results.

Field notes Data collection outside of a laboratory setting, in which the researcher takes notes systematically to record the behavior of interest.

Focus group A form of qualitative research in which a group of individuals is asked about their attitudes, perceptions, opinions, ideas, and beliefs about a concept, question, or survey.

Full participant Occurs when a researcher completely immerses themselves into the group they are studying.

Generalizability Results of one study being able to be observed in other samples or places, over time.

Going native Occurs when a researcher actually becomes a member of the group they are studying. There are a variety of dangers associated with a researcher going native.

Hawthorne effect The idea that changes in participants during the course of a study may be solely related to the special situation in the study and the treatments they receive.

Outsider When the researcher examines the phenomena of interest from an outside perspective without interaction with actors.

Overt observer One who identifies their position as a researcher to the subjects/participants they are observing. The researcher makes no effort to conceal his or her activity.

Qualitative research A method of inquiry in which researchers seek to gather an in-depth understanding of human behavior and the rationale behind such behavior.

Quantitative research The process of systematic empirical investigation of social phenomena in which the relationship between two or more variables may be quantified.

Rapport The idea of building trust with participants for the purpose of getting them to open up to the research in regard to whatever phenomena is being studied.

Social desirability bias The tendency of respondents to answer questions in a manner that will be viewed favorably by others, rather than providing the accurate response to the researcher. The purpose of this behavior is make themselves appear in a positive light before the researcher.

Transferability The degree to which the results of qualitative research can be transferred or generalized to other contexts and settings.

REVIEW QUESTIONS

1. How is reliability and validity addressed in qualitative research?
2. What are the benefits of being a full participant in field research? What are the drawbacks?
3. Develop a qualitative project to answer a criminal justice problem of your choice. How will you go about collecting the data?
4. What is the purpose of developing rapport in qualitative research projects?
5. Compare and contrast covert and overt observer roles and provide examples of each.

Useful Websites

www.ethnographic-research.com. A company that specializes in ethnographic research.

www.qsrinternational.com/what-is-qualitative-research.aspx. Website of an organization dedicated to qualitative research.

www.focusgroups.com. Website allowing individuals to find opportunities to be paid to participate in focus groups.

www.nova.edu/ssss/QR/QR8-4/golafshani.pdf. Link to article discussing reliability and validity in qualitative research.

http://writing.colostate.edu/guides/guide.cfm?guideid=61. Online guide to conducting qualitative content analysis.

References

Adair, J. G. (1984). The Hawthorne effect: A reconsideration of the methodological artifact. *Journal of Applied Psychology, 69*(2), 334–345.

Golafshani, N. (2003). Understanding reliability and validity in qualitative research. *Qualitative Report, 8*(4), 597–607.

Hayano, D. M. (1979). Auto-ethnography: Paradigms, problems, and prospects. *Human Organization, 38*(1), 99–104.

King, M. F., & Bruner, G. C. (2000). Social desirability bias: A neglected aspect of validity testing. *Psychology and Marketing, 17*(2), 79–103.

Krefting, L. (1991). Rigor in qualitative research: The assessment of trustworthiness. *American Journal of Occupational Therapy, 45*(3), 214–222.

Marshall, M. N. (1996). Sampling for qualitative research. *Family Practice, 13*(6), 522–526.

Maxwell, J. A. (1992). Understanding and validity in qualitative research. *Harvard Educational Review, 62*(3), 279–300.

Maykut, P., & Morehouse, R. (1994). *Beginning qualitative research: A philosophical and practical guide.* Bristol, PA: Taylor and Francis.

Morrow, S. L. (2005). Quality and trustworthiness in qualitative research in counseling psychology. *Journal of Counseling Psychology, 52*(2), 250–260.

Park, R., & Burgess, E. (1921). *Introduction to the science of sociology.* Chicago: University of Chicago Press.

Patton, M. Q. (1990). *Qualitative research & evaluation methods.* Thousand Oaks, California: Sage.

Rodgers, B. L., & Cowles, K. V. (1993). The qualitative research audit trail: A complex collection of documentation. *Research in Nursing and Health, 16*(3), 219–226.

Rossman, G. B., & Rallis, S. F. (2012). *Learning in the field: An introduction to qualitative research* (3d ed.). Los Angeles: Sage.

Shaw, R. L., Booth, A., Sutton, A. J., Miller, T., Smith, J. A., Young, B., . . . & Dixon-Woods, M. (2004). Finding qualitative research: An evaluation of search strategies. *BMC Medical Research Methodology, 4*, 1–5.

Tewksbury, R., Dabney, D., & Copes, H. (2010). The prominence of qualitative research in criminology and criminal justice scholarship. *Journal of Criminal Justice Education, 21*, 391–411.

Wolfinger, N. (2002). On writing field notes: Collection strategies and background expectancies. *Qualitative Research, 2*(1), 85–93.

12

THE INTERSECTION OF CRIMINOLOGICAL THEORY AND RESEARCH METHODS

This final chapter addresses how research methods and criminological theory are related. Although criminological theory and research methods in criminology and criminal justice are taught as distinct and separate courses, it is important that you understand and appreciate the intersections of these core topics. Criminological theory informs research methods, and research methods can be used to test criminological theory. With these interrelationships in mind, this chapter provides detailed examples of how the various research methods covered in previous chapters can be applied to test criminological theory and how the results from these theory tests can inform criminological theory as it relates to theoretical extensions and refinement.

DETERRENCE THEORY

Rooted in Enlightenment principles, **deterrence theory** assumes that crime can be deterred if the punishment is severe, certain, and swift. If individuals view the severity of punishment as sufficiently extreme, they will be deterred from committing a crime. For example, the crime of murder has the most serious punishment—death, or life in prison in some states. Therefore, most people who might want to murder someone are deterred from committing murder because the punishment is death or being locked up in prison for the rest of their lives. In a less extreme example, a $50 fine if caught shoplifting may not be viewed as a deterrent, at least in relation to the benefit afforded by stealing a $500 iPhone.

Certainty of punishment relates to the notion that certain crimes and circumstances are accompanied by varying degrees of punishment certainty. For instance, if you were to assault a police officer in the police station, then the certainty of detection and punishment would be obvious. However, if you were underage and drinking alcohol from an open container at a college football game, then the certainty of punishment would be less clear, as these types of crimes are often handled informally (e.g., the cops confiscate the alcohol, the cops give you a verbal warning, you get a ticket that is later dropped because of the relatively minor nature of the crime, etc.). Comparatively, the swiftness of punishment as it relates to deterrence is that the punishment should be applied soon after the commission of the crime. With the backlog in the criminal justice system due to resource constraints, plea-bargaining, and so on, the swiftness of punishment can be difficult to assess.

With these important elements of deterrence in mind, consider the following real-world legal example of a punishment intended to deter sex offenders from committing future offenses (specific deterrence) and deter all persons from committing sex crime in the first place (general deterrence). Specifically, recent legislation referred to as Sex Offender Registration and Notification (SORN) has been enacted federally and across all states to require sex offenders to register as sex offenders and have their personal information available to the public online. The deterrent elements are easily recognizable in this legislation—the punishment is severe, as sex offenders have to register as sex offenders (some for the rest of their lives); it is certain (if you are a sex offender, you will have to register as a sex offender); and it is swift (registration is required immediately after prison release).

Tewksbury and Jennings (2010) provided the first empirical test of the deterrence effect of SORN legislation. Relying on longitudinal data from a large *sample* of sex offenders who were released prior to the enactment of SORN and a large sample of sex offenders who were released after SORN was enacted in the state of Iowa, Tewksbury and Jennings performed a quasi-experimental design (pre-test and post-test) to determine if SORN deterred future sex crimes upon prison release. The measure of sex offending recidivism in this study was official data, specifically *conviction data*, in the 5 years following the sex offenders' release from prison. Their results suggested that sex offenders who were released before the SORN policy did not have different recidivism rates than those released after SORN. In other words, this study did not find a deterrence effect for the SORN policy because it did not reduce sex offenses.

More recently, Tewksbury, Jennings, and Zgoba (2012) conducted a similar longitudinal and quasi-experimental design with random samples of sex offenders matched according to demographic characteristics and released prior to and after SORN in the state of New Jersey. The findings from this research using official data, arrest data specifically, to measure recidivism for any crime in the 8 years following prison release revealed that SORN had little to no effect on recidivism, as the recidivism rates were similar between the pre-SORN and post-SORN sex offenders. Once again, this study did not find support for the criminological theory of deterrence.

LABELING THEORY

Labeling theory concerns the negative connotations ascribed to certain crimes by society and how these labels affect an individual's behavior. For instance, a juvenile who drinks a beer has committed a crime, because it is against the law to drink alcohol if you are underage. This behavior is considered primary deviance from a labeling perspective. Now, consider a police officer who just happens to be walking down the street and sees the juvenile drinking the beer. The officer confronts the juvenile and places him under arrest for minor consumption of alcohol. In this situation, society (a police officer or agent of formal social control in this case) has officially reacted to the juvenile's primary deviance by arresting her and labeling her as a criminal. As a result, the juvenile later pleads guilty and is convicted of underage drinking. By all accounts, the juvenile now is a delinquent and has been officially recognized and labeled as such. The juvenile now internalizes this negative label and its accompanied stigma, and in turn, decides to continue to commit crimes, or secondary deviance, and to escalate the seriousness of this criminal behavior in reaction to the label.

From a labeling perspective, consider the sex offender registration and notification example discussed above. In this regard, sex offenders are perceived to be at a high risk of recidivism, to specialize only in sex crimes, and to be dangerous. As such, legislation (i.e., SORN) has been enacted for the purpose of labeling these sex offenders, and this is a distinct criminal label that is not ascribed to other types of offenders. For example, drug offenders are not required to register as drug offenders and property offenders are not required to register as property offenders. Furthermore, this label is real in name and it is accompanied with public knowledge of the sex offenders' status as a sex offender, as their personal information is freely made available to the public online.

According to labeling theory, logic would follow that registered sex offenders may internalize this label and continue to commit more sex offenses in reaction to this negative label and associated stigma. However, two studies (Tewksbury & Jennings, 2010; Tewksbury et al., 2012) indicate little or no support for the criminological theory of labeling. Specifically, recidivism rates were not affected by being labeled a sex offender and being required to register as one. Nonetheless, the label of sex offender may generate other adverse reactions affecting or impeding successful reentry into society. For example, Jennings, Zgoba, and Tewksbury (2012) performed a longitudinal study on whether recidivism rates, measured via official arrest data, in the 8 years following release from prison, were similar or different between a random sample of sex offenders released post SORN compared with a random sample of non-sex offenders released post SORN in the state of New Jersey. Their results showed that the trends in recidivism were largely similar, but the group of offenders determined to be high-risk was considerably larger among the non-sex offenders. Furthermore, additional analysis by Jennings et al. (2012) revealed that although sex offenders recidivated less frequently, they experienced certain types of collateral consequences as a result of being labeled as a sex offender that the non-sex offenders did not face to the same extent (e.g., not living with friends, living in group facilities, and having to move frequently).

SELF-CONTROL THEORY

Gottfredson and Hirschi's (1990) **self-control theory** is among the most widely known and tested criminological theories according to a recent meta-analysis (Pratt & Cullen, 2000). According to the theorists, individuals with low self-control have the following attributes: (1) impulsive, (2) have a preference for simple tasks, (3) risk-seekers, (4) prefer physicality to mental tasks, (5) self-centered, and (6) have a bad temper. The theory relates the origin of low self-control to ineffective socialization of the child by the parent, who does not effectively monitor, recognize, and punish bad behavior, with the effect established by ages 8 to 10. Gottfredson and Hirschi maintain that children who develop low self-control by this age will maintain the same low level of self-control throughout life. Low self-control can lead to a higher likelihood of committing crime where the opportunity and motivation exists, and people with these tendencies have a greater likelihood of committing crime (Piquero & Tibbetts, 1996).

One of the main issues in testing self-control theory as a criminological theory for explaining crime is how to measure and operationalize the concept of self-control. Grasmick, Tittle, Bursik, and Arneklev (1993) are credited with establishing the most widely used self-report measure of self-control, which is a 24-item scale with four items measuring each of the six dimensions of self-control theory detailed previously. Each item in this scale has Likert-type response options that range from "strongly disagree" to "strongly agree." All 24 items that comprise the Grasmick et al. scale are displayed in Table 12.1.

As the questions from the Grasmick et al. (1993) self-control scale show, the items and scaled measure have face validity. For example, question 10 asks respondents to report their level of agreement to the question, "I take risks just for the fun of it," an item capturing the risk-taking element of self-control theory. Numerous studies have also supported the construct validity of the measure and its six dimensions in that the scale seems to measure what it intends to measure, although some studies find greater support for the impulsive and risk-taking dimensions (Piquero & Tibbetts, 1996). Research has also established the representative reliability of the Grasmick et al. (1993) scale across geographical context in countries, including Hungary, Switzerland, the Netherlands, the United States, and Japan (Vazsonyi, Pickering, Junger, & Hessing, 2001), and has revealing evidence in support of the test-retest reliability of the Grasmick et al. (1993) scale over time (Higgins, Jennings, Tewksbury, & Gibson, 2009).

Vera and Moon (2013) offer a recent example of a typical way to test Gottfredson and Hirschi's (1990) self-control theory. Relying on a cross-sectional research design, Vera and Moon administered a self-report survey to a convenience sample of adolescents in two junior high schools in the southwestern United States. They included the 24 items from the Grasmick et al. (1993) scale to measure low self-control as their independent variable of interest, and they reported that their measure of self-control had a high degree of reliability as indicated by a Cronbach's alpha coefficient of .90. Crime, the outcome variable or dependent variable, was measured with an additive scale, where

Table 12.1 Items in the Self-Control Scale

For the following questions please indicate your response by circling the most appropriate answer in the space provided next to the question. Use the following response options for your answers.

1= strongly disagree   2= somewhat disagree   3= somewhat agree   4= strongly agree

1. I devote time and effort preparing for the future.	1 2 3 4
2. I act on the spur of the moment without stopping to think.	1 2 3 4
3. I do things that bring me pleasure here and now even at the cost of some future goal.	1 2 3 4
4. I base my decisions on what will benefit me in the short run, rather than in the long run.	1 2 3 4
5. If I have a choice I will do something physical, rather than something mental.	1 2 3 4
6. I feel better when I am on the move, than when I am sitting and thinking.	1 2 3 4
7. I would rather get out and do things than sit and contemplate things.	1 2 3 4
8. Compared to other people my age, I have a greater need for physical activity.	1 2 3 4
9. I test myself by doing things that are a little risky.	1 2 3 4
10. I take risks just for the fun of it.	1 2 3 4
11. I find it exciting to do things for which I might get in trouble.	1 2 3 4
12. Excitement and adventure are more important to me than security.	1 2 3 4
13. I look out for myself first, even if it means making things more difficult for other people.	1 2 3 4
14. I am not very concerned about other people when they are having problems.	1 2 3 4
15. I don't care if the things I do upset other people.	1 2 3 4
16. I try to get things I want, even when I know it is causing problems for other people.	1 2 3 4
17. I try to avoid projects that I know will be difficult.	1 2 3 4
18. When things get complicated, I quit or withdraw.	1 2 3 4
19. I do the things in life that are the easiest and bring me the most pleasure.	1 2 3 4
20. I avoid difficult tasks that stretch my abilities to the limit.	1 2 3 4
21. I lose my temper easily.	1 2 3 4
22. When I am angry at people, I feel more like hurting them than talking to them.	1 2 3 4
23. When I am really angry other people better stay away from me.	1 2 3 4
24. When I have a serious disagreement with someone, it's usually hard for me to talk calmly about it without getting upset.	1 2 3 4

Source: Grasmick et al. (1993).

adolescent responses to how often they reported engaging in a series of 14 different delinquency behaviors were summed up to create an overall score on the scale. They also included several control variables such as gender, parental income, and family structure to rule out rival explanations for explaining crime. Their analysis yielded support for low self-control as a predictor of deviance, as adolescents with higher levels of low self-control reported a significantly higher frequency of involvement in delinquent behaviors.

SOCIAL LEARNING THEORY

Akers's (1998) **social learning theory**, similar to Gottfredson and Hirschi's (1990) self-control theory, has been the focus of a considerable amount of research in criminology and criminal justice according to a recent meta-analysis (Pratt et al., 2010). Social learning theory comprises four central elements: definitions, differential association, differential reinforcement, and imitation (Burgess & Akers, 1966). *Definitions* refers to the individuals' understanding of crime, including whether they see it in a favorable or unfavorable light and how they justify, excuse, or otherwise regard their commission of a particular act as being right or wrong, good or bad, desirable or undesirable, justified or unjustified, appropriate or inappropriate. For example, an individual considering stealing a candy bar from a grocery store will be influenced by his or her favorable and unfavorable definitions of shoplifting. If the definition assesses the crime more rather than less favorably, the person is likely to commit the act.

Other factors in addition to definitions influence these choices. Individuals are influenced by the definitions their peers hold toward certain crimes and behaviors (Thornberry, 1987). If an individual's peers are involved in crime and hold pro-criminal attitudes and beliefs, the individual is more likely to engage in crime. Rewards and punishments influence whether an individual will choose to participate in crime, with higher or greater rewards differentially reinforcing the probability that criminal behavior will occur and be repeated. Finally, imitation can play a part in the learning process as well. An individual may be more likely to engage in crime after having seen it modeled by another individual, either directly or indirectly through the media or other secondary sources.

The pioneering cross-sectional study done by Akers, Krohn, Lanza-Kaduce, and Radosevich (1979) provides the earliest and one of the most comprehensive tests of social learning theory. After administering a pilot test of the survey questionnaire in a district that was not included in the final sample, Akers et al. used a cluster sampling strategy where they selected schools within each school district and then classrooms within schools to administer a self-report survey to 3,065 seventh through twelfth graders in seven communities in three Midwestern states. The dependent variables in the analysis were (1) alcohol and marijuana use, operationalized and measured as a frequency-of-use scale ranging from nearly every day to never, and (2) alcohol and marijuana abuse, operationalized and measured as whether respondents had experienced more than one occasion an incident from a list of problems associated with alcohol and/or marijuana use (e.g., "had an accident," "couldn't remember later what I had done," and "used more than I had planned").

Comparatively, Akers et al. (1979) included measures of each of the four central elements of social learning theory for the independent variables. The operationalization of these concepts can be found in Table 12.2.

The analysis by Akers et al. (1979) demonstrated strong support for the relationship between social learning theory as a criminological theory to

Table 12.2 **Operationalization of the Four Elements of Akers (1998) Social Learning Theory**

Imitation	Respondents reported the number of "admired" models (parents, friends, other adults, etc.) whom they observed using substance/s.
Definitions Favorable or Unfavorable to Use	Respondents reported the use of definitions justifying or excusing their substance use by "denial of injury," "denial of responsibility," or "condemning the condemners."
	Respondents reported their attitudes toward the law in general and alcohol and drug laws in particular.
	Respondents reported their own approval or disapproval of substance use.
Differential Association	Respondents reported their perception of the attitudes toward substance use held by adults they know and value.
	Respondents reported their perception of the attitudes toward substance use held by other teenagers who they know and value.
	Respondents reported how many of their friends use substances.
Differential Reinforcement: Social	Respondents reported whether or not their friends, parents or both encouraged them not to use substances.
	Respondents reported anticipated or actual positive or negative sanctions of friends in response to their own substance use.
	Respondents reported anticipated or actual positive or negative sanctions of their parents in response to their own substance use.
	Respondents reported the likelihood that their parents would catch them if they used substances.
	Respondents reported the likelihood that the police would catch them if they used substances.
	Respondents reported the degree to which using substances would affect their involvement in activities such as sports or school work.
Differential Reinforcement: Combined Social/Nonsocial	Respondents checked the total number of "good" and "bad" things that may happen to them resulting from substance use.
	Respondents reported whether mostly "good" and "bad" things happened to them resulting from substance use.
	Respondents reported the general nature of the effects that substance use has on them.

explain crime, operationalized as alcohol and drug use and abuse in this study. Specifically, each of the four elements of social learning theory (definitions, differential association, differential reinforcement, and imitation) was significantly associated with the dependent variables, with the strongest effect being shown for differential association and the weakest effect being shown for imitation. This pioneering study has led to a considerably large number of studies since this original test of this theory, and the majority of this research has replicated earlier findings and revealed support for social learning theory's ability to predict a wide range of deviant behaviors. Furthermore, a series of studies has also found support for the generalizability of social learning theory for explaining crime across cultures and in different international contexts (Jennings & Akers, 2011).

GENERAL STRAIN THEORY

Agnew's (1992) **general strain theory** (GST) is another widely known and tested criminological theory for explaining crime and deviance, although it is more theoretically complex and contains a number of constructs in need of operationalization (or a direct method of measurement). According to Agnew (1992, 2006), strain results from one of three broadly defined causal processes: (1) failure to achieve positively valued goals (e.g., failure to graduate high school), (2) the removal of positively valued stimuli (e.g., death of a loved one), and (3) the presentation of noxious stimuli (e.g., being physically abused). Beyond these three sources of strain, Agnew discusses the role of negative affect or negative emotionality as a response to strain; these types of negative emotions include anger, depression, anxiety, fear, and guilt (Hollin, 1989). Agnew (1992, 2006) also considers cognitive, emotional, and behavioral coping strategies that individuals may utilize to adapt to difficult experiences and lessen their influence on experiencing negative emotion and in turn committing crime in response.

It should be apparent by now that strain requires a lot of survey data to measure all of its necessary components. Generally speaking, you need measures of strainful experiences, negative emotions, coping strategies, and crime. Furthermore, when you are testing GST, there is a step-by-step process that must be followed in order to test what is referred to as GST's **mediation** hypothesis and ways to evaluate its **moderation** hypothesis (Piquero & Sealock, 2004). Mediation implies some mediating variable that diminishes or eliminates an observed association between an independent variable and a dependent variable (Baron & Kenny, 1986). In the case of GST, negative emotions are theorized as the mediating variable in the strain-crime relationship. In other words, strain does predict crime, but once you include negative emotions in the analysis with the measure/s of strain, negative emotions are significantly associated with crime and the influence of strain on crime is either reduced (partially mediated) or completely rendered insignificant (full mediation) (Agnew, Brezina, Wright, & Cullen, 2002). In contrast, moderation implies that certain variables or measures interact with or condition the influence of other variables on your dependent variable/s (Fulton, Stichman, Travis, & Latessa, 1997).

Jennings, Piquero, Gover, and Pérez (2009) have provided a thorough and comprehensive test of GST and all of its related components and processes in order to evaluate its ability to explain crime. Using cross-sectional data from an earlier study designed to investigate school dropout and delinquency (Chavez, Edwards, & Oetting, 1989), Jennings et al. performed a secondary data analysis (Hagan, 1997) of Mexican American adolescents' responses to a *survey* that was administered in schools in three different metropolitan areas in the southwestern United States. Two types of dependent variables were used. First, interpersonal aggression was operationalized by a series of Likert-type questions that asked the youth about the number of times they had threatened to or engaged in scaring someone with a knife, scaring someone with a club or chain, scaring someone with a gun (e.g., threatening the use of interpersonal aggression) or cutting someone with a knife, hitting someone with a club or chain, and/or shooting someone with a gun (e.g., use of interpersonal aggression). Second, property crime was operationalized by responses to a series of Likert-type questions about their involvement in property crimes such as stealing a bicycle, breaking into a motor vehicle, breaking into a house, stealing something worth more than $250, stealing something worth less than $250, shoplifting something worth more than $250, shoplifting something worth less than $250, slashing someone's tires, and spray-painting something on a building or private property. The complete listing of how Jennings et al. (2009, p. 415) measured and operationalized all of the independent variables and components of GST (strain, negative emotions, and conditioning influences/coping strategies) is displayed in Table 12.3.

After conducting a secondary data analysis in the step-by-step fashion described above, Jennings et al. (2009) found the following:

1. Support for the relationship between strain and interpersonal aggression and property offending
2. Support for the role of anger (negative emotion) as a partial *mediator* of the link between strain and interpersonal and property offending
3. Limited support for depression (negative emotion) as a partial *mediator* in the relationship between strain and property offending
4. Some support for the interaction effect of coping strategies on the strain-crime relationship, particularly participation in sports and music and having peer social support

Many other studies have also found support for GST as a criminological theory for explaining various forms of crime, and most of these studies have identified anger as one of, if not the, most important negative emotion that mediates the strain-crime association (Jang & Johnson, 2003).

Table 12.3   Operationalization of the Components and Processes of Agnew's (1992) General Strain Theory

Independent Variables	Description
Strain	
Physical Abuse:	
Parent	Respondents had been beaten by their parents.
Sibling	Respondents had been beaten by their sibling/s.
Peer	Respondents had been beaten by their friends.
Stranger	Respondents had been beaten by someone other than their parents, sibling/s, or peers.
Sexual Abuse	Respondents had been sexually assaulted.
Academic Problems	Respondents had poor academic performance.
Future Expectations	Respondents reported that they anticipate getting what they want out of life in the future.
Negative Affect	
Depression	Respondents reported feeling low, lonely, sad, unhappy, bad, depressed, and lonesome.
Anger	Respondents reported feeling mad, angry, flies off the handle, and/or is quick-tempered.
Conditioning Influences	
Peer Delinquency	Respondents reported that their peers drank alcohol, got drunk, used marijuana, and/or used hard drugs.
Peer Support	Respondents reported whether they were liked be their peers.
Poor Family Communication	Respondents reported whether their family was supportive and concerned about their well-being.
Cognitive Coping Skills	Respondents reported their level of self-esteem and self-worth.
Physical Coping Skills:	
Athletics	Respondents reported involvement in athletics.
Music	Respondents reported involvement in non-required music.
Extracurricular Activities	Respondents reported involvement in extracurricular activities.
Spiritual Coping Skills	Respondents reported their level of religiosity.

DEVELOPMENTAL LIFE-COURSE THEORIES

Developmental life-course theories as criminological theories for explaining crime are a relatively recent addition to criminology and criminal justice (Laub, 2004). These theories offer a comprehensive approach to studying crime because they consider several factors that can affect an individual's criminal behavior with a particular emphasis on how these factors can influence criminal behavior over time and context (Farrington, 2003). Although there are many of these theories, one of the most recognizable is Terrie Moffitt's (1993) adolescent-limited and life-course-persistent **taxonomy** or typology of offenders.

Moffitt (1993) argues that there are two distinct types of offenders: adolescent-limited and life-course-persistent. Adolescent-limited offenders are those whose deviant behavior is confined to the period of adolescence, and their involvement in crime is primarily due to the maturity gap and to wanting to exert their independence and behave like adults. As such, most of their deviant behavior involves drinking alcohol, smoking marijuana, and being sexually promiscuous. In contrast, life-course-persistent offenders are offenders who began engaging in deviant behavior early in the life-course and who continue this behavior throughout life. For example, this type of offender may have bitten and hit other kids in preschool; been truant and stolen things in elementary school; stolen cars and used drugs in middle school; assaulted and robbed people during high school; and committed fraud, domestic violence, and other crimes during adulthood (Moffitt, 1993).

Adolescent-limited offenders may commit crimes during adolescence as a result of social mimicry of the behavior of life-course-persistent offenders and envy of the related social status rewards they gain (Elder & Giele, 2009). In some high schools the "cool kids" are the ones getting in fights, stealing cars, drinking alcohol, using drugs, skipping school, and so on (Farrington & Welsh, 2003). Other adolescents observe this behavior and decide to engage in some of the more minor forms of deviance to achieve similar status as a cool kid (Catalano, Kosterman, & Hawkins, 1996). But the difference is that these adolescent-limited offenders age out of this behavior, go to college, get a decent job, and go on to live successful and productive lives whereas the original "cool kids" (the life-course-persistent offenders) continue to commit crime the rest of their lives.

Moffitt, Caspi, Harrington, and Milne (2002) offer one such example of how to test the adolescent-limited and life-course-persistent offender taxonomy relying on longitudinal data from a large sample of males born between 1972 and 1973 in Dunedin, New Zealand. Based on previous research (Moffitt & Caspi, 2001; Moffitt, Caspi, Dickson, Silva, & Stanton, 1996), Moffitt et al. operationalized and categorized the offenders into life-course-persistent offenders if they met established criteria for extreme antisocial behavior during childhood and adolescence (47 males, 10 percent of the sample) and adolescent-limited offenders if they met these same criteria but only during adolescence and not during childhood (122 males, 26 percent of the sample). Utilizing this typology of offenders, Moffitt et al. compared these two offender groups across a range of 79 risk factors measured at age 26, and their results revealed that life-course-persistent offenders had more psychopathic personality traits, mental-health problems, substance dependency issues, children, financial problems, work problems, and drug-related and violent crime, including violence against women and children compared with the adolescent-limited offenders who showed more impulsive personality traits and a greater involvement in property offenses. This study, along with over a hundred others (Jennings & Reingle, 2012), have consistently found varying levels of support for Moffitt's (1993) taxonomy of adolescent-limited and life-course persistent offending.

SUMMARY

This chapter examined criminological theory and how it is intertwined with research methods. We discussed how deterrence theory, labeling theory, self-control, social learning, strain, the life-course paradigm, and research methods are used together to achieve a common goal of understanding criminals, crime, and criminal behavior. Examples of applications of criminological theory in research methodology were covered.

KEY TERMS

Deterrence theory A criminological theory that emphasizes the use of punishment as a threat to prevent individuals from offending.

Developmental life-course theories Multidisciplinary theories that evaluate criminal behavior as it changes throughout the life course. Some of the more prominent life-course criminological theories are Moffitt's dual taxonomy and Sampson and Laub's age graded theory of informal social control.

General strain theory Suggests that the inability to achieve positively valued goals, the removal or threat to remove positively valued stimuli (e.g., rewards), and the presentation or threat of presentation of noxious stimuli account for a person's decision to engage in criminal behavior.

Labeling theory The concept that deviance is not necessarily inherent to an act; rather, the societal response applies a deviant label to offenders. These activities are deemed to be deviant based upon cultural and societal norms.

Mediation Occurs when the underlying relationship between an independent variable and dependent variable is affected by a third variable, which is associated with both the independent and dependent variable. This third variable (the mediator) may mask the relationship between the observed independent and dependent variable.

Moderation In statistics, this refers to the relationship between two variables being dependent on a third variable. This variable is known as the *moderator* or *moderating variable*. The third variable may enhance or amplify the effect between the observed independent variable and dependent variable.

Self-control theory Asserts that criminal behavior is based on the individual tendency toward low self-regulation and control. Based on the idea of parent socialization, if an individual possesses a low level of self-control, that person will be more likely to engage in criminal behavior and delinquent acts.

Social learning theory Based on learning principles from psychology and differential association theory from sociology, the idea behind social learning theory is that criminal behavior similar to all other types of behavior is learned and reinforced through operant conditioning.

Taxonomy A concept derived from biology, which refers to grouping organisms based on shared characteristics and giving names to these groups.

REVIEW QUESTIONS

1. According to Moffitt's taxonomy, what are the two types of offenders? How do these offenders differ in the causes of their criminal behavior?
2. What are the primary principles behind deterrence theory?
3. What is the difference between mediation and moderation?
4. What are the four concepts incorporated within social learning theory?
5. Please explain the primary belief system behind self-control theory. In other words, how does the theory relate to criminal behavior? At what age does it believe that behavior is fixed?

Useful Websites

www.moffittcaspi.com. Official website of Terrie Moffitt, a great resource on life-course criminology.

www.umsl.edu/~keelr/200/ratchoc.html. Great resource on deterrence theory.

www.britannica.com/EBchecked/topic/1340874/Ronald-L-Akers. Encyclopedia entry on Dr. Ron Akers.

http://criminology.cbcs.usf.edu/facultyStaff/bio.cfm?ID=44. Link to biography and vitae of Dr. Wesley Jennings, one of the authors of this textbook!

www.criminology.fsu.edu/crimtheory/agnew.htm. Web resource and information on general strain theory.

References

Agnew, R. (1992). Foundation for a general strain theory of crime and delinquency. *Criminology, 30,* 47–87.

Agnew, R. (2006). *Pressured into crime: An overview of general strain theory.* Los Angeles, CA: Roxbury.

Agnew, R., Brezina, T., Wright, J. P., & Cullen, F. T. (2002). Strain, personality traits, and delinquency: Extending general strain theory. *Criminology, 40*(1), 43–71.

Akers, R. L. (1998). *Social learning and social structure: A general theory of crime and deviance.* Boston, MA: Northeastern University Press.

Akers, R. L., Krohn, M. D., Lanza-Kaduce, L., & Radosevich, M. (1979) Social learning and deviant behavior: A specific test of a general theory. *American Sociological Review, 44,* 635–655.

Baron, R. M., & Kenny, D. A. (1986). The moderator-mediator variable distinction in social psychological research: Conceptual, strategic, and statistical considerations. *Journal of Personality and Social Psychology, 51*(6), 1173–1182.

Burgess, R. L., & Akers, R. A. (1966). A differential association: Reinforcement theory of criminal behavior. *Social Problems, 14,* 128–147.

Catalano, R. F., Kosterman, R., & Hawkins, J. D. (1996). Modeling the etiology of adolescent substance use: A test of the social development model. *Journal of Drug Issues, 26*(2), 429–455.

Chavez, E. L., Edwards, R., & Oetting, E. R. (1989). Mexican American and White American school dropouts' drug use, health status, and involvement in violence. *Public Health Reports, 104,* 594–604.

Elder, G. H., & Giele, J. Z. (2009). *The craft of life course research.* New York: Guilford Press.

Farrington, D. P. (2003). Developmental and life course criminology: Key theoretical and empirical issues—The 2002 Sutherland Award Address. *Criminology, 41*(2), 221–225.

Farrington, D. P., & Welsh, B. C. (2003). *Saving children from a life of crime: Early risk factors and effective interventions.* Oxford: Oxford University Press.

Fulton, B., Stichman, A., Travis, L., & Latessa, E. (1997). Moderating probation and parole officer attitudes to achieve desired outcomes. *Prison Journal, 77*(3), 295–312.

Gottfredson, M. R., & Hirschi, T. (1990). *A general theory of crime.* Stanford, CA: Stanford University Press.

Grasmick, H. G., Tittle, C. R., Bursik, R. J., & Arneklev, B. J. (1993). Testing the core empirical implications of Gottfredson and Hirschi's general theory of crime. *Journal of Research in Crime and Delinquency, 30*(1), 5–29.

Hagan, F. E. (1997). *Research methods in criminal justice and criminology.* Needham Heights, MA: Allyn and Bacon.

Higgins, G., Jennings, W. G., Tewksbury, R., & Gibson, C. L. (2009). Exploring the link between self-control and violent victimization trajectories in adolescents. *Criminal Justice & Behavior, 36,* 1070–1084.

Hollin, C. R. (1989). *Psychology and crime: An introduction to criminological psychology.* New York: Routledge.

Jang, S. J., & Johnson, B. R. (2003). Strain, negative emotions, and deviant coping among African Americans: A test of general strain theory. *Journal of Quantitative Criminology, 19*(1), 79–105.

Jennings, W. G., & Akers, R. L. (2011). Social learning theory. In C. D. Bryant (Ed.), *The handbook of deviant behavior* (pp. 106–113). New York: Routledge.

Jennings, W. G., Piquero, N. L., Gover, A. R., & Pérez, D. (2009). Gender and general strain theory: A replication and exploration of Broidy and Agnew's gender/strain hypothesis among a sample of southwestern Mexican American adolescents. *Journal of Criminal Justice, 37,* 404–417.

Jennings, W. G., & Reingle, J. (2012). On the number and shape of developmental/life-course violence, aggression, and delinquency trajectories: A state-of-the-art review. *Journal of Criminal Justice, 40,* 472–489.

Jennings, W. G., Zgoba, K., & Tewksbury, R. (2012). A comparative longitudinal analysis of recidivism trajectories and collateral consequences for sex and non-sex offenders released since the implementation of sex offender registration and community notification. *Journal of Crime & Justice, 35*, 356–364.

Laub, J. H. (2004). The life course of criminology in the United States: The American Society of Criminology 2003 presidential address. *Criminology, 42*(1), 1–26.

Moffitt, T. E. (1993). Adolescent-limited and life course persistent antisocial behavior: A developmental taxonomy. *Psychological Review, 100*, 674–701.

Moffitt, T. E., & Caspi, A. (2001). Childhood predictors differentiate life-course persistent and adolescence-limited pathways, among males and females. *Development and Psychopathology, 13*, 355–375.

Moffitt, T. E., Caspi, A., Dickson, N., Silva, P. A., & Stanton, W. (1996). Child-onset versus adolescent-onset antisocial conduct in males: Natural history from age 3 to 18. *Development and Psychopathology, 8*, 399–424.

Moffitt, T. E., Caspi, A., Harrington, H., & Milne, B. (2002). Males on the life-course persistent and adolescence-limited antisocial pathways: Follow-up at age 26 years. *Development and Psychopathology, 14*, 179–207.

Piquero, A., & Tibbets, S. (1996). Specifying the direct and indirect effects of low self control and situational factors in offenders decision making: Toward a more complete model of rational offending. *Justice Quarterly, 13*(3), 481–510.

Piquero, N. L., & Sealock, M. D. (2004). Gender and general strain theory: A preliminary test of Broidy and Agnew's gender/GST hypotheses. *Justice Quarterly, 21*(1), 125–158.

Pratt, T. C., & Cullen, F. T. (2000). The empirical status of Gottfredson and Hirschi's general theory of crime: A meta-analysis. *Criminology, 38*(3), 931–966.

Pratt, T. C., Cullen, F. T., Sellers, C. T., Winfree, T. L., Madensen, T. D., Daigle, L.E., . . . Gau, J. M. (2010). The empirical status of social learning theory: A meta analysis. *Justice Quarterly, 6*, 765–802.

Thornberry, T. P. (1987). Toward an interactional theory of delinquency. *Criminology, 25*(4), 863–892.

Tewksbury, R., & Jennings, W. G. (2010). Assessing the impact of sex offender registration and community notification on sex offending trajectories. *Criminal Justice & Behavior, 37*, 570–582.

Tewksbury, R., Jennings, W. G., & Zgoba, K. (2012). A longitudinal examination of sex offender recidivism prior to and following the implementation of SORN. *Behavioral Sciences & the Law, 30*, 308–328.

Vazsonyi, A. T., Pickering, L. E., Junger, M., & Hessing, D. (2001). An empirical test of a general theory of crime: A four nation comparative study of self-control and the prediction of deviance. *Journal of Research in Crime and Delinquency, 38*(2), 91–131.

Vera, E. P., & Moon, B. (2013). An empirical test of low self-control theory: Among Hispanic youth. *Youth Violence & Juvenile Justice, 11*, 79–93.

GLOSSARY

2x2 table: The simplest method available for analyzing data in case-control studies; however, this method is not always applicable when more complex (e.g., matched) designs are utilized.

active consent: Requires the participant to directly acknowledge (via signature) the purpose of the research study, any harms and benefits associated with participation, and the participant's role in the research.

aggregate: A collection of items (in this case research items) gathered to form a total quantity, as opposed to items reported individually (e.g., the completion rate for a course may aggregate data from several terms).

alternative hypothesis: The opposite of the null hypothesis, the *alternative hypothesis* indicates the idea or possibility that an observed effect between variables or phenomena is real and not occurring due to chance alone.

anonymous: In the research context, an *anonymous* person's identifying personal information is concealed from public and often researchers' knowledge.

arbitrary scales: Summarize several variables. In the sense that such scales have different variables (i.e., they are all nominal), they are similar to the *variety index*.

attrition: The loss of participants from the original sample in a study; also known as *loss to follow-up*.

Belmont Report: The *Belmont Report*, issued in September 1978, proposed protections for research participants and subjects in clinical trials and research studies that give rise to ethics and health concerns. The report posits three guiding principles: justice, beneficence, and respect for persons.

bias: Reflects the degree to which survey questions are answered inaccurately or in unintended ways. Several types of bias can emerge in survey research, including response bias and non-response bias.

booster: A postcard, letter, or text message sent to remind a potential survey respondent to complete the survey.

booster session: Reintroduces a point later in the course of the research to reinforce treatment effects that may have atrophied over time.

bounding interview: Used frequently used in the National Crime Victimization Survey, the interviewer reviews with the respondent what the respondent reported in previous interviews. This procedure is intended to prevent duplicate reports.

break-off: Occurs when a respondent does not complete an interview (i.e., the respondent terminates the interview before answering all of the questions).

brief interventions: Experimental trials frequently as short as a few minutes in duration.

case: A study participant whose experience includes the outcome of interest (e.g., offenders). Cases are contrasted to *controls*. A researcher studying homicide, for example, selects cases who had committed homicide.

case-control study: A type of observational study in which two existing groups differing by the outcome measure are identified and compared on the basis of a supposed predictor or risk factor (often called a *retrospective study*.) Case-control studies are often used in health studies to identify factors that may contribute to a medical condition by comparing subjects with the condition/disease (the cases) with otherwise similar subjects without it (the controls).

case definition: A method used by researchers to select participants to be included as cases in a study.

causal inference: Posits one variable as the cause of another.

causation: The notion that events occur predictably, with one event leading to or causing another. To infer causation, variables must be statistically associated and ordered properly in time and all other possible causes must be ruled out.

census: Systematically acquires and records information about all members of a given population. In the United States, the term most frequently refers to the official decennial U.S. Census.

certificate of confidentiality: A legal document issued to researchers by federal agencies to protect the privacy and welfare of research subjects. The certificate prohibits release of identifiable and sensitive information about research project participants.

cluster: In statistics, a *cluster* is a grouping of individuals or units used for sampling purposes.

cluster sampling: Involves dividing a natural but homogenous population subgroup and then selecting these groups for study using simple random methods.

Cohen's *d*: The most commonly used effect-size measure. A Cohen's *d* of 0.2 is considered a small effect, 0.5 a moderate effect, and 0.8 a large effect.

cohort design: A type of longitudinal design that follows a group of people sharing a similar experience or characteristic, such as birth year, generation, Hurricane Katrina survivors, and so on, over time.

community-based participatory research: Conducted cooperatively between the community and experts in the field, with the community participating fully in all aspects of the research process.

community (or population) control: Control groups selected from the same community or geographic location as the cases.

computer-assisted personal interviewing (CAPI): A respondent uses a computer to answer interview or survey questions, typically with an interviewer present.

computer-assisted telephone interviewing (CATI): The interviewer follows a predetermined script provided by computer software. This structured system speeds up the collection and editing of survey data.

conceptualization: Concepts being derived from experience, observation, and data.

conditional logistic regression: A statistical command that uses an algorithm to identify an effect size of a treatment or an outcome, while holding other confounding variables constant. In other words, the statistical model is "conditioned" upon the variables matched upon it in the research design.

confidence interval: An interval estimate of the population parameter used to indicate the estimate's reliability. Confidence intervals include ranges of values that act as estimates of unknown population parameters.

confidence level: The *confidence level,* inversely related to the *confidence interval,* is a value set by the researcher to indicate the degree to which the researcher believes the observed relationship with the population to be a true one and not due to chance alone.

confidential: Research results or data that must remain privileged or secret.

confirmability: Represents the maintenance of quality controls during the data collection process or the certainty that qualitative research can be verified to minimize errors.

confounding: Variables that relate to both the exposure and the outcome of interest. This variable may be established as the "cause" of the outcome, but it is only associated with the outcome because of its relationship with the exposure measured. Potential confounds make it difficult to determine cause-and-effect relationships between variables. Alcohol use, for example, once thought to cause lung cancer, is now seen as a confounder between tobacco use and lung cancer: tobacco and alcohol use are highly correlated, leading to misinterpretation of that latter as a risk factor for lung cancer.

construct: A concept, model, or schematic idea established in a theory and examined through research.

construct validity: Refers to whether a scale measure correlates with the psychological constructs it is theorized and purported to measure.

contamination: Occurs when the control group is inadvertently exposed to some of the treatment. This might occur due to error, members of the experimental group sharing information or aspects of the treatment with the control group, or in some other way.

content analysis: Frequently used in the social sciences to study mass communication, includes the study of recorded human communications, books, websites, paintings, and laws.

content validity: Indicates the extent to which a measure represents all facets of the construct it is intended to measure.

continuous measures: A *continuous measure* is not discrete but takes on any range of values.

control: A research participant from the same population as that from which cases were chosen but does not have the outcome of interest (e.g., is not an offender). In a homicide study, for example, controls will not have committed homicide.

control group: A *control group* serves as a standard for comparison in a control experiment and receives no treatment, lesser treatment, or treatment for an unrelated problem.

control variable: A construct or measure held constant and unchanged within the course of an experiment (also known as *covariate*).

convenience sampling: A nonprobability sampling technique in which subjects are selected based on their accessibility or convenience to the researcher.

correlation: Indicates a functional or qualitative correspondence between two items or a statistical statement that two variables are related to each other.

covert observer: One who observes participants stealthily, without letting them know they are being observed. This may involve the researcher's participation in whatever activity is being observed.

credibility: Trustworthiness in qualitative research; refers to the degree to which a researcher can trust or believe in the truthfulness of the information being supplied by research participants.

crime rate: The ratio of total crimes in an area to the population of that area, expressed per 1,000 (or 100,000) population per year.

criterion-related validity: Indicates how well one variable or a set of variables predicts an outcome based on information from other variables.

dark figure of crime: A term used by criminologists and sociologists, refers to unreported and undiscovered crime, which calls into question the reliability of official crime statistics.

deduction: Represents the process of reasoning from a stated premise to a conclusion (i.e., reasoning from the general to the specific).

de-identified data: When identifiable markers are removed from data sets to preserve anonymity and allow the public to reuse the data.

dependability: *Dependability* in qualitative research refers to the degree to which consumers of qualitative research can trust that results are reliable and unbiased.

dependent variable: In an experiment, the *dependent variable* is modified by the independent variable.

deterrence theory: Emphasizes the use of punishment as a threat to deter individuals from offending.

developmental life-course theories: Multidisciplinary theories that evaluate criminal behavior as it changes throughout the subject's life. Two of the more prominent life-course criminological theories are Moffitt's dual taxonomy and Sampson and Laub's age-graded theory of informal social control.

discrete measures: Variables that exist as part of a countable set (i.e., they are not continuous).

disproportionate sampling: A type of stratified sampling. Within this process, the sizes of different groups vary and do not represent the percentage of the group with a larger population. This type of sampling is used when one or more subgroups are very small compared to other groups, and the researcher is specifically interested in small subgroups.

double-blind: An experiment conducted on human subjects in which neither the individuals participating in the experiment nor the researchers conducting the experiment know who belongs to the control group and who belongs to the treatment group. Double-blind structures help reduce bias in experiments.

dummy variable: Coded 1 or 0, it indicates either the presence or the absence of a quality (e.g., individuals living in the United States might be coded 1 and individuals living elsewhere coded 0).

effect size: Measures the strength of the relationship between two variables in a population.

empirical: Describes research questions verifiable by means of observation or experiment.

evidence-based practices: *Evidence-based practices* in clinical practice require that applications or programs used in practice be based on scientifically sound research.

exhaustive: The ability to cover the entire spectrum of a situation (e.g., measuring biological sex as male or female is an exhaustive category that covers all possibilities).

experiment: A research design conducted under controlled conditions for the purpose of demonstrating a known truth, examining the validity of a hypothesis, or determining the efficacy of something previously untried.

experimental group: A group of subjects is one exposed to the treatment condition of an experiment.

explanatory variable: An *explanatory variable* may be manipulated to explain the response variable; it is often called an *independent variable* or *predictor variable*.

exposure: Indicates being subject to some effect or influence.

extrapolation: The generalization of findings in a research study beyond the subjects actually participating in the study.

face validity: A property of a measure. An item on a survey has face validity if it measures what it is intended to measure.

field notes: Data collection outside a laboratory setting, where the researcher takes systematic notes recording the behavior of interest.

focus group: Elicits qualitative research by asking a group of individuals about their attitudes, perceptions, opinions, ideas, and beliefs about a concept, question, or survey.

full participant: A researcher completely immersed in the group being studied.

generalizability: A study's applicability to other samples or places over time.

generalize: To extrapolate findings from a sample to make inferences or conclusions about an entire population.

General Social Survey (GSS): A sociological survey used to collect data on demographic characteristics and attitudes of residents in the United States. The survey is conducted via face-to-face interviews by researchers at the University of Chicago.

general strain theory: Suggests that individuals decide to commit crime in response to an inability to achieve positively valued goals, the removal or threat of removal of positively valued stimuli (e.g., rewards), and the presentation or threat of presentation of noxious stimuli.

going native: When a researcher becomes a member of the group being studied, with resulting dangers to both the researcher and the reliability of the research.

Hawthorne effect: Changes in participants' behavior during the course of a study may be attributable to participation in the study itself because participants know that their behavior is being studied.

hierarchy rule: Individuals are charged only for the highest rated (generally the most severe) crime committed during one multicrime incident.

hospitalized controls: *Hospitalized controls*, or *institutional controls*, are drawn from a hospitalized or institutionalized population when the cases are drawn from such populations.

household survey: A survey conducted on a regular basis (varying by survey type to collect data from all household members).

hypothesis: A tentative explanation for an observation, phenomenon, or scientific problem.

incentive: Anything that motivates an individual to participate in research. Incentives may take the form of cash, gift cards, or other compensation such as gifts.

independent variable: A descriptor, such as age, height, and so on, that does not depend on another factor or variable (also known as *risk factor, predictor,* or *explanatory variable*).

in-depth interviews: These interviews are relatively longer unstructured interviews, typically with few prescribed questions and few survey respondents. These interviews are also used in exploratory research to gather a great deal of information about a very specific topic.

induction: Represents the process of deriving general principles from particular facts or instances.

informed consent: Requires researchers to inform research participants about their roles in a research study, the purpose of the research, and the possible risks (and benefits) associated with participation.

Institutional review board: A committee, designed by a high-ranking university official, that approves, monitors, and reviews medical and behavioral research conducted at that institution that involves human subjects and participants.

instrumentation: The development and use of measurement instruments for scientific purposes.

intensive longitudinal designs: These provide large databases with frequent, multiple measurements (typically 10 or more) of the same participants over time, including both before and after an intervention, behavior change, or policy change. They are more powerful analytically than other types of longitudinal designs.

intent to treat: A subtype of analysis that assumes that all participants received the optimal dose of treatment (regardless of how much treatment they actually received). This is a conservative method for evaluating the outcome of an experiment.

interactive voice response (IVR): This computer-based technology allows humans to interact with computers by speaking.

internal validity: Indicates the degree to which study results are actually true (i.e., are without systematic bias or confounding factors). A strong research design and a valid, reliable questionnaire increase the likelihood of internal validity in the study findings.

International Consortium for Political and Social Research (ICPSR): Housed at the University of Michigan, the International Consortium for Political and Social Research maintains and provides access to an archive of social science data for research and instructional use. ICPSR also offers training in quantitative methods to increase the efficacy of data use.

inter-rater reliability: Indicates agreement or concordance among raters, demonstrating the degree of homogeneity or consensus among them.

interval measures: Indicate the order of and size of intervals between data points.

interviewer effect: A physical or personal characteristic of an interviewer (race, gender, overt friendliness) that influences how an interviewee completes or answers interview questions.

intra-individual: Indicates a condition or event within an individual, including individual characteristics or performance on surveys or cognitive tasks.

item nonresponse: When a survey respondent leaves a particular question unanswered.

labeling theory: Posits that deviance is not necessarily inherent to an act; rather, the societal response to an act applies the label "deviant" to offenders, indicating the acts were deviant according to cultural and societal norms.

lagged effects: A treatment intervention or experimental condition emerge well after the fact, often after measurement and the experiment officially cease.

Likert scales: Commonly used in survey and other research, a Likert scale involves scaling responses from "strongly disagree" to "strongly agree."

literature review: When a researcher examines a body of texts to assess the state of knowledge, including substantive findings and theoretical and methodological contributions, on a particular topic.

longitudinal design: In a longitudinal design, participants, processes, or systems are studied over time and data are collected at multiple time points or intervals. A study must have at least two measurements to be considered longitudinal.

matching: Cases are paired with one or more controls based on the strongest hypothesized confounders.

mean: The arithmetic or statistical average for a given population or sample.

mediation: Occurs when the underlying relationship between an independent variable and dependent variable is affected by a third variable associated with both the independent and dependent variables. This third variable (the mediator) may mask the relationship between the observed independent and dependent variables.

meta-analysis: Identical outcomes from different studies are pooled to obtain one effect size to describe the strength of a relationship (e.g., pooling the literature evaluating the effect of bars' drink specials on impaired driving).

mixed-methods research: Combines collection and analysis of both quantitative and qualitative data.

moderation: The effect of a third, or moderating, variable on the relationship between the observed independent variable and dependent variable. The third variable, also known as a *moderator,* may enhance or amplify the effect between the observed variables.

Monitoring the Future (MTF): Provides a long-term epidemiological study surveying high school students on their licit and illicit drug use. Other risk behaviors, attitudes, and opinions about substance use are also measured.

multistage cluster sampling: A more complex form of cluster sampling in which researchers randomly select elements from each cluster instead of using all elements in the constructed clusters (e.g., randomly selecting classrooms within schools).

mutually exclusive: These variables occur when response options to a measure (or variable) are contradictory and thus cannot both be true at the same time.

National Crime Victimization Survey (NCVS): Administered by the Bureau of Justice Statistics, the National Crime Victimization Survey is a household-based survey conducted twice a year to measure the frequency, characteristics, and consequences of crime victimization.

National Incident-Based Reporting System (NIBRS): Based on the occurrence of criminal incidents, the National Incident-Based Reporting System is used by law enforcement agencies throughout the United States to collect and report data on crimes.

National Longitudinal Survey of Youth (NLSY): Consists of a series of surveys, conducted by the U.S. Department of Labor Statistics, to gather information at multiple time points about significant life events, specifically labor market activities, in several population samples of U.S. citizens.

National Survey on Drug Use and Health (NSDUH): Conducted by the National Institute on Drug Abuse (NIDA) to collect data annually on the prevalence of drug usage and abuse.

nominal measures: Enable the classification of variables in relation to quality features (i.e., grade, school, etc.).

nonequivalent groups design: Arguably the most frequently used design in social research; resembles a pretest, posttest randomized experiment, but without randomization.

null hypothesis: The general or default research hypothesis indicating that no relationship exists between two measured phenomena or that a potential treatment has no effect.

odds-ratio: An effect size that represents the magnitude of the relationship between the exposure and the outcome in question. The larger the odds-ratio (greater than 1), the stronger the relationship between the exposure and the outcome.

official data: Collected by government agencies or other public research agencies for use in policy and practice.

official statistics: Produced by governmental agencies to shed light on the prevalence of crime for general information and to guide policy creation.

operationalization: Through *operationalization,* empirical observation is used to render a concept measurable and understandable.

ordinal measure: Classifies and ranks the value of the variable from its lowest to highest value.

outsider: A researcher who examines the phenomena of interest without interacting with study subjects.

overmatching: Prevents associations between the variables of interest by matching to too many control variables.

overt observer: When researchers identify themselves as researchers to the subjects or participants they are observing and by making no effort to conceal their research activities.

panel design: A longitudinal design in which the same individuals are followed over time.

part 1 crimes: The eight most severe crimes indexed in the UCR. Violent and property crimes are considered part 1 crimes, such as homicide, burglary, and motor vehicle theft.

part 2 crimes: Another crime category in the UCR, part 2 crimes are considered less severe than part 1 crimes and include fraud, gambling, drug offenses, and sex offenses.

passive consent: Implies consent to participate in research. A signed refusal to participate in a study retracts consent; without a signed refusal, consent is assumed.

personalization: *Personalization* includes minor details (such as a person's name) added to survey communications to increase the participants' likelihood of responding.

pilot study: A small-scale preliminary study conducted to evaluate the feasibility, cost, validation of data collection methodology, and so on, of a planned study prior to full implementation.

population: A set of entities (individuals, institutions, etc.) from which statistical inferences may be drawn.

population parameter: A quantity or statistical measure for a given population.

posttest: A survey or other data collection method administered to research participants after completion of a treatment to determine change in behavior and effect of the treatment. This is used in conjunction with a *pretest*.

power: The probability that a statistical test will reject the null hypothesis when the null hypothesis is false. Generally, power is a function of possible distributions, typically determined by a parameter based on alternative hypotheses. This calculation is often used when planning a study to determine how many participants should be included.

predictor: Measures risk factors, or explanatory variables, for the dependent variable (crime).

prenotifications: Includes e-mails, postcards, or letters informing potential survey respondents that they were selected to participate in a survey and that they will receive the survey in the days or weeks to come. The prenotification is intended to increase the response rate.

pretest: A preliminary test administered to determine baseline behaviors and characteristics prior to treatment. See also *posttest*.

probability sampling: Involves selecting a participant sample through a form of random selection when all members of the population have a known and equal probability of being selected to participate in the study.

probe: Interviewers prod respondents with follow-up comments or questions to dig deeper into their experiences and to elicit more depth and detail in their responses. These comments or questions are known as *probes*.

property crime index: A summative measure created from the Uniform Crime Report, adds up incidences of the following crimes: burglary, larceny theft, and motor vehicle theft.

proportionate sampling: Used when a population consists of several subgroups that differ in their proportion of the population. The number of participants drawn from each subgroup is determined by the proportion they comprise in the entire population.

public-use data: Any information readily available for use by researchers and available to the public for consumption.

purposive sampling: Based on knowledge of the population and the purpose of the study, with subjects selected for a particular characteristic (sometimes called *judgmental* or *judgment sampling*).

qualitative research: Researchers seek in-depth understanding of human behavior and the rationale behind it.

qualitative variables: Variables that have no natural set of ordering and are typically measured on a nominal scale.

quality assurance: Researchers' ability to ensure a program is administered as expected.

quantitative research: Undertakes systematic empirical investigation of social phenomena in which the relationship between two or more variables may be quantified.

quantitative variables: Variables that are naturally measured as numbers for which meaningful arithmetic operations make sense.

quasi-experiment: An empirical study similar to an experiment in all respects with the exception of random assignment of participants.

quota sampling: In *quota sampling*, similar to *stratified sampling*, the population is selected into mutually exclusive subgroups and subjects are then selected from each group based on specific proportions.

random: Participants are chosen without basing their characteristics on any particular characteristic or trait.

random digit dialing: A sample selection method in which telephone numbers are generated at random to select research participants.

random start: Occurs when selecting a systematic sample at an interval. In this process, the first random number for selection within a survey is generated by drawing or fingerpoint.

rapport: In qualitative research, *rapport* indicates building trust with participants to get them to open up to researchers about the phenomena being studied.

ratio measures: *Ratio measures* are like *interval measures*, with the addition of a meaningful zero.

rebound effect: The disappearance of a short-term effect of a policy, law, or intervention—that is, a program may have had a short-term effect, but participants soon rebounded to normal levels.

recall problems: Inaccuracies or lapses in memory when reporting events.

reliability: The consistency of a measure.

repeated cross-sectional designs: Repeated at regular or irregular time intervals to estimate change at the aggregate or population levels.

replication: A primary principle of the scientific method, *replication* of a finding or an experiment verifies or expands on the results of a previous study.

representative reliability: The degree to which a measure demonstrates stability across subgroups or populations.

researchese: The specific language, terminology, and way of talking and writing used by researchers and the research community.

research method: The toolbox of processes used to collect information and data to obtain scientifically sound results.

research question: The methodological point of departure in scholarly research, the broad question the researcher seeks to answer through the research study.

response option: An answer provided in a survey that respondents may use to respond to the survey item.

response rate: The number of people answering a survey divided by the number of people selected to participate. Response rates are typically expressed as a percentage.

restricted use data: Any information that has previously been collected by researchers, the government, and so on, but is not available for public use.

retrospective design: A *retrospective design* looks for a relationship between an outcome more recent than an exposure. In other words, such studies "look backward" in time to identify causes and correlates of the outcome of interest.

retrospective longitudinal design: Attempts to remedy flaws in cross-sectional research by collecting several years after the behavior of interest occurred using recall methods.

sample: A subset of a population. Because it is usually not necessary to study an entire population, a representative sample of the population is used to make inferences about the entire population.

sampling: Researchers select a subset of individuals from a population to estimate characteristics of the whole population.

sampling frame: A list of the population from which a sample can be drawn. The sampling frame lists individuals, households, or institutions.

scaling: Involves construction of a numerical instrument associating a qualitative construct with quantitative measurements.

screening questions: Used prior to survey administration to determine an individual's eligibility to participate in a survey.

secondary data: Used for statistical analysis after having been previously collected for some other purpose by another researcher.

self-control theory: Asserts that criminal behavior is based on the individual tendency toward low self-regulation and control. If an individual possesses a low level of self-control, that person will be more likely to engage in criminal behavior and delinquent acts.

self-report data: Data collected by survey, questionnaire, or poll, with respondents reading questions and selecting the responses most appropriately reflecting their own behavior, without researcher assistance or interference.

series victimizations: According to the Bureau of Justice Statistics, in *series victimizations* respondents report more than one type of crime but cannot recall specific details relating to the event.

seriousness scale: Often used in criminology and criminal justice to account for the greater seriousness of some crimes over others. An example of such a scale is the Wolfgang Sellin Index.

simple random sample (SRS): A subset of individuals from a larger population. In this type of sample, each individual is selected randomly or entirely by chance, often using a random number table.

single-blind: An experiment in which information that could skew the results of the study (e.g., knowledge of the study's purpose) is withheld from participants but is completely known to the experimenter. The purpose of this is to reduce bias in the study results.

skip patterns: Guiding respondents to skip questions that, based on a previous answer, do not to apply to them.

snowball sampling: A type of nonprobability sampling, this is typically used by researchers to identify hard-to-locate subjects. The researcher gains access to an initial subject and from there or through that subject gets access to subsequent subjects.

social desirability bias: The tendency of respondents to answer researchers' questions by stating what they believe will be viewed favorably, rather than by providing an accurate response. Subjects thus intend to "save face," or make themselves appear in a positive light to the researcher.

social learning theory: Based on learning principles from psychology and differential association theory from sociology, *social learning theory* holds that criminal behavior, similar to all other types of behavior, is learned and reinforced through operant conditioning.

split-half reliability: The consistency of a measure when it is split in two and the scores of each half of the test are compared with one another. If the scores are comparable, they are likely measuring the same concept.

spurious: A false or factitious claim.

standard deviation: Measures how much variety or dispersion exists from the average in a given population or sample.

statistic: A single measure of some attribute of a sample.

stratified random sampling : Dividing a population into smaller subgroups called *strata* (such as a census block, school, or wing of a prison), with strata created based on members' shared attributes or characteristics. A random sample is then taken from each stratum in a number proportional to the size of the strata in relation to the population.

stratify: A method used to sample subpopulations within a population. When a study requires a large number of people with one characteristic that is rare in the population, it is advantageous to sample from this group at a higher rate, or to *stratify*. The sampling frame is divided into groups based on the characteristic of interest, and a (not necessarily equal) proportion of each group (strata) is selected into the sample.

structured interview: A quantitative research method used in survey research for the purpose of ensuring that each interview is composed of the exact same questions, asked in the exact same order. See also *unstructured interview*.

Supplemental Homicide Report (SHR): A complementary or supplemental report to the UCR. Law enforcement agencies complete this form separately to gather more specific information about homicides.

survey: Any measurement procedure that involves an investigator posing questions to and requiring self-report responses from research participants.

systematic random sample: Randomly selecting the first participant from the sampling frame and then selecting each (*nth*) subject from the sampling frame.

taxonomy: A concept derived from biology, *taxonomy* refers to grouping organisms based on shared characteristics and giving names to these groups.

testing effect: Indicates the tendency of a respondent who has been previously interviewed to remember the report given in the first interview when responding in a subsequent interview. This is typically a problem in the NCVS.

test/retest reliability: Assesses the degree to which test scores are consistent from one time period to the next.

test statistic: A numerical value that summarizes the information contained in the sample data; it is the primary basis for testing a given hypothesis.

theory: A set of statements or principles devised to explain a group of facts or phenomena that have typically been widely tested and accepted.

time-series design: A quasi-experimental research design in which periodic measurements are made on groups or individuals both before and after the implementation of an intervention or policy.

transferability: The degree to which the results of qualitative research can be transferred or generalized to other contexts and settings.

treatment as usual: The treatment received by the control group within an experiment. "Treatment as usual" may mean no treatment at all, another unrelated program, or a bare-bones version of the experimental condition treatment program.

underreporting: Refers to crimes not reported to law enforcement. This occurs for a variety of reasons and biases official crime statistics.

Uniform Crime Reports (UCR): Published by the FBI, these are police-reported data on crime in the United States.

unit of analysis: The entity studied in research. Units of analysis can be individuals, groups, artifacts (books, newspapers), geographical areas (towns, states, countries), or social interactions (marriages, divorces).

United States Census Bureau: The federal agency responsible for the US. census. The bureau also collects demographic and economic data.

unstructured interviews: Interviews that do not have predetermined questions or answers. Future questions are based on the responses from previous questions. These interviews, generally used for exploratory research, can be adapted or changed while under way to meet the needs of the interview respondent. See also *structured interview*.

validity: The idea that a concept, conclusion, or measurement corresponds accurately to the real world or measures what it is intended to.

variable: A condition subject to change; specifically, it is a characteristic allowed to vary during a scientific experiment to test a hypothesis.

variety index: A type of composite measure that summarizes and rank orders specific observations to represent a more generalized dimension.

victimization rate : The rate at which individuals are victimized in a given population. The rate is reported differently depending on survey type or data source.

violent crime index: A summative measure created from the Uniform Crime Report; it adds the following crimes: murder and non-negligent man-slaughter, forcible rape, robbery, and aggravated assault.

voluntary participation: The information provided to research participants to ensure their participation is voluntary and includes the specific point that failure to participate in or decision to withdraw from a study will not result in any penalty or loss of benefits.

vulnerable populations: Groups of people who are typically excluded, marginalized, or disadvantaged due to certain environmental, economic, social, cultural, or other characteristics. Women, children, and prisoners are examples of vulnerable populations.

weighting: Used in sampling designs with a stratified or proportionate multilevel sampling method. Each participant in the sample is weighted, so the sample is equivalent (based on the variables the researcher is interested in, generally demographics) to the characteristics of the population. Weighting is also frequently used in dealing with nonresponse, with participants demographically or behaviorally similar to those lost to follow-up counted more heavily.

INDEX